£21·00

PERSPECTIVES ON SOUTHERN AFRICA

Soldiers Without Politics

Soldiers Without Politics

Blacks in the South African Armed Forces

Kenneth W. Grundy

UNIVERSITY OF CALIFORNIA PRESS
BERKELEY   LOS ANGELES   LONDON

University of California Press
Berkeley and Los Angeles, California

University of California Press, Ltd.
London, England

©1983 by
The Regents of the University of California

Printed in the United States of America

1 2 3 4 5 6 7 8 9

Library of Congress Cataloging in Publication Data
Grundy, Kenneth W.
  Soldiers without politics.
  (Perspectives on Southern Africa; 33)
  Includes index.
  1. Soldiers, Black — South Africa.   2. Soldiers, Black — Namibia.
I.Title. II. Series.
UB419.S6G78 322.5 089968 82-2584
ISBN 0-520-04710-9 AACR2

TO MY MOTHER AND FATHER
whose gift of love made everything possible

Contents

Preface

"Soldiers without politics" may seem a harsh description of those men of color who have joined and participate actively and efficiently in the South African Defence Force, other armed South African forces, the homeland guards and armies, and the units of the South West Africa Territory Force. Because the career and economic choices of these individuals are severely bounded, any condemnation of them, no matter how implicit, is a bit unfair. Pressure to join, while indirect, has been nonetheless compelling.

Yet criticism is in order. All black participants in the armed defense of the status quo in white South Africa have been volunteers. Although the authorities in South West Africa have recently instituted compulsory national service in the newly formed Territory Force, South African black soldiers and a considerable percentage of South West Africa's black recruits have volunteered to soldier the region. Do they do so out of conviction that the status quo is worth defending or that the revolutionary opponents of the regime are politically or morally wrong? In a few cases these convictions may provide the motivation. But most feel no great affinity for the white regimes they are defending; nor do they identify with the revolutionary elements seeking to destroy minority white rule, or, if they do, such identification has not inhibited their obedience to orders. In short, in most instances political considerations do not play a significant part in their decision to fight: their purpose in serving in the armed forces is personal rather than political.

Samora Machel, the president of Mozambique and leader of the politico-military organization that led Mozambique to independence, disparaged the mobilization in his own country of fighting forces without sufficient political education or identification with the cause for which they are fighting. Fighting must be founded on a issue, not motivated simply by the need to earn a living. In Machel's damning words: "A soldier without politics is an assassin."[1] To those who choose revolutionary struggle, Machel believes, the only justification for the employment of violent means ought to be an end that transcends short-term, selfish motives. This political objective makes the struggle worthwhile. In Machel's sense, South Africa's black soldiers have no politics. This does not mean, however, that their actions have no political effects. In fact a good part of this study is devoted to the political impact of these black formations.

A note or two on terminology is in order. The word *black* is used to refer to all nonwhite South Africans and Namibians. It is a generic term that, in this study, fails to make important distinctions in discussing in detail political concerns and the composition of various units and formations. To facilitate more detailed examination, the terms *African* or *black African* are employed to designate the indigenous peoples of South Africa. Granted, some white people, all Coloured people (of mixed European and black African or Malay descent), and those of Asian descent, if they are born in Africa and regard a portion of Africa as home, ought to be considered Africans. But for our purposes, only people autochthonous to the continent are referred to as Africans, merely for convenience and

1. As quoted in the *Financial Times* (London), 23 May 1975.

accuracy of expression. There is no effort here to imply either unity or division among South Africa's black peoples or to enter into the emotional debate over official South African nomenclature.

Likewise, a number of other terms used in this study are ideologically loaded. Take the word *homeland*. Its usage would seem to imply acceptance of the South African government's policy of partitioning off and granting "independence" to territories ostensibly reserved for various black ethnic and national groups. Certainly, these territories are not and never have been "home" for large percentages of South Africa's blacks. Yet the alternative term *bantustan* is equally loaded. For want of a better expression, I shall therefore follow official usage and eschew repeated "so-calleds" or frequent use of quotation marks to demonstrate the doubts we may have about the viability, legitimacy, and efficacy of these territories, their governments, and their leaders.

The names *Rhodesia* and *South West Africa* are used here to refer to those respective territories during the colonial period and to the existence of white minority regimes. *Zimbabwe* and *Namibia* apply to the independent majoritarian governments and to the goal of establishing such regimes. The state established by a Unilateral Declaration of Independence in 1965 is known as Rhodesia, whereas the official designation, Zimbabwe, refers to the dream and reality that has motivated and continues to motivate the revolutionary forces under Robert Mugabe and Joshua Nkomo. South West Africa is the official title used by the South African government and by white politicians and people in that territory. Namibia is the appellation preferred by the United Nations and by elements working for genuine change in that land. These four place names, therefore, carry a racial connotation, and, just as important, refer to frames of mind as well as to political realities.

A word or two about some of the citations is in order. All citations to South African parliamentary debates are drawn from the weekly edition. Hence I preferred a shortened form that provides only the date and the column. One might also have referred to the particular parliament and the session

(South Africa is currently in its seventh parliament since the establishment of the Republic in 1961), but that can get cumbersome and does little to help one locate the material in question. In addition, during each business day members may address questions of fact to the ministers regarding matters under their responsibility. The questions and replies appear as a separate set of columns at the conclusion of each weekly edition. I have referred to these columns as "Q cols." in the footnotes to distinguish them from the ordinary daily proceedings. I also made extensive use of clip files compiled and generously made accessible by the *Cape Times,* the South African Institute of Race Relations, the Johannesburg Public Library, and the International Institute for Strategic Studies (London). Unfortunately these files did not include reference to the pages in which materials appeared. As a result, that information is missing from many of the newspaper citations in my own footnotes.

I was also most fortunate to be able to conduct interviews in South Africa and Great Britain with a number of individuals who are or have been associated with the South African Defence Force and with others who have followed defense matters closely. I have made reference to these interviews in the footnotes by indicating the place and date of the interview. In only one or two instances have I identified the respondent. This citation form is largely designed to protect the anonymity of sources yet to enable the reader to know when and where the information was secured. I regret not being able to provide a more complete citation, but such protection was required in order to gain access and secure informative interviews. Most informants asked that I not disclose who they were in the report of my findings.

I am deeply indebted to a variety of institutions and a great many individuals who assisted in the research and writing stages of this study. Financial assistance in small but important packages came from five quarters. First, I would like to express my appreciation to the Earhart Foundation of Ann Arbor, Michigan, for enabling me to conduct field work in southern Africa in 1979. A second source of support was the Joint Committee on African Studies of the Social Science Research Council, New York City. That body underwrote a part of my work in the United Kingdom in 1979 and during a brief trip to South Africa in 1980. The early drafting of this study would have been impossible without the Social Science Research Council's generous assistance. The third organization, the Council for International Exchange of Scholars, provided a Fulbright grant which, thanks to the Irish body, An Bord Scoláireachtaí Cómalairte, was spent at University College, Galway, Ireland. My colleagues there, particularly Fr. Edmund E.J. Dougan, O.F.M., deserve special thanks for the provision of adequate space, patient secretarial assistance, and blessed peace from administrative responsibilities. My own university, Case Western Reserve University, granted a sabbatical leave, secretarial assistance, and other small favors too numerous to detail, yet too important to overlook.

Help was also provided by the University of Essex in Colchester, the University of London's Institute of Commonwealth Studies, and the South African Institute of Race Relations in Johannesburg, each of which made available a quiet desk, fine library facilities, and a cheerful helping hand when materials proved hard to locate. I made use of the clip file at the *Cape Times* and the libraries at the South African Institute of International Affairs (Johannesburg), the University of the Witwatersrand, the International Institute for Strategic Studies, South Africa House, and the School of Oriental and African Studies (the last three in London).

Individuals in several cities helped immensely with patient ears, ideas, criticisms, and a genial willingness to arrange appointments and to provide transport, hospitality, and inspiration, to help with documentation and materials, and to offer encouragement. To them I can offer one large thank you that, in turn, assures their anonymity and thereby frees them from any responsibility for what follows.

Parts of this book were discussed, at various levels of formality, before several groups. Each in its way added something of value to my work. Two papers were presented at annual meetings of the African Studies Association (Baltimore, 1978, and

Philadelphia, 1980). Others were discussed at faculty-student seminars at the Foreign Service Institute (Washington, D.C., 1978), Columbia University (1979), the School of Oriental and African Studies (University of London, 1980), the universities of Bristol (1980), Leicester (1980), and Aberdeen (1980), and Miami University (Ohio, 1981). I owe an intellectual debt to those who organized these seminars and to those who participated in the discussions.

Parts of this study have already appeared in print, and I would like to express my gratitude to editors and publishers for permission to reprint slightly altered versions. Chapter 9 is a much enlarged version of an article that appeared in the January 1981 issue of *African Affairs,* the quarterly of the Royal African Society (London). An early summary of the work in progress was published in *The Societies of Southern Africa in the 19th and 20th Centuries,* Volume 11, Collected Seminar Papers No. 27 (University of London: Institute of Commonwealth Studies, 1981), which Shula Marks saw through a difficult birth. Parts of the concluding chapter appeared in an article for the *Journal of Strategic Studies* (September 1981). Finally, Chapter 10, dealing with the strategy surrounding the homelands forces, will appear in Thomas M. Callaghy's collection on *South Africa in Southern Africa* to be published by Praeger in 1983.

To all who assisted me, friends, acquaintances, and family, I extend thanks and absolution for any flaws embedded in this study.

1

Introduction

SOUTH AFRICA'S APARTHEID society and economy contain the hallmarks of a system of dominance and subjugation. That regime is sustained by a de jure and fundamentally de facto set of unequal relationships between racial groups.[1] Various South African governments have tried to convince us that race is not the crucial variable, that nationality is. But the propaganda message that South Africa makes policy and divides peoples solely on the basis of ethnic and national differences (as opposed to racial distinctions) has proven unpersuasive. In reality color and other biological, or racial, characteristics govern one's political, legal, and social freedoms, and one's obligations, rights, power, and status. But South Africa is not just a divided or segregated society. It is one based on the uneven distribution of power. Whether the system is called baasskap, segregation, apartheid, separate development, or plural democracy, in South Africa the white group

1. Guy C. Z. Mhone, "Factor Combinations and the Distribution of Product in a Dominance-Subjugation System: An Approach to the Allocation of Resources in the *Apartheid*-type Economy of South Africa," *Journal of Southern African Affairs* 1 (Special Issue, October 1976): 31–52.

is dominant. Social relationships, structures, and dispensations (when they are permitted) are made by white officials. In the process of securing a steady supply of inexpensive (meaning black) labor, white South Africa has fashioned political, social, and economic institutions and relationships so that virtually all facets of interaction work to the material and psychological advantage of the white people.

Thus South Africa is an exploitative, racist system in which social benefits are distributed according to unequal arrangements fashioned for and by a single racial group (itself to some extent cognizant of the social consequences of maintaining this system). The Pretoria regime is not entirely insensitive either to the wishes or to the political discontent of black people (*black* used here in the widest sense to mean all who are not white). Yet whites have institutionalized an economic arrangement of unequal appropriations and expropriations of economic surplus to the benefit of the dominant group.[2] Although the system may have evolved as a series of ad hoc responses founded on particular perceptions of social challenges, there is clearly a logic and order to it. The dominant Afrikaner's mind set, although it may admit inequities in the system, is not prepared to recast a social order that favors him and disproportionately disadvantages those with darkly pigmented skins.

Force is essential to maintain this inequitable order. Threat and submission are as much a part of the system as are physical separation and economic maldistribution. Blacks are disproportionately punished and incarcerated and disproportionately intimidated and coerced. The dominant group is able to sustain itself in power because it has consciously monopolized control of the coercive instruments of the state — the police, the armed forces, the intelligence services attached to civilian and military authorities, and the distribution of weapons to private individuals. The dominant group has retained its unequal power by assuring that only whites may bear arms; in those rare circumstances when blacks bear arms, they do so only under carefully controlled and monitored conditions.

2. Ibid., p. 32.

For white South Africans the raw nerve of the "colour question" is exposed by the emotional specter of well-trained and well-armed black soldiers in the country. Yet during periods of dire threat or far from South Africa itself, black armed men have been employed by the regime, even though the political ramifications would have been distressing to the government of the day had these men been permitted to function without overbearing supervision in white populated areas of South Africa. Gen. J. C. Smuts was not alone when he contended that "militarizing" the African "might prove a danger to civilisation itself."[3] One South African editorial writer described the emotion of his fellow whites: "The unspoken fear has always been 'Won't they turn the guns on us?'"[4] "Unspoken" is inaccurate, for that longstanding fear has frequently been expressed. It would be easy to locate dozens of quotations by alarmist groups and fearful white citizens indicating their determination to keep the "native" disarmed. Out of these expressions emerged an implicit doctrine that blacks ought not be placed in a position that might threaten white dominance—in short, blacks ought not be armed. In reality, this doctrine has never been totally adhered to.

Throughout South African history, before and since the establishment of the Union government, selected blacks have been employed in armed defense of the status quo. A record of that experience will follow in chapters 2 and 3. Almost from the beginning of white settlement on the Cape, white burghers and their Coloured servants defended the community and were used offensively in land seizures, cattle raiding, and "pacification" campaigns. When in the 1670s commandos were dispatched for frontier warfare, Basters and Khoikhoi were essential to the success of such expeditions. Many were fine marksmen and excellent horsemen, and they soldiered against the Xhosa and San, often outnumbering their burgher officers and mounted soldiers. Throughout the eighteenth and nineteenth centuries, black men served on commando and in colo-

3. J. C. Smuts, *War-Time Speeches: A Compilation of Public Utterances in Great Britain* (New York: George H. Doran, 1917), pp. 82–83.
4. *The Star*, (Johannesburg; Weekly Air Edition), 15 June 1974, p. 11.

nial formations as the burghers and the British Crown pushed northward. Africans were used as "auxiliaries" in military campaigns against the enemies of the Boer communities and the Boer republics. Controversy about their use and their loyalty surged then.

The Anglo-Boer Wars supposedly marked a turning point in the employment of black forces. By tacit agreement (although often abandoned, especially by Lord Kitchener), both sides claimed to refrain from involving the African peoples as combatants. However, blacks were employed in massive numbers as unarmed servants and armed scouts and, by the British, as guards. They were also attached to fighting units. It has been estimated that 10,000 or more blacks were armed by the British, who later sought to cover up this policy. Neither side wanted to weaken the principle of white control over the black population; however, neither wanted to lose the war.

Finally, after the founding of the Union in 1910 and the establishment of the Union Defence Force in 1912, a Coloured unit was later formed to fight in World War I. Although the Coloured people had been excluded from compulsory military service by Union legislation, by the end of 1915 the Cape Corps of Coloured volunteers, numbering some 25,000, was raised. It fought commendably in east and central Africa, in Palestine, and on the western front in Europe. A Native Labour Contingent of up to 25,000 black Africans also functioned as noncombatants in World War I. Again in World War II the Cape Coloured Corps was mobilized, but it was intended for noncombatant duties only. Some arms were issued to home units for guard duties and at the front for self-defense against enemy patrols. In most cases, the black forces were divided into small sections and attached to white units as drivers, dispatch riders, stretcher bearers, and laborers. In both wars blacks suffered heavy casualties.

After World War II black elements were disbanded, and it was not until 1963 that the Coloured Corps was reestablished for administrative jobs. Developments since then will be chronicled later in some detail. Yet a basic analysis must emphasize that although whites, both British and Boer, and various components of the black population have had a long history of military activity, each group has tended to arm itself against the others. Their military interactions were competitive rather than unified in response to external threats. Even after the independence of South Africa, military service was often a function of ethnic particularities, not a symbol of a South African nationalism, even an all-white nationalism.[5]

But situations change, especially the manpower needs of South Africa and the economic realities of a limited white work force. After considerable soul-searching the National Party government started to train and deploy small black units, but selectively. This is the primary focus of the present study — the debate on the issue, its partial resolution, and the implementation and consequences of that policy.

Before opening a discussion of the subject, I must provide a measure of perspective. Certain patterns of behavior and a confluence of important historical trends have combined to make this issue of security vital for contemporary South Africa. It would be helpful at this point to outline these trends in order to sharpen and make more intelligible the discussion that follows.

Since the rising tide of black nationalism pressed southward through tropical Africa, demands for national independence and majority rule, minority resistance to these demands, and consequently, violence in southern Africa have constantly escalated. The retreat of Portugal after the 1974 military coup in Lisbon, the military and electoral success of the Patriotic Front in Zimbabwe, and the improving field effectiveness of the fighters of the South West African People's Organization (SWAPO), aided by a Movimento Popular de Libertação de Angola (MPLA) government and Cuban soldiers in Angola, have added to South Africa's security woes. Pretoria is faced with a shrinking and increasingly hostile hinterland. Economi-

---

5. See Kenneth W. Grundy, *Defense Legislation and Communal Politics: The Evolution of a White South African Nation as Reflected in the Controversy over the Assignment of Armed Forces Abroad, 1912–1976,* Papers in International Studies, Africa Series, no. 33 (Athens: Ohio University Center for International Studies, 1978).

cally this has been apparent for some years, despite the periodic reliance by neighboring black states on South African products, services, and infrastructures during various crises.[6] Through the years Pretoria's sense of space and security has steadily eroded. Within the ruling party and the key policy-making bodies of the state and its auxiliary agencies, a debate rages on how best to conserve a fundamentally unstable regional and eventually local order, an order that is, at base, indefensible save possibly by coercion. Throughout the white establishment there are deep cleavages between *verligte* (enlightened) and *verkrampte* (narrow-minded) nationalists. They differ over tactics and to a lesser extent over strategy. There is little disagreement, however, over ultimate ends: to protect the Afrikaner nation (or, in *verligte* quarters, white society) and its social structures and, to the greatest extent possible, to preserve white political and economic dominance. The *verligtes* tend to be more flexible, pragmatic, and willing to accommodate in order to defuse tensions. To them it is not an issue of whether to change, but which changes are needed and which are least likely to disturb radically the essence of white dominance. The *verkramptes* place greater stock in displaying firmness. Each policy challenge is to them an opportunity to demonstrate determination and commitment to the status quo. Any change, to them, sets in motion a train of events that jeopardizes the present order. Both groups are conservative; they merely disagree on how to interpret the situation and whether to accept change. To a society unsure of itself, these become vital issues leading to profound social cleavages.

These divisions within the ruling establishment occur in an environment marked by a growing sense of international isolation. Governmental changes in the West, especially in Great Britain and the United States, may provide short-term reassurances, but the undeniable international trend is not lost on those charged with saving the *volk* and its racist order. In some

6. See Kenneth W. Grundy, "South Africa in the Political Economy of Southern Africa," in Gwendolen M. Carter and Patrick O'Meara, eds., *Southern Africa: International Issues and Responses* (Bloomington: Indiana University Press, 1982), pp. 148–78 and 242–45.

ways those in power are even too obstinate to realize that many of the diplomatic and political steps taken by Western governments (such as the activities of Great Britain regarding Zimbabwe or the Western Contact Group regarding Namibia) are designed to salvage a major capitalist presence in the region in the face of surface governmental changes. Instead, South Africa bemoans the loss of white regional allies such as Portugal and the Ian Smith government in Rhodesia and increasingly envisions the day of reckoning in violent terms.

The upshot for South Africa is that greater demands are placed on its defense establishment — to deter incursion from abroad, to prevent the flight of potential guerrilla trainees, to coordinate with the police in the control of internal unrest and sabotage, and to undertake preemptive operations beyond the borders of the Republic and Namibia. The terms "total war" and "total national strategy," designed to justify and popularize the war effort in South Africa, are not just rhetorical flourishes. They are reflected in state policies and attitudes and in the psychological shifts taking place in popular white responses to pressures from within and outside of South Africa.

Organizationally, a commitment to the violent defense of the status quo is reflected in structural changes at the top. This can be seen in the enhanced and central decision-making role of the State Security Council. This council appears to have superseded the Cabinet and the councils of the National Party itself in importance in planning and coordinating South Africa's military posture. In political terms Prime Minister P. W. Botha, a former Minister of Defence and National Security, has assumed control of the government and, although less securely, of the party. As minister he was a hawk, and he now works closely with SADF brass, especially his new Minister of Defence, Gen. Magnus Malan (who had been the Chief of the SADF), to modernize, enlarge, and upgrade the armed forces. Senior military officers are increasingly involved in political decisions, and they often make political, although not necessarily partisan, speeches. In the field of intelligence work, the Department of Military Intelligence has been raised to a status equal to that of the civilian intelligence arm, the National Intelligence Service (formerly BOSS, the Bureau of State Security), which had been preeminent under Prime Minister J. B. Vorster and his close confidant, Gen. Hendrik van den Bergh.

Quantitatively, this military emphasis can be seen in the growth of SADF force levels (from a total of 101,800 in 1970–71 to 351,050 in 1980–81; see table 7), in the rapid escalation of defense expenditures (from R257.1 million in 1970–71 to R2,465 million in 1981–82),[7] and in the calculated development and expansion of the local armaments industry, organized along para-statal lines and coordinated carefully with private industry to emerge as an effective military-industrial complex.

What, exactly, is the relationship between the South African state and the South African military? Although this question will be addressed in detail in chapters 5 and 12, and in less direct terms throughout the study, we might summarize the key linkages here. Conflict and violence have been the most conspicuous operative characteristics of South African history since its founding. *Die Boer met sy Bybel en sy Roer* (the Boer with his Bible and his rifle) has become a symbolic expression of the Afrikaner's role in history. The state, especially in the forms of the Boer republics and trekboer communities, was dependent entirely on part-time, voluntary (subject to peer pressure) citizen involvement in defense. This usually consisted of the formation of mounted units of burghers riding their own horses, firing their own rifles, and choosing their own leaders. These commandos became the organizational mode of defense, and, as such, military organization was relatively democratic and participatory. Not since then have defense matters been so close to the Afrikaner people. The commando was practically a representative institution, and it dealt with very specific security assignments. Today, the military has sought to combine the idea of a ready Citizen Force in reserve, based on the Boer concept of commando and involving virtually every able-bodied white male citizen, with the British, or Western, concept of

7. International Defence and Aid Fund, *The Apartheid War Machine: The Strength and Deployment of the South African Armed Forces,* Fact Paper on Southern Africa, no. 8 (London: International Defence and Aid Fund, 1980), p. 10; and *Financial Mail* (Johannesburg), 14 August 1981, p. 747.

a professional Permanent Force, additionally assisted by full-time conscript national servicemen. The trade-off for preparedness and efficiency has been a loss of voluntarism and representativeness. These formations provide the South African state and its white nation with a formidable fighting force capable of mobilizing on short notice an optimum number of trained white men.

The SADF seeks to be regarded as a citizens' army kept at the ready by a professional, full-time cadre that provides technical expertise, organizational support, and a training arm. But in another respect, the SADF has a dual existence. For Afrikaner nationalists, the SADF is a primary component of the coercive arm of the *nation,* the Afrikaner *volk.* As such they see little harm in the armed forces identifying with the government that they, through their National Party, control. English speakers, however, are more likely to see the SADF as the defensive and coercive instrument of the *state* as distinct from the nation or the government. Hence, they would be determined to keep the armed forces divorced from partisan politics. The SADF's role, in their minds, is to defend the state and to help in the execution of state policy.

Since the ascendency of the Afrikaner nationalists in 1948, steps have been taken to gather the reins of power into National Party hands, and this has involved bringing loyal nationalists into positions of command in the SADF. Once this was accomplished (by key appointments and promotions, pressured resignations and early retirements, and so forth), steps were successfully taken to improve the professional capabilities of the SADF.

Today the SADF is more intimately involved with real authority in South Africa than at any time since the establishment of the Union. The SADF is prepared to defend the status quo, but the question is: what exactly is the nature of that status quo? Does it include all current facets of apartheid policy? The SADF leadership wants, and apparently has secured, a greater voice in the definition of the status quo it must maintain. This is a crucial shift in the role and emphasis of the SADF under the Botha government.

These shifts of emphasis, role, and policy have not been

brought about without resistance. Much of the change has necessitated a greater involvement in defense by the white citizenry. Expansion of part-time military formations such as the Citizen Force and the Commandos has accompanied greater defense expenditures. More young white men are spending more of their time in military pursuits. The authorities have also widened the civil defense activities of citizens and have begun to indoctrinate white youth earlier (through the formation of cadet paramilitary units in the schools) on the need for military preparedness. Women as well have been more efficiently tapped to share the security burden. Finally, various groups of black South Africans have been drawn into the armed forces, in larger and larger numbers, to supplement manpower shortages, as well as for other socioeconomic and political reasons; that process is the subject of this detailed study. As a result, virtually every member of the white and the black populations is immersed in the militarization of society, either as wielders of coercive and restrictive power or as objects of or respondents to that power. Black South Africans have not been and are not passive, but more often than not, their immediate alternatives are limited.

This mounting preoccupation with coercion, this mobilization of the people behind the war effort, in turn, conflicts directly with even the South African conception of a democratic system of government. The institutions of democracy, so long an alleged special feature of political life for white society, are being restricted. There is a serious challenge to the parliamentary form of government. Top officials of the National Party, in seeking constitutional revision, argue openly that the Westminster model is no longer viable (if they ever thought that it was) for South Africa. In other ways (some directly involving the SADF), life is made rough for the opposition, even the "loyal" opposition that shares many of the same security goals as the government. In short, the current domestic and international pressure on the apartheid order has consequences in practically every facet of South African life and on every population group.

In this state of flux, the issue of race relations must, of necessity, occupy center stage. There appear to be growing opportunities for carefully selected and trained blacks (in the economy as in the armed forces), where few existed in the past. This, of course, is a relative assertion and reflects merely the token or partial accession of blacks into selected and "safe" occupations that do not threaten the dominant minority, a process generally approved by the white community. It is itself part of the process of the opening of other areas of South African life to "acceptable" blacks. To understand why this process has begun at this historical juncture is far beyond the scope of this study.

South Africa has been, throughout its history, a marginal country. It has rested on the periphery of the larger world capitalist order, supplying raw materials and foodstuffs and absorbing capital generated in the developed countries. Only recently, as its economy has begun to expand, has South Africa sought to broaden its role, to become an active semi-peripheral or intermediary capitalist state, particularly in relation to its own, albeit shrinking, regional hinterland. The process is marked by paradoxes and inconsistencies, but they need not trouble us here. Key to our understanding is an appreciation of the marginality of South Africa in many phases of the capitalist world's economic life. The gold mines survive because of the cheap black labor. If the owners had to pay the going rates that apply for mining labor elsewhere in the capitalist world, many of their facilities would be unprofitable. The same can be said for much of South Africa's economy, its agriculture, manufacturing, and so forth. The reason whites live so well in South Africa (materially speaking) is that they have forced the blacks to live so badly. To constrain all South Africans to think of the economic issues in racial terms contributes to the provision of a labor force more easily mobilized and managed.[8]

But the historical persistence of the use of racial designations for economic exploitation does not mean that the pattern is immutable and perfectly consistent. The impact of acceler-

---

8. George M. Fredrickson, *White Supremacy: A Comparative Study of American and South African History* (New York: Oxford University Press, 1981); and Stanley B. Greenberg, *Race and State in Capitalist Development: Comparative Perspectives* (New Haven: Yale University Press, 1980).

ated capitalist development on racial and ethnic questions is
not altogether clear. Capitalist development would tend to ex-
pose the class character of a racist order, but it does not necessarily undermine it, certainly not in the short run. To conclude
that modern capitalism leads to the destruction of apartheid
would be tantamount to acceptance of the liberal argument for
the withering away of racism.[9] Liberal analysts argue that the
demands of a flourishing capitalist economy necessitate a "rational" arrangement involving the free flow of labor and capital predicated on the optimal utilization of the forces of production. But the South African economy is not a market
economy in which goods are allocated solely according to the
dictates of supply and demand. Despite its unabashedly capitalist foundations, South Africa's economy functions as a
segmented, quasi-market economy. Given the reinforcing sym-
biosis of politics and economics, how else could a minority-
dominated settler society be structured? According to the liberal view, race as a basis for the division of labor is an irrational,
"pre-modern" reversion that must be weakened by the logic
of economic growth. The race variable inhibits the economic
process, contributing to inefficiencies and outcomes that defy
the logic of market economics.

In contrast a well-developed racist state, such as exists in
South Africa, can be seen as a product, not an anomaly, of
capitalist development.[10] "But," as Stanley B. Greenberg maintains, "in the absence of clearly articulated class interests in the
dominant section [or racial group], the racial order and the
racial state tend toward an amorphous racism, 'mere dominance' in the face of the dominant class actors' diminishing
interest in the racial framework and the subordinate population's increasing resistance to it."[11] Although those in power in

9. Herbert Blumer, "Industrialisation and Race Relations," in Guy Hunter,
ed., *Industrialisation and Race Relations* (London: Oxford University Press,
1965); and Ralph Horwitz, *The Political Economy of South Africa* (London:
Weidenfeld and Nicolson, 1967).

10. A good exposition of this thesis may be found in Frederick A. John-
stone, "White Prosperity and White Supremacy in South Africa Today," *African Affairs* 69 (April 1970): 124–40.

11. Greenberg, *Race and State,* pp. 27–28.

Pretoria seem to be less and less taken with a rigid and thoroughgoing racist order, they are still insistent on white dominance. The polity and the economy are, if not seamless, at least of the same fabric. Conflict theory would seem to shed more light on race relations in this setting than a pluralist or a liberal capitalist theory. Increasing political challenge and disorder threaten the survival of the apartheid system. Racism may be irrational per se, but in South Africa and other racist societies it is rational insofar as it succeeds as an ideology that legitimizes and organizes the exploitation of blacks. Failing to achieve these ends, racism may be abandoned. Some elements of the business community, which throughout South African history supported or else adapted to the prevailing racist ideas and practices, may today be prepared to work for significant changes in the system. The racist apparatus of the state, in some eyes, has failed to provide for labor and capital needs and for commercial outlets. The mounting expenses of forceably maintaining an illegitimate regime eat into profits. Defense expenditures add markedly to the costs of doing business. So do the hidden and open manpower needs of the economy as they relate to the defense of the system. South Africa has always been short of skilled labor, and racism has contributed to these shortages. But under severe military and political pressure, South Africa is nearly pressed to the limits of its capacity. To shift to a total war footing would hobble the economy still further. Therefore, some think that state structures stripped of their racist base and drawn along patently class lines may serve their purposes better. The decision to tap the black manpower pool must be viewed in this context, along with other explanations and rationalizations, as will be discussed in chapter 6.

In like measure, the readiness of some blacks to join the armed forces clearly grows out of a perception of their economic prospects offset by their sense of political and social alienation and their assessment of peer pressures regarding their decision. An SADF career is not, by any means, a free market decision. But blacks are not a totally passive, manipulable mass. The numbers of blacks currently needed in the armed forces are sufficiently small as to pose no recruitment problem for the authorities. The economy can be counted on to provide an adequate supply of black enlistees, but this condition may be short-term. If military manpower needs increase markedly, if police repression of blacks grows, if the polity and the economy continue to fail to satisfy black wants and needs or, conversely, if economic opportunities should open for blacks and thereby remove what has been called "the economic draft" of blacks into the armed forces, then greater coercion would be necessary to fill military ranks. For black South Africans the sense of citizen responsibility to defend "their" state is dubious. A willingness to risk life, limb, and social standing among peers is strictly a function of limited economic alternatives.

Focusing more explicitly on matters of military sociology and the related theoretical concerns would place South African political and security concerns into a larger picture. The study of the armed forces is absolutely central to a knowledge of politics within nation-states and between independent states. Long before Mao Tse-tung's maxim that "political power grows out of the barrel of a gun" scholars and politicians had noted that the key distinction between domestic politics and international politics is that the sovereign state enjoys a legal monopoly on coercion within its territorial boundaries but that no such corner on legal coercion exists in the interstate arena. While such a simplistic and spurious dichotomy does not, in fact, apply in today's world, it does serve to point up the crucial consideration that, for conservators and revolutionaries alike, access to the means of coercion dictates, in large measure, the configuration of political power in any given context. As Michael Howard observed, "No community of any degree of complexity has succeeded in existing without force, and the manner in which that force is organized and controlled will largely determine the political structure of the state."[12] The reverse may also be the case — the way in which political power is distributed may also determine how military force is orga-

12. Michael Howard, ed., *Soldiers and Governments: Nine Studies in Civil-Military Relations* (London: Eyre and Spottiswoode, 1957), p. 11.

nized and controlled. In the case of a society more dependent on force and coercion than most, such as South Africa, a knowledge of the armed forces and how they relate to the rest of society and to the power elite is indispensible.

In societies with scarce resources planning is an essential tool to make the most efficient use of society's assets. From the perspective of white South Africa the scarcity of white man-power, in economic and military terms, limits the effectiveness of that society in a number of ways. We know that elaborate thinking has gone into the formation of the apartheid eco-nomic system with its arrangements of living and working con-ditions, job reservation, growth points, border areas, migra-tory labor, influx control, pass laws, and so forth. Yet despite Marion Levy's grand generalization that "throughout the his-tory of mankind few things have been as explicitly structured as religious ritual, magical practice, and armed force organiza-tions,"[13] the fact is that South Africa's defense establishment grew piecemeal. The planning that went into it was at times ex post facto and crisis-oriented. The use of black forces has not been entered into lightly, but caution is no substitute for care-ful thought, consistency, or design. It is my aim in this study to explore that decisional process critically in order to under-stand how and why such an important step was taken.

The sociology and political science of the military have been largely neglected fields until relatively recently. Historically the study of the armed forces, particularly as it applies to South Africa, has emphasized accounts of battles, key personalities, and regimental histories. But social questions relating to the composition of the armed forces; the social differentiations within those organizations; and the relationships between the armed forces, the society in general, and the ruling classes thereof have too often been left to speculation. When it comes to the study of racial and ethnic issues relating to the sociopo-litics of the armed forces, comparatively little serious research has been conducted outside the intelligence services of various major powers.

13. Marion J. Levy, Jr., *Modernization and the Structure of Societies: A Setting for International Affairs*, 2 vols. (Princeton: Princeton University Press, 1966), 2:576.

The study of race and ethnic relations in the armed forces and the larger society may well be the ideal prototype of Winston Churchill's proverbial "riddle wrapped in a mystery inside an enigma." First of all, the topic is baffling because of the double sensitivity of race and ethnic questions, on the one hand, and military and security affairs, on the other. Both issues are essentially linked to the integrity and continuity of the state, the society, and the various segments thereof. Because of these sensitivities both the regime and its violent critics consciously seek to deny the relevance of these issues, to obfuscate the facts, and to deny access to these facts to those who seek to understand them.

Because of these difficulties it is necessary for researchers to devise means to get around barriers imposed by those who would hide reality. One example of this can be found in Jorge I. Dominguez's paper "Racial and Ethnic Relations in the Cuban Armed Forces." Cuban authorities deny the existence of the topic on ideological grounds, and thus they make research on it virtually impossible. This is why Professor Dominguez unflinchingly and sarcastically subtitled his paper "A Non-Topic." In a similar manner the unavailability of data forced Douglas L. Wheeler to piece together by great effort disparate snippets of information on the racial composition of the Portuguese army in Africa.[14] But despite these difficulties, this important research was completed, often with detective-like ingenuity, by means of persistent library work and correspondence. As a result, composite pictures were developed about environments that sought to deny scholarship the full picture.

Conscious obscurantism is only part of the problem. In some instances comparable data are not only difficult to come by, they may not even exist. Perhaps in the vague hope that racial and ethnic differences and antagonisms will evaporate if notice

14. See the special symposium "Race and Ethnic Relations in the Armed Forces," edited by Kenneth W. Grundy, in *Armed Forces and Society* 2 (Winter 1976): 227–304. Dominguez is at pp. 273–90; and Wheeler, "African Elements in Portugal's Armies in Africa (1961–1974)," is at pp. 233–50. See also Cynthia H. Enloe, *Ethnic Soldiers: State Security in Divided Societies* (Athens: University of Georgia Press, 1980).

is not drawn to them, relevant data may not be collected by a regime. This may be the case in contemporary Cuba. It may also be the situation in many African regimes. Data collection and statistics are characteristically Western (especially American) preoccupations. In other societies they may be regarded as luxuries serving no social purpose or, worse, as spotlights focusing attention on society's defects. Data on intergroup behavior and characteristics often convey the very worst impression of society. No wonder the dominant elites are anxious to sweep such conditions under the carpet or to give them a romantic gloss.

For South Africa the situation is slightly different. That regime has emphasized, if not gloried in, cultural, racial, and national differences. For them to deny such differences at this stage would be out of character. Thus, it is a matter of open debate, even pride in some quarters, that the racial composition of South Africa's armed forces is becoming more diverse. South African authorities argue that this reflects a widespread support for the present regime among all social groupings. Yet inconsistency faces them. Elsewhere, in an era of the nation-state, elites seek to hammer a single nation from diverse mixes of ethnic groups. South Africa continues in its commitment to an exclusive nationalism in which other groups are merely peripheral to the racist enterprise. In Rhodesia a multiracial yet unintegrated security force enabled the government to claim that the war against the liberation movements had nothing to do with racial discrimination. Rather they contended that it was a cooperative struggle of black and white Rhodesians against "communist insurgents." On the other hand, it had been widely claimed with characteristic bravado that the South African military was entirely white. So rather than deny the realities of diversity the South Africans have instead burdened race and ethnicity with an interpretative baggage of self-delusion and myth that is troublesome to penetrate. To be sure, South African officials are not about to publicize all details of the racial composition, state of readiness, deployment, intergroup relations, and so forth of various armed units. Even if we had access to this information, our chief challenge is how

to interpret South African policy intentions and the socioeconomic and political importance of the racial issues involving
the armed forces.

Much of the scholarship on the matter of social and racial
differences in and about the armed forces has heretofore focused on the officer corps. In studies of military intervention in
politics, coups, military organization, recruitment patterns,
the social background of elite groups, and the political and
social attitudes of the military, the officers are the primary
focus of analysis and sometimes, especially in attitudinal
studies, the unit of analysis. Amos Perlmutter, for example,
writes only about officers in his recent study. In his eyes military ideology is "the sum of the orientations of the officer class
(whatever its degree of cohesion) toward society, regimes, and
politics."[15] Study after study of the military emphasizes the
officers' marked conservatism.[16] But contemporary officers do
not function in a vacuum. Not only the military organizational
and social environment but the external political and social
environment shape the character of the officers themselves as
well as of the larger military. Marvin Fletcher has demonstrated how the growing climate of legalized racism in the
United States and the intensified discrimination in the civilian
life of blacks at the end of the nineteenth and early twentieth
centuries have analogues in the treatment and career prospects of blacks in the U.S. armed forces. The vehicle through
which these white racist views were expressed was the officers

15. Amos Perlmutter, *The Military and Politics in Modern Times: On Profes-
sionals, Praetorians, and Revolutionary Soldiers* (New Haven: Yale University
Press, 1977), pp. 7, 17.

16. Seminal works include Samuel P. Huntington, *The Soldier and the State*
(Cambridge: Harvard University Press, 1957); Alfred Vagts, *A History of Militarism* (New York: Meridian Books, 1959), esp. chaps. 9 and 12; Gordon A.
Craig, *The Politics of the Prussian Army* (Oxford: Oxford University Press,
1955); Morris Janowitz, *The Professional Soldier* (Glencoe, Ill.: Free Press,
1960), chap. 12; George A. Kourvetaris and Betty A. Dobratz, *Social Origins
and Political Orientations of Officer Corps in a World Perspective*, University of
Denver Monograph Series in World Affairs, vol. 10, no. 4 (Denver: University
of Denver Press, 1973); and B. Abrahamsson, "Elements of Military Conservatism: Traditional and Modern," in Morris Janowitz and Jacques van Doorn,
eds., *On Military Ideology* (Rotterdam: Rotterdam University Press, 1971), pp.
61–74.

(almost exclusively white), who probably shared these prejudices but who, for professional reasons, found it convenient in earlier times to repress them.[17]

In large measure this focus on the officer corps is understandable. The officers as a group are more identifiable and accessible. Their numbers are manageable in terms of scholarly research. Moreover, given the hierarchy of military command structures, the vast majority of political acts by the military involve the officers almost in direct relationship to their rank, although it may, in fact, be a curvilinear relationship. Those at the very top of the command ladder are less likely to contemplate a coup than those near to yet blocked from the top for various reasons. Military involvements in civil affairs tend more to be problems of palace revolution than of mass mutiny. As Marion J. Levy correctly argues, "The problem of control of the general membership of an armed force organization never reaches considerable proportions save under conditions of extremely general breakdown of the society of which the armed force organization is a sub-system."[18] There are, however, conditions when it is important to know about the rank and file. Mass mutinies, desertions, and apathy in the armed forces do occur in cases of generalized social disorganization and widespread civil unrest. The potential for them should certainly contribute to any appraisal of force effectiveness. Thus the social composition of the armed forces becomes important in relation to the social composition of the society in disarray. Perhaps this fact has not been sufficient inducement to stimulate scholarly interest in the rank and file as well as the officer corps, but it should be.

When it comes to the study of the rank and file in armed force organizations the principal focus has been on class differences or on regional variations rather than on racial differences. Only the armed forces of the United States have been studied in any depth on racial questions.[19] There are nu-

17. Marvin Fletcher, *The Black Soldier and Officer in the United States Army, 1891–1917.* (Columbia: University of Missouri Press, 1974), especially pp. 28–31 and 153–60.

18. Levy, *Modernization,* 2: 590–91.

19. Ironically, the study of blacks in the U.S. armed forces "has focused

merous questions that might be raised around racial issues. Morris Janowitz has provided us with several insights into the social meaning of military service in an era of mass popular armies.[20] Among other things he deals with the democratizing impact of military service and the relationship of military service to citizenship, parliamentary government, nationalism, social stratification patterns, and social sources of recruitment. The argument is that for Western liberal democracies, citizen military service has been seen as a device by which excluded segments of society could achieve political legitimacy and rights.[21] Such subjects might be explored in racial terms. For example, in the American Revolutionary War the Rhode Island legislature passed a law by which every slave who enlisted in the Continental Army was immediately discharged from the service of his master or mistress and was made "absolutely free." Other states adopted similar practices.[22] The same applied in the War of 1812 for slaves from New York. But most observers have tended to see this phenomenon more as a class process than as a racial or ethnic one. Depending on the quality and rigor of their class analysis, this is as it should be. But nationalism, in the cases of the Western democracies, was widespread, ideally coinciding roughly with state boundaries. Hence, though the grant of increased political rights may have been grudgingly tendered, nationalism was often inclusive rather than exclusive, at least insofar as all inhabitants of the state's territory were concerned.

To be sure, it was not an easy task arriving at this inclusivity. Indeed, Cynthia H. Enloe refers to the "myth of integrative conscription." She thinks that we can just as fruitfully analyze conscription as a "last-resort solution" to the problem of obtaining sufficient manpower. Conscription was designed to

almost entirely on the enlisted ranks as though black officers were non-existent" (Alvin Schexnider, "The Black Experience in the American Military," *Armed Forces and Society* 4 [February 1978]: 329–30). Enloe, *Ethnic Soldiers*, devotes some attention to these issues.

20. Morris Janowitz, "Military Institutions and Citizenship in Western Societies," *Armed Forces and Society 2* (Winter 1976): 185–204.

21. Ibid., p. 192.

22. Fletcher, *The Black Soldier*, p. 13.

supply cannon fodder, not to heighten soldiers' participation in the social and political regime.[23] In the middle of the 1848 turmoil the Prussian General von Roon boasted: "The army is now our fatherland, for there alone have the unclean and violent elements who put everything into turmoil failed to penetrate." That same nineteenth-century mentality was expressed five decades later by a French writer: "The army embodies in itself its morality, its law and its mystique: and this is not the morale nor the mystique of the nation."[24] Professional military men saw the citizen forces, those recruited for cannon fodder, as hotbeds of revolution, as "unreliable elements." Later, when it became clear that mass armies were necessary for modern warfare as then conceived, command opinion divided between those who were willing to enlarge the forces in the interests of national defense and those, preoccupied by political stability and unrest, who wished to keep the ranks relatively exclusive. At that point, the exclusivists found it necessary to retreat to the officer corps as the select repository of virtue. As one Prussian officer stated: "Our power finds its limits at the point where Junker material proves inadequate to fill the officers' billets."[25]

The South African experience is similar but not entirely analogous. Citizen armies were both British and Boer traditions, one on a more regularized and structured pattern and the other on a voluntaristic and ad hoc basis. Their command and organizational structures were considerably different, too. But citizenship itself was and is a privilege open only to selected white elements, those who have, so to speak, served their apprenticeship. And with the ultimate fulfillment of the homelands policy, according to former Minister of Bantu Administration and Development, Dr. C. P. Mulder, there will be no black African people with South African citizenship.[26] Each

23. Enloe, *Ethnic Soldiers*, pp. 53, 63, and 83.
24. Both quotations are from Howard, *Soldiers and Governments*, p. 16.
25. As quoted in ibid.
26. Republic of South Africa, *House of Assembly Debates* (Hansard), 7 February 1978, col. 579 (hereinafter cited as *Assembly Debates*). See my explanation of the notation style in the preface. See also *The Star*, 5 April 1978, p. 8.

black will be a citizen of an ethnic homeland and thereby will be deprived of any claim to a voice in the political life of South Africa as a whole or to a share in the economic wealth of the republic.

Manpower for military purposes had not been a problem for white South Africa until recent years. Sufficient volunteers were found for both world wars, albeit with some difficulty. The problem for the whites in regard to the black population was to organize blacks economically and to force them to participate in the cash economy on terms favorable to white farmers, foreign and settler industrialists and miners, and the organized white laborers.[27] In many respects South Africa today is going through the same debate most Western democracies went through in the second half of the nineteenth century. To what extent can the establishment employ the *untermensch* to defend the status quo without undermining that status quo? What concessions, if any, must the dominant white community make to force and entice black people to defend an order which obviously exploits them? For the Western democracies an inclusive nationalism was a helpful ally. For the South African regime appeals to anti-communism and to the defense of "our country" as distinct from "the nation" have proved less convincing.

For South Africa the question of expanded recruitment is both a racial and a class issue. In the nineteenth-century European context, governments that were relatively representative often opposed and cajoled the professional militarists, who were antirepresentative. In South Africa the government is generally representative only of white society. The armed forces, once they had become an Afrikaner institution, were transformed entirely into an instrument of partisan government. But professional military men, however unified in their desire to defend the civil order, have different life experiences. Some may see or consider different means to achieve the same end. Should that occur, differing attitudes on the use of black forces may emerge among various segments of the white elites.

Answers to the key theoretical questions relating to the di-

27. Greenberg, *Race and State*.

verse racial components in the South African armed forces are critical to any appraisal of the future of that country. These questions are particularly difficult to deal with in that empirical data relating to personnel, numbers, organization, responsibilities, deployment, and structure have been hidden from public view. Thus the data are incomplete, and answers to the theoretical questions must be speculative. Even less sensitive issues, such as the relationship between the armed forces and the economy, are clouded. For example, an inquiry regarding a newspaper account about a conference on "Manpower and Defence" involving a number of business leaders and the South African Defence Force brought back the courteous but frustrating response that the conference had been held in camera and that the military authorities had thus far restricted distribution of the transcription of the proceedings.[28] Most published accounts about the Defence Force are sadly lacking in substantive data about racial issues. These accounts tend to be phrased in the most general and uncritical terms. Understandably this is a product of extensive legislative curbs on reporting military affairs and of the Official Secrets Act (1965). Popular literature on the military ignores the real racial issues and, instead, includes laudatory puffery on black units. Few regimental histories mention Africans or Coloureds. Few honor rolls include blacks by name. Considering that in other social matters the dominant racial segment is obsessed by race, such an omission appears more than accidental. The white populace would seem more interested in insignia, medals, uniforms, colors.[29] Official materials are even more flavorless, as though everyone in the military were living in frictionless coexistence. Serious scholarly work on the sociopolitics of the South African Defence Force is almost nonexistent.[30]

28. Letter to the author from the National Development and Management Foundation of South Africa, Johannesburg, 26 May 1978.

29. Representative examples include Reginald Griffiths, *First City: A Saga of Service* (Cape Town: Timmins, 1970); and A.C. Martin, *The Durban Light Infantry*, vol. 2, *1935–1960* (Durban: Headquarter Board of the Durban Light Infantry, 1969).

30. In the South African literature there is nothing resembling E. A. Azambuja Martins, *O Soldado Africano de Moçambique* (Lisboa: Divisão de Publicações

For South African scholars this reticence to risk regime sanction is understandable. The line between studying and criticizing the armed forces and police and subverting the "national interest" is thin indeed. It is defended by a battery of legislation specifically designed to shield these institutions from serious scrutiny. To some extent this is comprehensible given the protective tendency of South African social scientists to sidestep contentious issues or to treat them in legalistic, institutional, philosophical, or historical and largely descriptive fashion. This overall observation is less applicable to sociologists and historians, and thus it is disappointing that more work on this subject has not been undertaken. Despite obstacles to research and analysis first steps will be taken in this study.

Although it does violence to the holism of the social sciences it is possible to divide the subject into disciplinary categories — social, political, and economic issues — at least for the purpose of posing questions. Of course, each impinges on the others, but for the sake of organization, at the risk of some distortion, one could examine the social (as distinct from the political or economic) implications of the use of armed black men in the military. Is the relationship between the armed forces and society a consequence of a different racial or ethnic composition of the armed forces compared to that of the larger society? Are the armed forces a racial and ethnic microcosm of the society, or are the armed forces distinctive? Why? In the sense that the armed forces usually reflect the real distribution of power in society, armed force organizations are, in the words of Marion Levy, "as much a mirror of general social structures as any other subsystem in a given society."[31] South Africa's all-white regular armed forces of the past mirrored and, in fact, anchored the political center of gravity in that country. They may not have reflected population distributions, but the armed forces reproduced and reinforced power distributions. Such organizations need not be a cross section of society; that would be difficult to achieve even in a widely representative state.

e Biblioteca, Agência Geral das Colónias, 1936). The closest to it can be found in J. V. Martin and Neil Orpen, *South African Forces, World War II,* vol. 7, *South Africa at War* (Cape Town: Purnell, 1979).

    31. Levy, *Modernization,* 2:593.

Despite this reality, to what extent can the armed forces now serve as agents of social mobility for black members? Levy generalizes that "armed force organizations in societies undergoing modernization will become major leaders ... of social mobility."[32] Moreover, "if mobility is not on predominantly universalistic grounds, the price paid in terms of efficient, loyal, and dependable armed force personnel will be heavy."[33] To what extent do these points apply to South Africa and other racially divided states? What is the trade-off between "efficiency" and "reliability" in a racist state?

How do answers to these questions relate to levels of stability and violence in a country? Despite the well-formed ideological biases of the present South African government, there is a pragmatic situational component to the South African use of black forces. Wartime needs, with their pressing immediacy, often set in motion policies not clearly favored in more tranquil times. Morris Janowitz, in referring to the French and American revolutions, noted that participation in armed conflict had been "an integral aspect of the normative definition of citizenship."[34] Political leaders, anxious to further their own conception of the state, armed extensive segments of the civilian population and thereby broke decisively with traditional patterns. Is this at all possible given South Africa's circumstances? Is the citizen-soldier, a concept that originated with the Greeks, a viable alternative for all race groups in South Africa, in spite of the past?

We have thus arrived at a number of political considerations. If we wish to explore the role of the armed forces in South Africa's politics and government, a great deal depends on whether the forces are regarded as an elite organization with a fundamentally coercive posture toward the populace or as an armed citizenry playing a socializing role. If they are an elite organization, how do the armed forces compare with other relevant elites in racial and ethnic terms? If there are differences, why? It may be that in a racist state such as South Africa,

32. Ibid., p. 600.
33. Ibid., p. 601.
34. Janowitz, "Military Institutions," p. 190.

the armed forces are, at one and the same time, a coercive elite organization toward the blacks and a citizen army for the white populace or, looked at from a slightly different vantage, an elite organization of professional soldiers close to the circles of power and a citizen force involving differing components of the populace.

Numerous writers have dealt with the role of armed force organizations in revolution. Most focus on the social backgrounds of the personnel (especially at command levels) in attempting to explore this issue. If the coercive instruments of the state remain loyal to the government, does this assure continuance of the regime? Is armed force (or some segment of it) support necessary for a revolution to succeed? If it is, could South Africa conceivably be sowing the seeds of its own demise by arming some blacks? It is D. E. H. Russell's conclusion that, among the seven successful mass rebellions she studied in some detail, "in no case of successful rebellion did the regime retain the loyalty of the armed forces." But in applying her thesis to South Africa she concludes that "it seems extremely unlikely that the armed forces of South Africa will be disloyal to the regime."[35] It must be recalled, however, that she was writing at a time before South Africa had enlisted and armed a number of blacks.

Opponents of the South African regime are not unaware of this thesis. The South African Liberation Support Committee (SALSCOM), a group of white South Africans in exile (they since have been reorganized into a South African Military Refugee Aid Program and other groups), developed a program to encourage desertion and draft resistance among South African white conscripts. Their rationale is close to Russell's words. In their bold capitals: "NO SUCCESSFUL REVOLUTION HAS TAKEN PLACE IN THIS CENTURY WITHOUT THERE HAVING BEEN A SIGNIFICANT LEVEL OF DISLOYALTY AMONGST THE DEFENDING TROOPS."[36] Al-

35. D. E. H. Russell, *Rebellion, Revolution, and Armed Force: A Comparative Study of Fifteen Countries with Special Emphasis on Cuba and South Africa.* (New York: Academic Press, 1974), pp. 77 and 54.

36. South African Liberation Support Committee, *Towards an Understanding of the Role of Whites in the South African Struggle* (London: South African Liberation Support Committee [1977?]), p. 37.

though they seem to accept her thesis, they reject the substance of her application of it to South Africa. They do not, however, mention the potential of black disenchantment within the Defence Force.

Would it be necessary to modify Russell's view today? Related to this is Katherine Chorley's assertion that political revolution cannot occur in a modern state with a highly trained army unless control of the officer corps is eroded, usually through the solvent of unsuccessful large-scale war. She adds that "no revolution will be won against a modern army when that army is putting its full strength against the insurrection."[37] But Chorley, like so many before, focuses on the officer corps, not the ranks. High disloyalty scores as developed by Russell, however, may be a necessary but not conclusive condition for rebellion.[38] To what extent does racial and ethnic diversity affect the unity and morale within the armed forces? How are the forces organized, and does that organization maximize positive intergroup relations? Various techniques have been utilized by military forces to assure organizational cohesion and obedience. Some carefully recruit and select. Others employ indoctrination. Still others control by structural devices, especially the balkanization of the armed units into separate ethnic formations. The South Africans have attempted all three techniques, but for years they have concentrated on the first of these in recruiting an all-white force. But with the use of blacks, the second and third techniques have also come into play, especially the latter, in which the unified all-white command structure is maintained by creating separate units of racial and ethnic groups.[39] Whatever control device is utilized, it is clear that the authorities are conscious that they may have a tiger by the tail. Intergroup diversity and the techniques used to neutralize it may diminish the field effectiveness of the armed forces.

Questions of control lead to the question of praetorianism—

37. Katherine Chorley, *Armies and the Art of Revolution* (London: Faber and Faber, 1943), pp. 241–47.

38. Russell, *Rebellion, Revolution, and Armed Force*, pp. 77–89.

39. Jacques van Doorn, "Political Change and the Control of the Military," in van Doorn, ed., *Military Profession and Military Regimes: Commitments and Conflicts* (The Hague: Mouton, 1969), pp. 11–31.

the involvement of the military in government to such an extent that the military serves as the arbiter of political affairs.
South Africa is a society that has been established by naked
force. It is one maintained by violence or the threat of it.
Stanislav Andreski argues that "the armed forces are more
likely to be arbiters of politics if they are the main pillars of
authority; that is to say, if the government rests principally on
naked force and not on the loyalty of the subjects."[40] A good
deal depends, of course, on which subjects in a heterogeneous
state one is referring to. Gaetano Mosca, furthermore, maintains that socially homogeneous armies are more likely to dominate politics than those split into different, mutually exclusive
strata.[41] Andreski seems to agree when he notes that "ethnic
homogeneity also contributes toward making mercenary
armies more dangerous to their employers."[42] If these general-
izations are valid, then South Africa is vulnerable to a military
takeover, although the use of black troops would seem to diminish that prospect. The military in South Africa, as elsewhere, seems committed to order. It would be more likely to
intervene if the system were to become precarious or unstable.
Just how the diverse racial components of the armed forces
would affect the ability to maintain order is an issue I wish to
explore.

Finally, the economic dimensions merit scrutiny, especially
in that the regime being defended is characterized by a particular distribution of economic values and advantages. In one
sense the presence of blacks in South Africa's armed forces
might be examined in terms not unlike those which affect mi-
gratory labor flows—"push/pull" factors. To be sure, the enlistment of blacks may also be informed by political factors and
in that sense may not be mainly a function of market factors.
But political support for the regime would be quite rare as a
motivation. A decision to enlist is always a product of a highly
personal perception of one's overall career and social pros-

40. Stanislav Andreski, *Military Organization and Society*, 2nd enl. ed. (Berkeley: University of California Press, 1968), p. 105.

41. Gaetano Mosca, *The Ruling Class* (New York: McGraw-Hill, 1939), pp.
222–43; and Andreski, *Military Organization*, pp. 106–7.

42. Andreski, *Military Organization*, p. 107.

pects in the context of a particular set of situational determinants. Black recruitment is a two-way process involving the absence of opportunity in civil society and the attractions of the armed forces. Blacks are not passive, even less so today than a generation ago. The study of blacks in the armed forces must, therefore, be ever cognizant that the citizenry, even in a repressive, white-dominated society, cannot be viewed as objects who obediently do the bidding of the authorities at every turn. It has taken South African leaders a long time to realize this. It seems to be taking some scholars an even longer time.

On the other hand, the governmental decision to use blacks has also been situationally induced. As the white military manpower pool decreases or as the economy becomes less able to manage itself without sufficient skilled labor, which heretofore had been reserved for whites, authorities are driven to consider arming select blacks. Certain groups of blacks, especially those in the homelands and in rural areas, may find employment in the military as a viable, indeed the only significant form of entry into the cash economy. They may have no sense of loyalty to the regime (indeed they may be hostile to it) and may possess no desire for citizenship or politically high-status employment. Thus, certain economic "push/pull" factors may lead the government to accept black soldiers and in turn compel blacks to consider armed employment. Although this may be portrayed as a voluntary system for blacks, it has been referred to as an "economic draft," in which many unemployed blacks are forced, in a fashion, to volunteer.[43] Such economic considerations deserve further study.

As can be seen, the prospect of blacks in the armed forces of South Africa opens a pandora's box of questions all vital to the future. We have, in this introduction, merely raised some of them. These and other issues will be discussed in considerable detail in the succeeding pages.

43. "Army and Politics," part 3, *Sechaba* (June 1980), p. 11.

2

The Historical Roots of
Black Military Service

THE FOLLOWING TWO chapters are intended to set
the scene for the shifts in National Party (NP) defense policy
after World War II. It must be stressed that, despite the NP
rhetoric, there was not a complete break with the past. Indeed,
even after the NP took firm command of the defense establishment and reconsidered its total condition, there has been a
good deal of historical continuity in terms of defense policy.
There are patterns that run through all South African military
history, and these deserve to be accented here so that the nar-
rative and analysis that follow can more effectively inform the
later chapters.

First, despite a presumed ideological but merely rhetorical
rejection of the idea, whites in South Africa have regularly and
willingly accepted the use of blacks for military purposes. Since
blacks were most often deployed against other blacks regarded
as threatening by the whites, these decisions have been thought
to be necessary and therefore tolerable. Further, the use of
blacks in the military may be regarded as a facet of an issue
central to race relations, that of labor politics. So much of
black-white relations has revolved around white efforts to se-

cure an adequate labor force for the farms, mines, and industries. It is not segregation or separation that really matter; the bottom line of race relations is labor exploitation. Racial domination became a means to assure an adequate supply of compliant labor. Skilled and trained manpower has generally been inadequate for the needs of exploitative capitalist development in South Africa. Defending and expanding a white-dominated order has likewise demanded more manpower than was readily mobilizable without turning to a reluctant black labor pool. The employment of blacks for military purposes, though frequent, has never been regarded as more than a lesser of evils. It has never been seen as a transitory stage that would enable blacks to enhance their political and social standing outside of the military. Likewise, in each stage of South African history there has been a voice warning against both the spillover of this precedent into nonmilitary fields and against the more direct danger of armed black men breaching the control mechanisms designed to keep them in check. An element of white South Africans has never been reconciled to armed black soldiers.

Second, to facilitate control, blacks have usually been carefully selected, either in terms of groups or individually. Whether it was the time-honored ploy of playing off one tribe, ethnic group, or nation against another; the equally classic device of dividing a group by supporting individuals or factions; or the more modern modes of individual selectivity based on testing, a period of apprenticeship, and the demonstration of loyalty, blacks have not been enlisted without first deciding which blacks are more likely to fight efficiently and loyally and which are the most manipulable.

Third, the deployment of blacks has ordinarily been under the most controlled and modulated conditions. Even though the use of black soldiers has been a policy of last resort, mobilization has been marked by caution and experimentation. In terms of absolute numbers and of ratios of white to black personnel; in terms of organization and command structure; in terms of roles and combat expectations; in terms of weaponry issued; or in terms of assignment and deployment patterns, white authorities have taken pains to prevent control from slipping from their grasp. In short, when blacks are enlisted to do white bidding, every possible precaution must be taken to reduce the range of unanticipated developments. In most instances, regime safeguards have proved adequate to the task.

Fourth, with the regularization and increasing professionalization of the South African defense forces, ad hoc usage of black fighting forces has proved to be more difficult. The desire for readiness, professionalization, and efficiency on the one hand are frequently offset by political and ideological considerations on the other. Divisions between generals and civilian politicians occasionally arise on these matters. They are usually resolved in favor of the politicians' perspective. This, however, is no longer an automatic outcome, especially with professional military men being brought into councils of state at high levels and with others building high and respected political profiles among white South Africans. Many of these questions are addressed in detail in chapters 3, 5, 6, 8, and 9.

Pre-Union Use of Blacks

Amid the current discussion about arming blacks and deploying them in defense of the white-dominated regime, it is easy to overlook or to be beguiled by conflicting accounts of the historical role of various groups of blacks in establishing and maintaining the racist order. In most important respects racial lines and battle lines were coterminous as white interests and those of the indigenous populations clashed. But white groups were often willing to engage any help they could find to do their fighting and to provide the physical support services for the fighting forces. Nor were whites above playing on already established cleavages between indigenous peoples or on the insecurities of the Coloureds as a dark-skinned proletariat nonetheless identified (especially by black Africans) with various settler and colonial interests and thereby alienated from their African origins. Such entanglements enabled settlers to set group against group and nation against nation. The Coloured group did not always know what their national or group interests were in particular disputes, and occasionally some were found on both sides in a conflict, sometimes switching sides as the struggle unfolded. In such settings, whites became the material and political beneficiaries of much inter- and intraracial conflict.

Settler and colonial interests were particular in their choice of military allies and auxiliaries. Not only did the whites have to consider various numerical combinations and the racial and social reactions of diverse groups in their response to kaleidoscopic security problems, but they had to weigh the potential military effectiveness and loyalty of contending groups. The result was a confusion of organizational forms and uses for diverse black and mixed fighting groups.

In the early settlement period the pattern was that of the commando, a formation designed in the 1670s initially for frontier defense and for defense against native cattle raiding and later for settler cattle raiding, for the kidnapping of children for labor, and for satisfaction of the insatiable settler hunger for land. The commando evolved into a form by which, officered by burghers, mounted burghers and their servants (Khoikhoi and racially mixed individuals) could engage in military-police actions against indigenous peoples.[1] The local authorities provided ammunition for the whites and guns for the Coloured members of the commando. These arrangements became increasingly formalized with the use of regulars and army officers, and after 1774 a "general commando" was established, consisting of about one hundred "Christians" and one hundred and fifty Basters and Khoikhoi, on the frontier.[2]

1. For an outline of this early period see "Notes on the Military History of the Coloured: Notas Mbt die Militêre Geskiedenis van die Kleurling," a typescript dated 31 October 1973 found in the clip file "Cape Corps" of the *Cape Times*, Cape Town. See also G. Tylden, *The Armed Forces of South Africa: With an Appendix on the Commandos*, Frank Connock Publication no. 2 (Johannesburg: Johannesburg Africana Museum, 1954). Some background on this and subsequent periods is in S. Horwitz, "The Non-European War Record in South Africa," in Ellen Hellman, ed., *Handbook on Race Relations in South Africa* (Cape Town: Oxford University Press, 1949), pp. 534–55, a flattering, uncritical account.

2. M.F. Katzen, "White Settlers and the Origin of a New Society, 1652–1778," in Monica Wilson and Leonard Thompson, eds., *The Oxford History of*

In fact, not infrequently blacks outnumbered whites on commando. During the first half of the eighteenth century regulations were laid down for registers to be maintained of all Khoikhoi able to bear arms. These men were required to serve on commando in case of attack by hostile outsiders and are, perhaps, the first example of black conscription in South Africa.

In the economic life of the Cape Colony the Khoikhoi and Coloured servants may have been relegated to menial tasks. But on commando and with other formations, in addition to the usual assignments as cooks, herdsmen, laborers, wagon drivers, and interpreters, many were fine horsemen and marksmen. Some, therefore, hunted for the commando, and many soldiered against the San and Xhosa.

Organizationally, a breakthrough occurred in 1781 when a regiment known as the Pandoere or Pandours was established in the Cape. It consisted of liberated slaves and Khoikhoi and was a part of the Permanent Force. When the British occupied the Cape in 1795 they retained this unit and gave it their own uniform. In 1787 a "Korps der Vrijen" was established, the first full-fledged Coloured Corps, and in 1796 the Cape Corps (1796–1803) was formed under the command of Lt. Col. John Campbell.[3] It was enlarged and in 1803 became the Hottentot Light Infantry (1803–6) when the Cape was returned to the Dutch. By this time they numbered around six hundred. In 1806 it was redesignated the Cape Regiment (1806–17) when the Cape reverted again to British control.[4] The Cape Regiment fought faithfully in the Fourth Kaffir War until 1812, after which they were moved to a location on the present site of

South Africa, vol. 1, South Africa to 1870 (Oxford: Oxford University Press, 1969), pp. 226–27. Additional information on early Coloured military activity can be found in J. S. Marais, The Cape Coloured People, 1652–1937 (Johannesburg: Witwatersrand University Press, 1959), especially pp. 131–34; and in J. Ploeger and F. J. Jacobs "Die Kleurlingsoldaat," Paratus 27 (September 1976), pp. 15–16 which deals with the period 1795 to 1916.

3. For details see G. Tylden, "The Cape Coloured Regular Regiments, 1793 to 1870," Africana Notes and News 7 (Johannesburg; March 1950): 37–59. Tylden regards the Cape Corps as a re-raising of the Pandoers, which he says were begun by the Dutch East India Company in 1793.

4. J. deVilliers, "Die Kaapse Regiment, 1806–1817," South African Historical Journal, no. 7 (November 1975): 10–32.

Grahamstown. In 1814 the strength was increased to eight hundred in order to release from duty burghers serving on the frontier.

Still, the governor was aware of white hostility to Coloured troops in the upcountry districts. Farmers objected to the employment of ex-slaves, slaves, and farm hands and resented their presence on the frontier. Although imperial authorities probably sympathized with the white farmers, there were few troops available to replace the blacks. This, plus the financial saving in fielding infantry rather than cavalry units, prompted the authorities to keep the unit together.[5] All was not well on the frontier, and black detachments were employed out of desperation. Settler misgivings were to be borne out later.

In 1817 the Cape Regiment was reorganized under the old name, the Cape Corps, although various other names, the Cape Light Infantry, the Cape Corps Cavalry and Infantry, and even the title Pandoere were used. In late 1827 the Cape Corps infantry was disbanded and the cavalry was retained under the new title, Cape Mounted Riflemen. This formation saw action in the Frontier Wars and in the Anglo-Boer War before being disbanded in 1870. When first formed the Regiment was reduced to 222 privates, officered by Europeans. It grew until 1847, when it numbered eight hundred.[6]

Despite this extensive history, the Boers could not bring themselves to trust Coloured soldiers, even when the latter acquitted themselves well on the march and in battle. Prejudice, fear, and distrust were deep. Some "Basters" or "Bastards," those descendants of Khoikhoi mothers and white fathers, fled to Namaqualand to avoid serving on commando. Others drifted to the frontiers, particularly to Griqualand, where they established a small state. Because of their military experience, organization, and location on the frontier, the Griqua were repeatedly involved in battles and skirmishes with other blacks and with Boers, often independently and some-

5. Tylden, "Cape Coloured Regular Regiments," p. 41, felt it was a mistake to employ Coloured men as infantry, especially on the frontier. He argued that their skills served best in the cavalry, where they were fully occupied and were less likely to get into idle trouble.

6. Marais, *The Cape Coloured People*, pp. 133–34.

times allied with other peoples. There was a continual fear on
the part of the Boers that the Khoikhoi and the Coloureds
might join forces with the Xhosa in various frontier wars, a fear
that was not without substantiation. Between 1799 and 1802
such an alliance emerged, and together the black peoples
made life dangerous for homesteaders along the Gamtoos
River and down the Long Kloof.[7] Later, during the Sixth Kaffir
War of 1834, part of a detachment of twenty-five levies at Fort
Willshire plotted to deliver the fort to the Xhosa.[8] Mutinies and
group desertions occasionally were reported. Nonetheless,
through the years, Coloureds and Khoikhoi proved indispensible to white rule. They helped tip the battle of Grahamstown
in 1819 and in the twenties through the fifties protected white
settlements on the eastern frontier. J. W. D. Moodie said they
were "found to be by far the most efficient troops for dealing
with the Kaffres."[9] In the 1840s Coloured units served effectively against the Boer Voortrekkers. This was all the more
reason for Boers to regard them with suspicion. Later, in the
Xhosa Wars of 1846–47 and 1850–53, the Coloured people
played, in the words of one Afrikaner historian, "a greater part
in the defence of their country than the European burghers,
who responded badly to the calls for service."[10] That may be a
romanticized version, for when the war broke out in 1850, the
Cape Mounted Riflemen were in a state of mutiny. The so-
called Kaffir Police deserted to the Xhosa, some fifty or more
Cape Mounted Riflemen deserted, and another three hundred had to be disarmed. To add to the imperial difficulties,
the Coloured clans on the frontier went over to the Xhosa, and
together they occupied an abandoned fort. Although this rebellion was put down, the military situation was so delicate that
prisoners and disarmed Cape Mounted Riflemen were re-
armed to defend the frontier.[11]

7. Monica Wilson, "Co-operation and Conflict: The Eastern Cape Frontier," in Wilson and Thompson, eds., Oxford History, 1: 247; and Marais, The
Cape Coloured People, pp. 113–15.
8. Tylden, "The Cape Coloured Regular Regiments," p. 42.
9. J. W. D. Moodie, Ten Years in South Africa, vol. 2 (London: 1835), p. 304;
as quoted in Wilson, "Co-operation and Conflict," p. 247.
10. Marais, The Cape Coloured People, p. 131.
11. Tylden, "The Cape Coloured Regular Regiments," pp. 47–48.

At other times, even when blacks fought reliably, their armed presence drove whites to opposition. For example, in the first Anglo-Boer War some 786 Basters were enrolled by the British in the northwest Cape. European farmers, in protest, rallied to the Boer cause. Either they fought badly, in which case whites regarded blacks as worthless or untrustworthy, or they fought well, fanning white fears of armed blacks. Things were not all that smooth in the use of black soldiers. But the frontier held a congeries of racial admixtures. Politicians and militarists of all pigmentations were not loath to exploit the racial confusion that prevailed.[12]

Whereas Coloureds on the frontier had displayed a greater independence and hence were more suspect, those who remained back at the Cape must have evoked a greater sense of confidence from their Boer and British masters. Reliable fighters they might have been, but on whose behalf they fought apparently depended on who treated them decently. The majority of the rank and file were, to put it directly, mercenaries. They held few bonds of attachment to their officers, units, or even to the community which paid them save their meager pay, other perquisites, and the capacity of their officers to command them. It was in most units a rugged existence, and discipline was strict. Their loyalty was often a function of who was in power, how well they were paid, and what grievances specific groups of blacks harbored. It is for these and other reasons that G. Tylden concludes that "in the long run the enlistment of Coloured men and Hottentots had proved a failure."[13] But this seems to miss the vital point that in some situations the colonial and settler authorities had little choice but to turn to the manpower available. Using blacks was, in their eyes, the lesser of evils. Without the blacks within the forces, holding the eastern frontier may have been far more costly to the government.

After 1822 frontier defense was also taken up by regulars, assisted from time to time by volunteer colonial units composed of white and Coloured troops. Coloured commandos fought against Mvilikazi in the 1820s. The British used large

12. Wilson, "Co-operation and Conflict," p. 248.
13. Tylden, "Cape Coloured Regular Regiments," p. 51.

numbers of African levies against Cetshwayo's Zulu army in
1879. Blacks were used as "auxiliaries" in military operations
against enemies of the first Republic of South Africa in the
1880s. In the second Anglo-Boer War some Coloureds fought
alongside the burghers in the Transvaal and in the Orange
Free State. But black forces were never really trusted by the
Boers. The "strong prejudice that exists against the organisation and arming of the Coloured classes" led to the Burgher
Force and Levies Act of 1878. Coloured persons were catego-
rized as "levies," and what limited rights they may have possessed were further constrained.

By the time of the Anglo-Boer War (1899–1902), white
leaders had individually arrived at the tacit understanding that
blacks should not be armed. Whether they reliably conformed
to that accord invariably depended on the situation. Some
88,000 men fought on the republican side. Another 450,000
were mobilized by the British. But when it came to using
blacks, both sides willingly exploited the accessible, coercible,
and not-so-willing labor force. Blacks were enrolled as transport drivers, carriers, trench diggers, porters, watchmen, cattle guards, and drovers by both sides. One "conservative" estimate was that 40,000 laborers were used during the war on
each side.[14] But there was also, despite public protestations and
denials, a large-scale use of armed blacks. In this the British
seemed less reluctant. Sir Alfred Milner, Gen. Sir Redvers Bul-
ler, and Gen. Lord Kitchener were all inclined to arm the natives. Kitchener, in particular, used black Africans with rifles in
large numbers, over ten thousand as he later confessed in private. He armed black Africans to serve as "watchmen" on rail-

14. Thomas Pakenham, *The Boer War* (London: Weidenfeld and Nicolson,
1979), p. 547. A number of other works are useful in assessing the roles of
blacks in the South African War; among them are Peter Warwick, "African
Labour During the South African War, 1899–1902," in *Collected Seminar Papers on the Societies of Southern Africa in the 19th and 20th Centuries*, vol. 7 (London: Institute of Commonwealth Studies, University of London, 1977), pp.
104–16; Warwick, "The African Refugee Problem in the Transvaal and Orange River Colony, 1900–1902," in *Collected Papers*, vol. 2 (York: Centre for
Southern African Studies, University of York, 1977), pp. 61–81; and
Warwick, ed., *The South African War* (London: Longmans, 1982), particularly the
chapters by Warwick and Brian Willen.

ways and blockhouse lines. He armed Coloureds as "scouts and police." He claimed that these men had only been armed for their own defense and to protect property, but in fact these "watchers" took an offensive role. Many other blacks served as armed scouts for the mobile columns, and they were the main source of each column's intelligence and advance work. The result was that this policy, especially in the Transvaal, enraged and frightened the Boers.[15]

The first use of blacks to fight helped in the defense of Mafeking. Col. R. S. S. Baden-Powell, in command of the garrison of that town, which had been besieged altogether for seven months, organized three hundred black Africans armed with rifles to guard the perimeter of the defenses.[16] Afterward, he refused to acknowledge their contribution. Most villages in the Cape organized "town guards" using Coloureds and black Africans in separate companies. These units were indispensible in maintaining order behind the lines.[17]

What truth is there, then, in calling this a "white man's war," as so many commentators insist? To be sure, neither side wanted to jeopardize continued white dominance. A "white man's war"? Yes, in the sense that black civilians suffered more than the whites during the early sieges, in concentration camps, and at the hands of marauding Boer and British flying columns. Yes, too, in the sense that black participation consisted largely of the unheralded and frequently involuntary performance of gruelling labor to keep the white fighting formations fed, on the move, and entrenched. Yes, as well, in the sense that whites alone were in command at every turn, and that white objectives had little to do with, indeed, were contrary to black needs and values. Black status and material conditions were no better after than before the war, and they were a great deal worse during the struggle. But it was a black man's war in one overriding sense — the war affected the future of black people in southern Africa at least as much, if not more,

15. Pakenham, *The Boer War,* pp. 537, 540, and 547.

16. Ibid., pp. 402, 418.

17. S. Horwitz, "The Non-European War Record in South Africa," in Hellman, *Handbook on Race Relations,* pp. 534–55.

than it did that of whites. The Anglo-Boer War was, in sum, a fitting application of Willem van Heerden's aphorism that in the titanic struggle between the twin millstones of Boer and British all else is ground to paste.[18]

Throughout the war the masses of Africans remained largely unrebellious and meek. Why had they not sought to take advantage of the situation and thereby recover lost territory or settle old scores? Perhaps awed by the military might surrounding them, few blacks exploited the vulnerabilities of the white society. Yet although this generalization held throughout most of the war, near the end there were signs that natives were stirring. General Louis Botha perceived a growing animosity felt by blacks for the Boers. Although most blacks remained neutral through the war, in the western Transvaal there had been news of an armed black African commando that had risen up against the Transvaal Republic and had struck at Boer farms. Families and farms had been left undefended. Botha, like many of his compatriots, was haunted by this ominous prospect.[19] In addition, when some Bastards were armed by the British, whites in the Northwest Cape rose up in sympathy with the Boers of the republics. Many Bastards had been pro-British, and when 786 Bastard "border scouts" were enrolled, they took advantage of the situation to settle old scores with the Boers. This led to a Boer rebellion in 1901, in which it became license for Boers to kill Bastards and confiscate their property. Until January 1902, when the British threatened retaliation, many armed Coloured persons captured by the Boer rebels were shot without ceremony.[20] In

18. W. van Heerden, "Africa and South African Politics," in *South Africa in the African Continent: Papers Read at the Tenth Annual Conference of the South African Bureau of Racial Affairs (SABRA), 1959* (Stellenbosch: South African Bureau of Racial Affairs [1959?]), p. 126.

19. Harold Spender, *General Botha: The Career and the Man* (Boston: Houghton Mifflin, 1916).

20. Marais, *The Cape Coloured People*, p. 96. See particularly Bill Nasson, "'These Natives Think this War to be Their Own': Reflections on Blacks in the Cape Colony and the South African War, 1899–1902," in *Collected Seminar Papers on the Societies of Southern Africa in the 19th and 20th Centuries*, vol. 11 (London: Institute of Commonwealth Studies, University of London, 1981), pp. 36–47.

Natal, during the postwar rebellion, a large section of blacks offered their services to the British forces to demonstrate their loyalty to Queen Victoria. Some were enrolled, uniformed, and equipped as the Natal Native Horse to fight in the Zulu Wars. Another black African unit known as the Edendale Horse also excelled at several important battles.[21]

Related to the use of black troops and white concern for frontier security, of course, is the issue of black access to firearms. Almost from the beginning Khoikhoi found sources of muskets. Later in the 1830s traders fanned out through Xhosa territory selling muskets, sometimes openly. On a still larger scale, the diamond rush of the 1870s turned the area around Kimberley into a Wild West scene, with a heavy traffic in arms and ammunition. The diamond fields required black labor, some of whom were attracted by free trade in firearms. "Guns brought labourers," writes historian C. W. de Kiewiet, and "guns stimulated trade with the interior tribes. . . ."[22] During the last nine months of 1873 over 18,000 guns were introduced into Griqualand West. Most of the weapons that found their way into African hands were obsolete models dumped on the market by European manufacturers. Rarely were blacks adequately supplied with ammunition or organized to make the most effective military use of their firearms.[23] So anxious was the government to sustain its trade with the interior that it made little effort to determine who was receiving these weapons. It even failed to enforce its own laws.[24] When the

21. Horwitz, "The Non-European War Record," p. 535.
22. C. W. de Kiewiet, *The Imperial Factor in South Africa: A Study in Politics and Economics* (Cambridge: Cambridge University Press, 1937), p. 18.
23. Leonard Thompson, "The Subjection of the African Chiefdoms, 1870–1898," in Wilson and Thompson, eds., *Oxford History*, vol. 2, *South Africa, 1870–1966* (Oxford: Oxford University Press, 1971), p. 253.
24. E.g., The Law of the Land (Law 5 of 1859) forbade the possession of firearms by blacks without the express sanction of the lieutenant governor, but the law was inconsistently and slovenly enforced. The Bloemfontein Convention of February 1854, which released the inhabitants of the "Orange River Territory" from their allegiance to the Crown and transfered government to representatives of those people, included a number of arms clauses by which Afrikaners could openly acquire arms and ammunition from the British Colonies, but black Africans were forbidden to gain them legally. A president of the Orange Free State was dismissed in 1855 because he failed to enforce this

Boer republics objected, the British prevented the Free State, for example, from controlling traffic in weapons through its own territory. This could be done by manipulating British elements among the white population and by threatening to cut off the supply of arms and ammunition to the republics' white inhabitants. The republics were upset to see their own farm laborers lured to the diamond fields; one can imagine their anger on seeing some return with firearms. The Boers protested to the British, but to no avail. It wasn't that the British were keen to see blacks armed — on the contrary, provisions of law in both the Cape Colony and Natal opposed that. Rather, it was that key British elements valued expanded trade with blacks more, and they felt that guns were the stimulant needed to facilitate commerce.

Later, however, when the situation had got out of hand and after the end of the Xhosa War in June 1878, a general disarmament of all indigenous peoples in the Cape Colony was ordered. In April 1880 an attempt was made to disarm all Sotho. But the British failed to enforce this militarily and tried to save face by declaring that the Sotho merely had to register and license their guns.[25] In the Constitution of the Transvaal Republic the lines were drawn more graphically. That document stated expressly that "the People will countenance no equality between Black and White in Church and State." Thus black Africans were deprived of all civic rights, and they were forbidden to possess firearms, ammunition, or horses, or to be abroad without a pass signed by an employer or state official.[26] The same applied in the South African Republic, the laws of which, concerning black African subjects, were derived from those of the Natal Republic. In short, blacks were deprived of all means necessary to execute an uprising or to mount resis-

embargo. Missionaries were also ejected on suspicion of trading in arms with the Africans. See Leonard Thompson, "Co-operation and Conflict: The High Veld," in Wilson and Thompson, eds., *Oxford History*, 1: 422 – 25.

25. The Peace Preservation Bill; see de Kiewiet, *Imperial Factor*, pp. 18 – 19, 36 – 37, and 174. In Natal the government acted sooner. In 1872 it ordered the chiefs to see to the registration of all arms held by their people. Thompson, "The Subjection of African Chiefdoms," pp. 260 and 268 – 69.

26. Albie Sachs, *Justice in South Africa* (Berkeley: University of California Press, 1973), p. 70.

tance, and in an important sense the process of conquest had been completed.

At present, the possession of firearms by South Africa's blacks is virtually nonexistent, except, ironically, among bona fide criminals and among opponents of the regime. In contrast, the white population is armed to the teeth. For example, the 1947 annual report of the Department of Justice reported the number of licenses issued under the Arms and Ammunition Act as around 70,000 for Europeans and 34 for Coloureds.[27] By 1976, 154,305 licenses were issued to whites, and almost that many were issued in 1977.[28] The number declined slightly in 1978 and again in 1979, indicating that licensing was very much a result of the immediate post-Soweto anxieties among whites. As of the end of 1979, 791,210 white people were licensed to possess firearms, and almost 1,500,000 firearms were registered at that time.[29]

A variety of laws make it difficult for blacks to own weapons legally. According to the Dangerous Weapons Act (No.71 of 1968), anyone found in possession of a weapon which could cause bodily injury if used in an assault or of an object liable to be mistaken for a firearm is guilty of an offense unless the accused can show that at no time was it intended to be used for an unlawful purpose. Furthermore, the Minister of Justice may prohibit any person or class of persons from being in possession of any object which in his opinion is a dangerous weapon. Proclamation R135 of 1958 provides that, unless required by law or authorized in writing by a senior official, no African may, outside the plot on which he resides, carry or use any firearm, spear, or other dangerous weapon or instrument.[30] That proclamation may be applied to any African area

27. Cited in Sheila Patterson, *Colour and Culture in South Africa: A Study of the Status of the Cape Coloured People Within the Social Structure of the Union of South Africa* (London: Routledge and Kegan Paul, 1953), p. 219, n. 100.

28. Republic of South Africa, *House of Assembly Debates* (Hansard), 18 April 1978, Q col. 634.

29. *Assembly Debates,* 28 March 1980, Q col. 540. See also *Rand Daily Mail* (Johannesburg), 17 January 1979 and 19 October 1976; and *The Star* (Johannesburg), 14 August 1976.

30. See Muriel Horrell, *Legislation and Race Relations,* rev. ed. (Johannesburg: South African Institute of Race Relations, 1971), pp. 108 and 93. Efforts

(the homelands, for example) determined by the Minister of Bantu Affairs and Development (from 1978 called the Minister of Plural Relations and Development and still later, since 1979, the euphemistically named Minister of Cooperation and Development). The Arms and Ammunition Act of 1969 indicates that, unless the Minister of Police directs otherwise, no application for a license to possess arms by "any person other than a natural or White person" shall be granted, except with the approval of the Minister.[31] To be sure, illegal weapons are circulating, but the numbers in the hands of blacks are not great enough to threaten the political order. When blacks are found to be illegally in possession of firearms, the judges usually proclaim maximum sentences.[32] Today, however, stolen guns surface during faction fights and armed robberies, and guns have replaced knives and knobkeries in tribal fights.[33]

However averse to it they may have been, white settlers in early South Africa were compelled to arm and use black men in military capacities on ad hoc, selective bases. At the same time, however, they feared a restive black population and sought eventually to disarm them and to prevent their military employment. It was felt in the Cape Colony, for example, that "the methods of native warfare are barbarous at all times" and that it was impossible "to restrain natives and keep them under control, even if officered by Whites." And in Natal, the feeling was expressed that "arming the Zulu would give them false ideas of their own powers ... and create a position which would render much more difficult the ultimate settlement of Europeans in the province."[34] The paradox is that to control blacks in general some blacks had to be enlisted to assist whites. But Boers allowed their experiences, no matter how effective

by black traders in the townships to obtain firearm permits have grown out of increased armed burglaries and robberies (*The Star*, 5 July 1979, p. 9).

31. Arms and Ammunition Act, no. 75 of 1969, sec. 3(4).

32. On judicial attitudes, see Sachs, *Justice*, chap. 5, pp. 123–60. See also Rex v. Mhlauli, 1954, (I) S.A. 87 (c).

33. *Rand Daily Mail*, 17 January 1979.

34. Prime minister to governor general and governor to secretary of state, as quoted in Shula Marks, *Reluctant Rebellion: The 1906–8 Disturbances in Natal* (Oxford: Oxford University Press, 1970), pp. 157 and 113.

as fighters or loyal as comrades in arms blacks may have proven to be, to confirm their deep-seated prejudices. Those attitudes followed white South Africa into the twentieth century.

In this early stage the pattern of pragmatism, caution, and fear emerged. Before the establishment of the Union, fear was almost raised to an article of ideology. Afrikaners and English speakers alike shared these views. Blacks, mostly Coloureds, were armed and deployed in defense of the status quo only because the authorities could devise no better substitute in a country short on skilled white manpower. But the perceived alternatives were even more threatening to the white order. Boer and British administrator alike had pressing economic responsibilities, either on the farm, at the office, or at the mine. A supply of exploitable manpower was available. How desperately whites perceived their security situation and how much they were alarmed by the prospect of a black uprising ultimately determined whether they employed blacks for military purposes.

The Defence Act of 1912

By the time the Union was formed in 1910 and its leaders were ready to provide for the defense of the state, white fears of militant and armed blacks were deeply ingrained. Whether these were individuals and groups opposed to white dominance or blacks mobilized by the state in support of the regime made little difference. One is reminded of George Orwell's statement: "But there is one thought which every white man ... thinks when he sees a black army marching past. 'How much longer can we go on kidding these people? How long before they turn their guns in the other direction?'"[35] Learned and reinforced racism led South Africa's white population to think in color categories; whites were unable to see that the Coloured population of South Africa would probably have identified with *Het Volk* if treated in a fashion that approached

35. George Orwell, "Marrakech," in Sonia Orwell and Ian Angus, eds., *The Collected Essays, Journalism and Letters of George Orwell*, vol. 1, *An Age Like This, 1920–1940* (New York: Harcourt, Brace and World, 1968), pp. 387–93.

fairness and equity. When it came time to draft enabling legislation to create a South African defense force, racist views
prevailed. Efforts were concentrated on the raising of a black
labor force, not an armed force.

An omnibus bill, drafted by the Minister of Defence, General Smuts, was gazetted, along with an official explanatory
commentary by the department, in November 1911.[36] The bill
was officially introduced into the House of Assembly in February 1912. The full scope of the bill cannot be discussed here.
Suffice to say that only one clause dealt with the racial issues.
Although the bill, in its opening passages, referred to "the
liability of every citizen to defend his country in time of grave
danger," another section of chapter 1 (clause 7) made provision
for excluding Coloured persons from wartime service in a
combatant capacity and from the peacetime training or financial contribution expected of white citizens.[37] This clause, however, became the subject of some criticism, especially by Coloured spokesmen, who were offended by the implied affront
to their loyalty and courage, and by some white supporters,
who wanted to have access to black manpower for defense. Col.
C. P. Crewe, for example, felt that although clause 7 did not
exclude black Africans and Coloured people "for all time, the
House had no right to exclude any volunteers at present,"
especially in light of the role of Coloureds as artillery drivers
in the Cape Mounted Rifles and as assistants in the Cape
Mounted Police then. Crewe felt that this clause would have to
be altered in Select Committee. Although he recognized that
"the chief burden of defence must for some time to come fall
upon the Europeans," he definitely wanted provision for voluntary service for blacks.[38] Smuts apparently was of the same
mind, and this bill ultimately reflected it. He had no intention
of "hurting the feelings of anyone in South Africa," he said. So
he took pains to point out that all that clause 7 provides "is
simply that no compulsion shall be laid on any coloured citizen

    36. Union of South Africa, Department of Defence, *Memorandum Explana-
tory of the South African Defence Bill (As Published in the Gazette, November 1911)*.
(Pretoria: Government Printing and Stationery Office, 1911).
    37. Ibid., p. 3. This was the only mention of race in that document.
    38. *Assembly Debates*, 23 February 1912, col. 651.

to serve or train in any military capacity, unless Parliament has otherwise decided. But no provision was laid down by which coloured citizens may not volunteer and offer services to the country, and a proposition like this will always be considered by the Government."[39] Nonetheless, such a guarantee would be meaningless if there were no units to which Coloureds could be assigned. The wily Smuts fully appreciated that for the opportunity to volunteer to have any practical meaning, a unit would have to be created in which Coloureds might serve. Thus the government would have final say on the use of Coloureds in a voluntary capacity. Smuts was to get the best of his opponents on this issue — by excluding Coloured persons from compulsory service he satisfied his Afrikaner critics who were wary of arming blacks. Yet by keeping voluntary service open to Coloureds, Smuts was able to harness their desire to bear arms on behalf of either the British empire or of South Africa, a country with which many wished to be identified. It must be recalled as well that in 1912 the issue in South Africa was not military manpower but economic manpower. Thus the government was not prepared to press the issue of bringing Coloureds into the Defence Force at that time.

The fact is that, as far as the Defence Bill was concerned, the issue of race as a matter of color as it is normally understood in the English-speaking world, had not exercised the white citizenry. By and large the bill passed easily. Where there had been controversy, it turned on other issues.[40] A more compelling and contentious question had been how to resolve the still

39. Ibid., col. 623. The precise wording of clause 7 is that "the liability" to render combatant service in wartime or to serve in various military training schemes "shall not be enforced against persons not of European descent, unless and until Parliament shall by resolution determine the extent to which any such liability shall be enforced against such persons: but nothing in this section contained shall be deemed to prevent the voluntary engagement at any time of such persons for service in any portion of the Defence Forces in such capacities and under such conditions as are prescribed." Union of South Africa, *Statutes, 1912,* act no. 13, clause 7.

40. See Kenneth W. Grundy, *Defense Legislation and Communal Politics: The Evolution of a White South African Nation as Reflected in the Controversy over the Assignment of Armed Forces Abroad, 1912–1976,* Papers in International Studies, Africa Series, no. 33 (Athens: Ohio University Center for International Studies, 1978), pp. 8–14.

smoldering ethnic split between Afrikaners and English speakers. It is ironic that South African society, obsessed as it is by race qua issues of color, should have labeled its chief division between whites a question of "race." Thus the meaning of *race* in the Defence Bill debate generally referred to the white ethnic schism. In Colonel Crewe's view, the bill "was going to weld the two races of South Africa together in the defence force. (Cheers.)"[41]

This meaning of *race* was the common South African usage in those days. Illustrative of this was General Smuts's congratulatory speech on the return of the victorious forces from South West Africa. Noting that the numbers of English and Dutch names were approximately equal among the fallen on the government side in both the expedition and in the rebellion that preceded the expedition, Smuts called it: "The first achievement of a united South African nation; both races have combined all their best and most virile characteristics."[42] This specific usage eventually faded in South Africa. But it does give one a perspective on what white South African elites regarded as the more pressing defense concern of that day. To what extent would Boers be compelled to fight on behalf of the empire they had just resisted so bitterly ten years before? Issues of voluntarism and compulsory service, taxes and levies, duration and terms of service, geographical limitations of service outside the borders of South Africa, and the command structures of various formations became more heated than the color issue, which seemed, at least for the time, to be settled and quiescent. Boers rightly sensed the danger of being pressed into service in defense of the British Empire. They saw a global conflict on the horizon (as did the English speakers). When it came, many Afrikaner nationalists sought to use the opportunity to reassert their independence of Great Britain.

World War I

Although South Africa now had its own defense force, it must be recalled that South Africa was technically not a sovereign

41. *Assembly Debates,* 23 February 1912, col. 651.
42. N. Levi, *Jan Smuts* (London: Longmans, Green, 1917), p. 256.

state but a part of the British Empire.[43] Within the terms of the
Defence Act of 1912 South African troops could be sent to
other territories of "South Africa" when it was deemed necessary by the British government. Britain's declaration of war,
therefore, included South Africa as a part of the empire. Of
course, the Union government was empowered to determine
the extent of South Africa's involvement, and since support for
Britain was a stated policy of the Botha government, South
Africa played an active part in the war. This revived the En-
glish-Afrikaner schism and led, in part, to a war on two fronts,
one external and one domestic.

Botha offered to help Great Britain by releasing the imperial
garrison. The British government accepted the offer and also
requested the Union to seize the harbors in German South
West Africa, immobilize German radio stations there, and occupy Windhoek. This involved mounting an expeditionary
force to fight outside the Union. Realizing that this would be
domestically explosive, yet under intense British and English-
speaking South African pressure, to say nothing of that from
General Smuts, Botha agreed to cooperate with the imperial
authorities and to send an expedition to South West Africa.

That decision precipitated an Afrikaner nationalist rebellion
that was suppressed within two months but at a cost of considerable and long-lived political enmity, both between ethnic
groups and within Afrikanerdom. It eventually led to the fall
of the Botha-Smuts government. The government's victory
against the rebels did little to suppress animosities. Afrikaners
did not rally to the flag.[44] And through this all, volunteer forces
were being raised to fight in South West Africa.

If one important segment of the white population was not
supportive of the South African war effort, the same cannot be
said of most blacks. The latter, for the most part, remained

43. S. B. Spies, "The Outbreak of the First World War and the Botha Government," *South African Historical Journal*, no. 1 (November 1969): 47–57.

44. T. R. H. Davenport, "The South African Rebellion, 1914," *English Historical Review*, 77 (January 1963): 73–94; and N. G. Garson, "The Boer Rebellion of 1914," *History Today* 12 (February 1962): 132–39. According to the
official Rolls of Honour in the House of Assembly, only 770 Afrikaners died in
World War I, compared to 7,544 English speakers. *The Star* (Weekly Air Edition), 12 November 1977, p. 6.

loyal to Britain during the war. If blacks occasionally resented their wartime duties, it was largely because the Union government invariably interceded. That government certainly sensed that it would have to keep a tight rein on any black contributions to the war effort. This they attempted to do with persistence, much to the consternation of the British and of the blacks themselves.

At the war's outbreak, for example, mineworkers pledged themselves to refrain from industrial strike action. The African Native National Congress (the predecessor of the African National Congress) decided not to criticize the government publicly, while continuing its campaign to secure a fair distribution of land under terms of the Natives Land Act of 1913.[45] Its leaders left a special conference on the Natives Land Act to offer their services to the government of Pretoria. They too wanted to be allowed to "cast a few stones at the Germans."[46] The Rev. W. B. Rubusana in 1914 offered to accompany a force of 5,000 "able bodied men" to German South West Africa. The Secretary of Defence, citing section 7 of the Defence Act, stated that the "Government does not desire to avail itself of the services, in a combatant capacity, of citizens not of European descent in the present hostilities." The Secretary went on, "The present war is one which has its origins among the white people of Europe and the Government are anxious to avoid the employment of its native citizens in warfare against whites."[47] Little did these offers achieve. Pretoria did not budge and London refused to intervene in South Africa's "do-

45. S. E. Katzenellenbogen, "Southern Africa and the War of 1914– 18," in M. R. D. Foot, ed., *War and Society: Historical Essays in Honour and Memory of J. R. Western, 1928 – 1971* (New York: Barnes and Noble, 1973), p. 114.

46. H. J. and R. E. Simons, *Class and Colour in South Africa, 1850 – 1950* (Baltimore: Penguin, 1969), p. 176.

47. Department of Defence to W. B. Rubusana, 6 November 1914, quoted in B. P. Willan, "The South African Native Labour Contingent, 1916– 1918," *Journal of African History*, 19 (March, 1978): 63. Note as well a reference to this rejection in the ANNC's memorial to George V in 1918, reprinted in Thomas Karis and Gwendolen M. Carter, eds., *From Protest to Challenge: A Documentary History of African Politics in South Africa, 1882 – 1964*, vol. 1, *Protest and Hope, 1882 – 1934*, ed. Sheridan Johns, III (Stanford, Calif.: Hoover Institution Press, 1972), p. 138.

mestic" racial affairs, either during the war or upon its termination.

As for the Coloured community, the African Political Organization (APO) pledged to be loyal to His Majesty's Imperial
Government and to maintain the security and integrity of the
empire. The APO had been founded in 1902 as a national
political party open to persons of all races, but throughout its
existence it was predominantly Coloured, centered in the
Western Cape, and concerned mostly with Coloured affairs.
The APO declared in 1914 that black citizens must endure
their domestic burdens in silence and prove themselves no less
worthy than the empire's other sons.[48] Leaders of the APO
undertook to raise a Coloured war relief fund and offered to
organize a corps of 5,000 men for active military service. Some
13,000 volunteered within a month.[49] The government turned
down their offers to serve, insisting that this was a "white man's
war." More importantly, the government appreciated the dangerous political costs associated with steps to arm blacks in
white South Africa.

Then, with the outbreak of the rebellion in October 1914,
the APO repeated its offer to raise a corps and was again
refused. The Coloureds in the northwest Cape requested arms
to defend themselves against the rebels. That too was politely
declined. The familiar "white man's war" argument (the same
as from the Anglo-Boer War) was reiterated.[50] A "white man's
war" to be sure, but elsewhere in Africa and in Europe blacks
were being deployed.[51]

In reality the government most feared the political reverber-
ations. South African whites were especially sensitive to the
symbolism and precedent attending the arming of blacks. According to the *East Rand Express:* "The empire must uphold the
principle that a coloured man must not raise a hand against a
white man if there is to be any law or order in either India,

48. 8 August 1914; cited in Simons, *Class and Colour*, p. 176.
49. 5 September 1914; ibid.
50. 14 November 1914; ibid., p. 177.
51. See the special issue of the *Journal of African History* 19 (March 1978)
devoted to this subject.

Africa, or any part of the Empire where the white man rules over a large concourse of coloured people. In South Africa it will mean that Natives will secure pictures of whites chased by coloured men, and who knows what harm such pictures can do?"[52] Had it not been for the government's skittishness in employing armed blacks, large numbers might have signed on. Some Coloureds, passing for white, did enlist in white units. A few, at their own expense, embarked for England, where they enlisted for active combat. A frustrated APO lamented that South African whites would rather see the empire fall than place Coloured men in the firing line.[53] But they kept trying, taking the occasion of each rebuff to make propaganda points: "Thrice we offered our services, and thrice they were refused. We can not do more." So they prayed for a peace that would bring "true British liberty and justice" and not the sort of system that would enact a Natives Land Act, take away franchise rights, or ban men as outcasts.[54]

After the rebellion Botha led an expeditionary force into South West Africa. There some 33,556 Coloureds and Africans served in noncombat capacities.[55] All but 1,326 from Bechuanaland and 58 from Basutoland were South Africans. Additional South African blacks were engaged independently and were taken to South West Africa by units or as individuals. One must also include the Native Artillery Drivers in the South African Field Artillery and other gunner units. Likewise, South Westers, including Herero and Bondelswart, served as scouts and laborers. The Germans, of course, made wide use of black forces in both South West and East Africa. But South Africa's victory in that territory did not help either the black population of South West Africa or that of South Africa itself.

The conclusion of hostilities in South West Africa did free up

52. As quoted in Willan, "The South African Native Labour Contingent," pp. 63–64.

53. 12 June 1915; Simons, *Class and Colour,* p. 178.

54. 7 August 1915; ibid.

55. Union of South Africa, General Staff, Defence Headquarters, *The Union of South Africa and the Great War, 1914–1918: Official History* (Pretoria: Government Printing and Stationery Office, 1924), p. 218. A further 18,000 laborers later served in East Africa. See W. M. Bisset, "Unexplored Aspects of South Africa's First World War History," *Militaria* 6 (1976): 55–61.

troops for operations further afield, and the more distant from South Africa proper, the more latitude commanders might have felt they had in permitting blacks and especially Coloureds a more active combat role. Coloureds hoped that in East Africa, the Middle East, or Europe Coloured combatants would be less obvious and perhaps less offensive to white racial susceptibilities and domestic political constraints. Again Coloured leaders petitioned for the right to fight. After all, they posited, no South African army would be representative of that country unless it included a Coloured contingent.

In September 1915 Coloured leaders were informed that Pretoria had relented. The government had offered, with British agreement, the formation of a volunteer Coloured infantry corps for active combat duties under the Imperial War Council. South Africa, however, insisted that it was to be officered by white South Africans. Dr. Abdul Abdurahman, the president of APO from 1905 until 1940, was appointed to a recruiting committee, and he urged his people to join the ranks. "Today the Empire needs us. What nobler duty is there than to respond to the call of your King and Country?"[56]

Under the name Cape Corps eventually two battalions of infantry were raised. Altogether, almost 18,000 members of the Cape Corps were in East Africa.[57] These men were technically regarded as imperial troops and were paid by the British government. At first, in February 1916, the First Battalion Cape Corps was sent to East and Central Africa, where it gained valuable noncombatant experience under arduous conditions.[58] This first group consisted of 32 European officers and 1,022 Coloured in other ranks.[59] Upon return from the East African theater in 1917 the regiment was reorganized and prepared for combat services, and a second battalion was es-

56. 18 September 1915; Simons, *Class and Colour*, p. 179.

57. Most accounts put the figure at 18,000, but J. Ploeger and F. J. Jacobs, "Die Kleurlingsoldaat (2)," *Paratus* 27 (October 1976): 23, mention 7,000. Eric Rosenthal lists 1,925 Coloured troop enlistments (Rosenthal, ed., *Encyclopaedia of Southern Africa*, 4th ed. [London and New York: Frederick Warne, 1967], p. 626). I have been unable to reconcile these discrepancies in the published accounts.

58. Ploeger and Jacobs, "Die Kleurlingsoldaat (2)," pp. 22–23.

59. "Notes on the Military History," p. 8.

tablished. Later, after its role in East Africa slackened, the Second Battalion was disbanded, and members were transferred to Egypt in April 1918 to strengthen the First Battalion. From the Egyptian base it participated in the Palestinian campaign. At the battle of Square Hill in September 1918, the First Battalion fought commendably.[60] They captured the position and suffered 152 casualties during the engagement. When General Allenby paraded triumphantly through Jerusalem he gave the Coloured troops the place of honor behind his white horse and said: "No man can have the honour to command men of better fettle than the men of the Cape Corps of South Africa."[61] The Corps and many of its members earned honors and decorations, as well as statements of appreciation from diverse quarters. In the war 450 officers and men of the First Cape Corps died in action.

The Cape Auxiliary Horse Transport (around 2,800 drivers) and the Cape Coloured Labour Corps were also raised and sent to the Western Front in Europe. Some members of the Cape Corps also served with the South African Field Artillery. After the war, in 1919, all these units were demobilized and disbanded. As a meek gesture of gratitude the band alone was allowed to continue in existence through the interwar period.

The other large scale black contribution to the war effort came in the form of the South African Native Labour Contingent (SANLC).[62] Between September 1916 and January 1918 some 25,000 black Southern Africans (including men from the High Commission Territories) enlisted for noncombatant labor in support of the British forces in France, and 21,000 were assigned to Europe. British authorities were quite pleased with their work, which was mostly work on the docks in French ports, work building roads, work on railways, and other behind-the-lines assignments. Formation of the SANLC originated in an Imperial War Council session in June 1916, when it

60. Ibid., pp. 8– 11.
61. Quoted by H. W. Holland in *Assembly Debates,* 5 May 1969, col. 5308. See also Ploeger and Jacobs, "Die Kleurlingsoldaat (2),"pp. 22– 23; Tylden, *The Armed Forces,* p. 50. That battle is still memorialized each year in Cape Town.
62. Most of the data in this section come from Willan, "The South African Native Labour Contingent," pp. 61– 86.

was suggested that black African laborers from South Africa and other parts of Africa should be recruited and sent to France to relieve labor shortages there. The South African government agreed to form such a unit, provided it could maintain direction and control of the force. This was a hot issue. But because the expenses of the "experiment" (both the Cape Corps and the SANLC were referred to as "experiments") were to be assumed by Great Britain, General Botha was able to begin to mobilize blacks without referring the matter to the South African House of Assembly, where opposition was bound to be voiced.

Despite initial enthusiasm for the project among blacks and their leaders, and despite the government's involvement of black leaders in consultative and recruiting capacities, the recruiting campaign met with poor response. By mid-1917 the South African authorities began lacing appeals to patriotism with heady dollops of compulsion. In some cases local chiefs were required and enticed to supply a quota of recruits. Yet in addition to superstition about service beyond the seas, most Africans rightly realized that this was a South African government effort, not strictly an imperial one. The Department of Native Affairs had organized the recruitment, and many of their most disliked officials (at local as well as provincial and national levels) were associated with the drive. The workers reasoned that their conditions would be substantially the same abroad as in South Africa. Why, then, leave home and family for little additional gain? Moreover, many employers, farmers, and the Chamber of Mines, inter alia, resisted the enlistment campaign. They feared labor shortages, and they discouraged their workers and the recruiters. To many employers, including those of British origin, the war effort and the profit motive were two sides of the same coin. In conditions of finite manpower, in their minds, the profit motive took precedence. Since this was a period of economic boom, as South African products helped sustain the British economy and, hence, war effort, keeping black laborers in South Africa was not so unpatriotic, after all.

In France pains were taken to maintain strict segregation

between the SANLC workers and other forces and civilians. Still, SANLC personnel could not be totally isolated, and many blacks returned "contaminated" with foreign notions about race relations and other social grievances. Such dissatisfactions led to a premature decision by the South African government to end the "experiment" in January 1918. Although the government insisted that it arrived at its decision for "reasons of a purely military nature," many saw politics underlying it. Parliament was soon to reassemble. National Party members had already in the preceding session raised awkward questions indicating their opposition to SANLC. Reports from Europe indicated that in practice South African control of the Contingent was not as complete as they had wanted. "Incidents" of disciplinary and racial confrontation had been reported by officers. African political consciousness was being awkwardly raised and the authorities aimed to nip it early. Despite continuing labor shortages in Europe the South African government decided to terminate their SANLC experiment. Official appreciative expressions of praise and of "the high commendation earned by the contingent"[63] notwithstanding, the experiment had not ended as had at first been expected. Praise words are cheap. Many Africans in SANLC were bitterly disappointed, and they resented the fact that despite their sacrifices they were awarded no medals or ribbons. There was no tangible demonstration of gratitude for their contribution. This was compounded by the fact that blacks from the High Commission Territories who served in the same and similar units were issued medals, as were blacks who served in South West Africa and those attached to the South African Artillery and the S.A. Mounted Rifles.

Most South African blacks must have realized that their service in World War I, in whatever unit they were eligible for, would have been in positions subordinate to whites. If traditional South African segregation patterns would prevail in the military, why risk one's life fighting or working on behalf of either the Crown or the South African government? Certainly all blacks did not volunteer for the same reasons, and the re-

63. General Staff, *Official History*, pp. 218–19.

cord shows that not all blacks were persuaded to sign up. Among various leaders different factors mattered. Many were patriotic and identified with the imperial war effort. War often brings out heretofore unrealized patriotism. Loyalty in these cases was genuine and spontaneous. Duty, adventure, and escape beckoned, and the prospect of a new beginning and of social mobility might have blossomed in these circumstances. Black African and Coloured leaders were, by and large, drawn from the ranks of intellectuals, clergymen, and small businessmen. Their desire to participate may not have always represented the wishes of their kinsmen and followers. Some leaders might well have been trying to ingratiate themselves to the authorities — seeking, in a way, future favors for current services rendered. Their exertions in recruitment cost them little and may actually have earned them direct payments while demonstrating their loyalty to the regime. Some surely hoped for personal advancement as a reward. Others may have hoped for and expected their people to be compensated in social and economic terms for their war efforts. Some indeed spoke of expected improvements in their economic, political, and civil rights on their return. Some made their message even more direct.

The African Native National Congress sent a deputation to England in 1919, and they submitted a memorial to George V. In it they reminded him of the contributions of African workers in various campaigns and of the loss of over six hundred men when the S.S. *Mendi* was sunk in the Channel. They quoted to the king his 1917 speech to the SANLC in Abbeville, in which he called them "part of my great Armies which are fighting for the liberty and freedom of my subjects of all races and creeds throughout my Empire." They also reminded him of the words of the governor general of the Union, Lord Buxton, who promised that such loyalty "will not be forgotten."[64] The ANNC were, in effect, calling his hand. But the Congress

64. On the *Mendi* disaster see Marischal Murray, *Ships and South Africa: A Maritime Chronicle of the Cape* (London: Oxford University Press, Humphrey Milford, 1933), pp. 113– 14. Full text of the memorial is in Karis and Carter, eds., *From Protest*, 1:137–42.

deputation was not permitted to be heard at Versailles. Instead, it was informed by the British Colonial Office that the
government could not interfere in the internal affairs of the
Union of South Africa.[65] So much for patriotism, loyalty, and
sacrifice. Black political leaders repeatedly made reference to
their people's role in the war and contrasted that to their treatment at the hands of the South African authorities. "Look, we
have been assisting the Kingdom [note: not the South African
government] in these great wars and many of our children,
fathers, and brothers have died in the war or have sunk in the
sea. So why can't we have our freedom just the same as any
other nation?"[66] Officially, 5,635 "Non-Europeans" died in the
war.[67] Yet conditions back home were not improved for the
black Africans or for the Coloureds.

   In other respects the impact of war service upon blacks was
not inconsequential. The psychological dimension mattered,
too. As one member of the SANLC put it:

> We were aware, when we returned, that we were different from
> the other people at home. Our behaviour, as we showed the
> South Africans, was something more than they expected from a
> Native, more like what was expected among them of a white
> man.[68]

Some whites must have sensed the change. One white officer
was reported to have uttered: "When you people get back to
South Africa, don't start thinking that you are whites, just because this place [France] has spoiled you. You are black, and
you will stay black. . . ."[69] Indeed, South African race relations
had changed little because of the war, and although the black
effort may have been appreciated by some whites, it didn't
bring about a change in the way most whites dealt with "their"
blacks.

   65. Leo Kuper, "African Nationalism in South Africa, 1910–1964," in
Wilson and Thompson, eds., *Oxford History,* 2:439.
   66. From a police report of a meeting of the Transvaal Native Congress,
1919, quoted in Willan, "The South African Native Labour Contingent," pp.
84–85.
   67. *The Star* (Weekly Air Edition), 12 November 1977, p. 6.
   68. Jason Jingoes, in John and Cassandra Perry, eds., *A Chief Is a Chief by the
People* (Oxford: Oxford University Press, 1975), p. 92.
   69. Ibid., pp. 92–93.

How did the government evaluate its "experiments"? The early end to the SANLC and the demise of the Cape Corps are two examples of their continued distrust of blacks organized for military purposes. For some officials, the experience was favorable. Their impressions of blacks as fighters and laborers had been positive. Lt. Commander W. Whittall said that he had "great respect and admiration for the native soldier; whether he be King's African Rifleman or German Askari, he is as good a fighting man as you would ask to have beside you in a tight corner. . . ."[70]

In letters from the war zones these views were repeated. Capt. A. J. Molloy, for example, wrote to a friend in April 1916:

> We have a lot to learn in the way of bush fighting from our black enemies, and that in spite of all talk to the contrary, we have found them an enemy to be fully reckoned with. He is resourceful, brave and well trained for this kind of fighting. I have heard he is a bad shot, but the casualties in action prove the opposite. He is however a brute and does not hesitate to mutilate and kill all wounded or prisoners. I don't think the Germans put much restraint on this peculiarity. They would be nowhere without him, the "Askari" as he is called.

He also praised the soldiers produced in India and the King's African Rifles from East Africa as "excellent soldiers."[71] In Molloy's account, however, there is conspicuously no mention of various black units fielded by the South Africans.

Smuts also spoke of the value of native troops, their ability to resist disease in tropical climes, and their "great military value."[72] The General Staff's *Official History* of the "Great War" and a number of regimental histories usually speak in positive and sometimes glowing terms when they do refer to black soldiers and laborers. Yet at the bottom line prejudices seemed only to be reinforced. Smuts repeatedly warned against the use

70. W. Whittall, *With Botha and Smuts in Africa* (London: Cassell, 1917), pp. 184–86.

71. Letter from Capt. (later Maj.) A. J. Molloy to Middleton dated 7 April 1916 (Military Museum, The Castle, Cape Town), as quoted in Bisset, "Unexplored Aspects," p. 59.

72. René Kraus, *Old Master: The Life of Jan Christian Smuts* (New York: E. P. Dutton, 1944), pp. 253–54; and Jan Christiaan Smuts, *Toward a Better World* (New York: Duell, Sloan, and Pearce, 1944), p. 15.

of blacks. He feared drilling them and "teaching them the arts of war, as the Germans were doing."[73] After he returned from the East African campaign, he warned a British audience:

> I must say that my experience in East Africa has opened my eyes to many very serious dangers that threaten the future, not only of Southern Africa, but also of Europe. We have seen, as we have seen before, what enormously valuable material lay in the Black Continent.

He went on to speak of the German plan to create a great Central African Empire,

> in which it would be possible to train one of the most powerful black armies of the world.
> We were not aware of the great military value of the natives until this war. This war has been an eye-opener in many new directions . . . . I hope that one of the results of this war will be some arrangement or convention among the nations interested in Central Africa by which the military training of natives in that area will be prevented, as we have prevented it in South Africa. It can well be foreseen that armies may yet be trained there, which under proper leading might prove a danger to civilisation itself.[74]

There are hints here of the so-called African Charter proposed by D. F. Malan in the late 1940s and 1950s. Although the government had agreed, out of necessity and because of external pressures, to employ blacks in various military capacities, there had been little real satisfaction on the part of the government with the experiment. It merely had been a lesser of evils to be ended as soon as possible and to be resisted again should the need arise.

Throughout this early period of South African history military formations and structures emerged from a dualistic heritage of political domination. South Africa is a society founded by settlers from Europe who conquered and dominated the indigenous black peoples in the region. In addition to the settler presence, however, there has been a considerable imperial presence from Great Britain, possessing a different conception of dominance and a different set of economic and political

73. A 1915 speech; see Levi, *Smuts*, p. 281.
74. Speech at the Savoy Hotel, London, 22 May 1917, in Smuts, *Toward a Better World*, pp. 14–15.

objectives. No wonder, then, that these two overbearing forces should have evolved slightly differing approaches to the governance of the indigenous peoples and to their military utility.

Imperial and colonial authorities have historically made wide use of an indigenous soldiery to defend selected parts of their empires. The crucial variable has been control, not necessarily the pigmentation of the ranks. Whether the command structure remained firmly in imperial hands was chiefly what mattered. Questions of expense, convenience, manpower shortages, metropolitan political considerations, and efficiency and speed in fielding an armed force all have prompted imperial use of "native troops." Such troops were hardly mercenaries. They were not well paid, except purely in the context of the colonial or indigenous economies. Nor were they always free agents. Indeed, they were occasionally press-ganged into service by compliant traditional leaders in the pay of or anxious to ingratiate themselves to the imperial authorities. In most respects they were compelled, either physically or by existing circumstances, into serving foreign masters against what many indigenes might have regarded as equally foreign peoples who just happened to live in the same territory or to have the same color skin but who were of different nations or ethnic groups.

Through much of the Boer and British settler history a similar colonial pattern prevailed. It is true that the Boers would have preferred not to have to use the indigenous peoples for military manpower. But for various purposes they felt they must. As long as this use was against other indigenous peoples their misgivings could be put to rest. But, nonetheless, given their sense of permanence in the area, settlers were most reluctant to have to depend on black military assistance and were positively fearful of the psychological and political precedents that might be read into such steps. So they resisted such policies unless they were absolutely necessary to defend their own settlements. In this important respect Boers and British imperialists came upon the issue from opposing directions.

Greater divergence in approach emerged as a result of the issue of the use of blacks to defend the empire against fellow whites. If the empire's enemies also used black forces, some of this resistance might have fallen away. But in the Anglo-Boer War a sort of instinctive racial sympathy grew up among white contestants. The Boer War was a "white man's war," and little would be gained in the long run by enlisting blacks to fight whites, even if other whites were the immediate "enemy." In such a struggle the long-range enemy was identified, at least tacitly, by the policies that emerged, and the ultimate enemy was clearly not always the groups of whites that pointed the rifles at one another from across the line.

As such a mentality became increasingly shared by Boer and British settler and by the British authorities who were influenced by their "kith and kin" in Africa, it became easy for white South Africans to refer to a "tradition" of not arming the blacks, the record notwithstanding. This set the tone for the establishment in the interwar period, although in fact it had been begun with the Defence Act of 1912, of what Pierre van den Berghe has called a "Herrenvolk army." In his view such an army is a "relatively egalitarian natural vigilante system for the perpetuation of a racial caste society" and is one with a relatively low degree of professionalism.[75] To a large extent this formula was breached in World War I by the insistence and sheer desperation of the British Empire, which was accustomed to the pattern of imperial armies based on indigenous manpower. To call the Union Defence Force during the interwar period a "Herrenvolk army" may be premature, for in South Africa of this time the idea of an Afrikaner-dominated white "nation" had itself not as yet congealed.[76] Still, the ideal of a "nation-at-arms" or of a white "people's army" was not unpopular with whites in South Africa. It is a term, strangely enough, that is used by the government today. To be sure, the Union Defence Force was maintained at a very low state of readiness during the interwar years, and it made few demands on the white citizenry. But the military and the police represented the coercive arm of the state and, as such, assumed an integral part in the imagery of white dominance.

75. Pierre van den Berghe, "The Military and Political Change in Africa," in Claude Welch, ed., *Soldier and State in Africa* (Evanston: Northwestern University Press, 1970), pp. 252–66.
76. See Grundy, *Defense Legislation,* passim.

3

The Manpower Crisis of
World War II and
the Government's Dilemma

AFTER WORLD WAR I the various black formations,
except for the Cape Corps band, were discontinued with the
general demobilization. The South African armed forces fell
on hard times during the interwar period. Budgetary shrink-
age regularly hampered the development of a permanent military organization. Pay scales were reduced to the point that the
Union Defence Force (UDF) could not compete with jobs in
the civil sector. Regulars resigned in droves. The depression
compounded the problem.

Except during the 1922 campaign in which some 14,000
Active Citizen Force members were deployed to control the
striking mine workers on the Witwatersrand, and during some
harshly punitive expeditions against various peoples in South
West Africa, the military appeared to many a somewhat expensive indulgence. In 1938 the Minister of Defence announced
plans to reorganize the Defence Force, but before his plans
could be acted upon, the war in Europe exploded, and South
Africa quickly became involved.

The fact is that the Defence Force was in an abominable state

of readiness.[1] Minister of Defence Oswald Pirow had allowed it
to deteriorate. At the beginning of the war the army consisted
of only 313 Permanent Force officers and 3,040 men in other
ranks (it was supposed to contain 5,385 men), plus around
14,631 Citizen Force men. There were another 1,800 in the air
force and 432 in the navy.[2] Equipment and supplies were inadequate, obsolete, and not well-maintained. In short, when
Gen. Smuts assumed leadership of the government and took
over the defence portfolio in September 1939 he had to re-
build his Defence Force practically from scratch.

The Debate

The drama that accompanied South Africa's decision to reject
a wartime policy of neutrality and to declare war on Germany
should not concern us here. What is important is that the
depths of rancor and hatred caused by the war issue and the
way it had been resolved, not just between English speakers
and Afrikaners but within Afrikanerdom itself, meant that
virtually every policy issue, either in Parliament or, if somehow
Parliament could be bypassed, outside those chambers, became divisive and threatening to the parties concerned.[3] Gall
and wormwood attended every confrontation. So Smuts's job
of organizing the defense forces was complicated by the
conflict of unreconciled nationalists throughout the land.

When the idea was broached that blacks might be pressed
into military service the nationalists became enraged. It was
bad enough for the nationalists that South Africa should be

1. J.S.M. Simpson, *South Africa Fights* (London: Hodder and Stoughton,
1941), pp. 94–101; G.H. Calpin, *There Are No South Africans* (London:
Thomas Nelson and Sons, 1941); Alexander Campbell, *Smuts and Swastika*
(London: Victor Gollancz, 1943); Leslie Blackwell, *Farewell to Parliament: More
Reminiscences of Bench, Bar, Parliament and Travel* (Pietermaritzburg: Shuter
and Shooter, 1946), pp. 94–104; and W.K. Hancock, *Smuts,* vol. 2, *The Fields
of Force, 1919–1950* (Cambridge: Cambridge University Press, 1968), pp.
328–32.

2. Deon Fourie, "South African Forces in World War II," *New Nation* 2 (July
1969): 19.

3. An account of the decision appears in Kenneth W. Grundy, *Defense
Legislation and Communal Politics: The Evolution of a White South African Nation as
Reflected in the Controversy over the Assignment of Armed Forces Abroad, 1912–*

mobilizing for a war in support of the hated British and against the National Socialist Reich, whose ideas so paralleled some of their own. That a South African government should even consider employing blacks in this war alarmed them just as much. The nationalist view, expressed by Pirow in 1933 when he had been Minister of Defence, was infused with the general spirit of resistance to the first hints of decolonization and liberalism throughout the colonies to the north.[4] In those "vast territories," he lamented, were governments "diametrically opposed to our policy of differentiation between black and white." There, "hundreds of thousands of black men [were] being trained into some of the finest fighting material in the world." It stood to reason that conflicting policies might lead to armed clashes between South Africa and its African neighbors. The time might come when whites would have to be protected against "black invaders."

The nationalists opposed any devolution of authority or responsibility to blacks, either in the civil or in the military service. In reality this position varied little from Smuts's view that blacks should not be armed lest civilization itself be placed in jeopardy. The nationalists wanted absolutely no military use made of blacks. This followed from their ideological concerns at that time. Smuts probably arrived at this position pragmatically, politically, as he tested the waters of white South African opinion. Smuts himself saw positive utility in using black manpower, but he realized that he could never sell white voters on the need for blacks to be armed.

South Africa was a country with limited white manpower, and all parties recognized that. In the past, volunteer brigades and units could not possibly have been maintained without the input of black manpower. A calculation of white manpower available in October 1940 re<koned that there were 251,519

1976, Papers in International Studies, Africa Series, no. 33 (Athens: Ohio University Center for International Studies, 1978), pp. 23 – 24; and in Newell M. Stultz, *Afrikaner Politics in South Africa* (Berkeley: University of California Press, 1974), pp. 60 – 66.

4. Oswald Pirow, quoted in Sam C. Nolutshungu, *South Africa in Africa: A Study in Ideology and Foreign Policy* (Manchester: Manchester University Press, 1975), pp. 62 – 64.

men in the 18 – 44 age group. Initial requirements for a Mobile Field Force (including coastal and home defense) were set at 140,973 men.[5] Taking into account possible casualties, it was felt that at least 209,000 white males would be needed for the first year of active service. Although initial white recruitment met with some success, it was clear to all that the services of blacks were urgently needed. Moreover, by early 1941 it became apparent that the Defence Force was scraping the bottom of the barrel as the twin demands for military as well as industrial manpower began to be felt.

When pressures were brought to bear on the government to permit "natives and coloured people to take part in the war," Smuts said that due to "the circumstances prevailing in South Africa" there was no choice but to bring them into the service. Still, he insisted, "it was out of the question to arm them."[6] Instead, he argued that it "has become customary" in South Africa "for natives to be used for that kind of work" [i.e., menial labor behind the lines]. At that point, under Nationalist prompting, Smuts promised unequivocally that blacks would not be armed. "I cannot conceive of anything which would have the effect of creating even greater discord among us, greater quarrels and greater division among the people than the arming of coloured people or the native population of the Union."[7] But South Africans should, he went on, recognize that their views are rather "unique," not shared by many others in this world. He hinted that a reconsideration might be in order if in the future "a great nation were to attack us with the aid of black armies."[8] Yet no matter what he said, he could not assuage the distrust and sense of betrayal the Afrikaner nationalists felt for him. Even within his own camp plenty of English speakers and Afrikaners would not abide the arming of nonwhites. Smuts knew well that he had to move warily around the issue.

From the beginning blacks pressed for a larger role in de-

5. H. J. Martin and Neil D. Orpen, *South African Forces, World War II*, vol. 7, *South Africa at War* (Cape Town: Purnell, 1979), p. 70.
6. *Assembly Debates*, 15 April 1940, col. 5007.
7. Ibid., col. 5008.
8. Ibid., col. 5009.

fense. The APO was weak by this time and provided no leadership to the Coloured community, but Coloured ex-servicemen promised Smuts their unqualified support, although they also made clear that they would prefer to serve as combatants. Some light-skinned Coloureds enlisted as whites in the Cape Scottish Highlanders.[9] Some Indians, on the other hand, were impressed by Nehru's dictum not to fight on behalf of the empire until full independence was promised.

Three days after war's outbreak the National Executive Committee of the ANC (African National Congress) issued a circular stating that it would support the war on condition that: (1) the government provide "military training whereby our men shall not only be used as labourers but as soldiers" and (2) "the African people are included in the South African Body Politic and Defence Schemes."[10]

The ANC had difficulty throughout the war formulating a consistent and widely acceptable policy on black involvement in the war. At their December 1939 meeting the Resolution Committee took a hard line — the ANC would not support the government unless the government granted "full democratic and citizen rights" to blacks and until the government armed African soldiers.[11] That proposal was drastically amended by the President-General, Rev. Z. R. Mahabana. In the end, a less forceful Congress declared that:

> The African National Congress ... desires to record its conviction that the decision of the Union Parliament in favour of a declaration of war on the side of Great Britain was correct. Further, Congress endorses the action of representatives of the African people in Parliament in voting against the neutrality motion. ...
>
> The time has arrived when the Union Government and Parliament should consider the expediency of admitting the African

9. H. J. and R. E. Simons, *Class and Colour in South Africa, 1850–1950* (Baltimore: Penguin, 1969), p. 531.

10. 6 September 1939; quoted in Brian Bunting, *Moses Kotane, South African Revolutionary: A Political Biography* (London: Inkululeko Publications, 1975), p. 101.

11. Edward Roux, *Time Longer than Rope: A History of the Black Man's Struggle for Freedom in South Africa* (Madison: University of Wisconsin Press, 1964), pp. 304 – 5; and Bunting, *Kotane*, pp. 101 – 2.

and other Non-European races . . . into the full citizenship of the
Union. . . .

The territorial integrity of the Union of South Africa can only
be effectively defended if all sections of the population were
included in the defence system of the country on equal terms,
and that those who are or may be eligible for military service shall
receive military training in all its aspects. Further, the Defence
Act should be so amended as to remove all colour bar restrictions
in the recruitment for the Defence Forces.[12]

In the Native Representative Council set up by a 1936 act,
Councillor R. H. Godlo moved that "Council requests the Union Parliament to consider the advisability of amending the
Defence Act of 1912 so as to open the door to all loyal South
Africans, irrespective of race and colour, to take part in any
sphere of hostilities for the defence of their common country."
Despite the advisory, nonbinding character of Council resolu-
tions, the motion was thrown out.[13] Other bodies tried to add
their voices. In December 1939 the Non-European United
Front demanded the right of blacks to bear arms and fight on
an equal basis alongside Europeans. In July 1940 the execu-
tives of the ANC and the All African Convention jointly passed
a resolution calling for a number of improvements in the rights
of blacks and repeating a call for full participation in defense.[14]

On a number of occasions the ANC sought to embarrass the
government. They pointed out inconsistencies between the
call to support the war effort and the repressive racial policies
within the Union. They made their declared support of the
war effort conditional upon the arming of blacks in the Defence Force. They called for some installment of expanded
citizenship rights in return for their action in good faith. But
there was no large-scale movement by blacks to withhold cooperation. Such a step might have had important political effects
domestically in Smuts's hour of need. But government still
could ignore their pleas, and instead it signed on thousands of
black Africans in noncombat roles.

12. *Guardian* (Cape Town), 26 January 1940; quoted in Bunting, *Kotane*,
p. 102.
13. Bunting, *Kotane*, p. 103.
14. Ibid., pp. 101–3.

If ANC was unsure of its position, especially early in the war, the Communist Party of South Africa (SACP) was worse — weak, inconsistent, and externally manipulated. Before the war, in keeping with the international communist doctrine, they pushed for a "popular front" policy of cooperation with all democratic forces opposing fascism. After the Nazi-Soviet Pact of 1939 South African Communists began to campaign against the military recruitment of black laborers.[15] Several leading Communists were prosecuted and interned for hampering the war effort. But in June 1941 the Wehrmacht invaded the Soviet Union, and, as if on signal, the SACP rallied to the defense of Moscow. Propaganda against black recruitment was terminated, and in its place came the slogan "Arm the non-European soldiers" and a "Defend South Africa" campaign.[16] Listeners were told to defeat the fascists first, and then oppression in South Africa could be shattered. If Hitler were to win in Europe, the oppressed people elsewhere in the world would suffer even more. Moses Kotane's speech to a May Day rally in Johannesburg in 1942 was representative:

> I say: Africans must be armed! Africa is your country. Where else can you go? If you say it was stolen from you, see that no one messes around with it! Demand arms for its defence!
> Only if you know how to use a gun can you fight those who will not give you freedom. Some may tell you that the Japanese are Coloured people and will give you freedom. But it is not a question of colour — Japan oppresses her people. . . .
> Stand together! Demand arms![17]

This was not simply supportive of the war effort; it was a call to arms, and some whites were alarmed that it had gone too far. They demanded government action against the Communist Party on the grounds it was inciting blacks to rebellion.

Meanwhile, Smuts and his government may have been wavering. At the time when Smuts assured Parliament that blacks

15. See, for example, the June 1940 SACP pamphlet *Must We Fight?* cited in Bunting, *Kotane*, p. 97; Roux, *Time Longer than Rope*, p. 308.

16. Roux, *Time Longer than Rope*, p. 309; note the SACP pamphlet *Arm the People* (1942) in Bunting, *Kotane*, pp. 109–10; see also the SACP's *Communist Plan for Victory* (1943) cited in Simons, *Class and Colour*, pp. 537–38.

17. As quoted in Bunting, *Kotane*, p. 110.

would not be armed, he was also taking steps to reestablish the
Cape Corps and the Indian Service Corps. Black Africans were
organized a short time later. Late in 1941 and early in 1942 the
strategic situation appeared to be desperate. Australia was preparing for a Japanese invasion. Rangoon and Singapore had
fallen. The Japanese had broken into the Indian Ocean, and
nothing the British or Americans did seemed to stop them.
South Africa braced for an attack. At this point Smuts made his
famous "retreat from segregation" speech at the Cape Town
City Hall. "Isolation has gone," he declared, "and I am afraid
segregation has fallen on evil days."[18] Liberals took this as a hint
that changes in South African race policies were imminent.
Smuts followed this speech by declaring in Parliament that
"before Japan, before the enemy, takes this country, I shall see
to it that every native and every coloured man who can be
armed will be armed. It will help us to know that if the struggle
comes to our coasts and frontiers, we will not be alone. I will
train and arm any non-European prepared to help defend
South Africa. I have not the slightest doubt whatsoever that the
bulk of our people agree with me in this attitude."[19] In fact he
must have harbored many doubts about his white compatriots'
views. But his statement was not made without prior contem-
plation. The danger from Asia was real. Many nationalist journalists were writing of the collapse of the British Empire in
Southeast Asia. Smuts had on his desk a memorandum from
Col. P. B. van der Westhuizen favoring a massive enlistment of
black troops because, he wrote, the existing military force was
inadequate to defend the Union's 1,500-mile coastline. If government failed to arm blacks, van der Westhuizen argued, the
Japanese could be counted on to arm them for conquering the
Union.[20] Smuts's hint of almost two years earlier that the traditional policy of not arming blacks might have to be reconsidered if "a great nation were to attack us with the aid of black
armies" seemed about to become a reality.

18. Quoted in Roux, *Time Longer than Rope*, p. 306.
19. Union of South Africa, *House of Assembly Debates* (Hansard), 11 March
1942, col. 3572; René Kraus, *Old Master: The Life of Jan Christian Smuts* (New
York: E. P. Dutton, 1944), pp. 420 – 21; Hancock, *The Fields of Force*, p. 370.
20. Hancock, *The Fields of Force*, p. 371.

But he hadn't yet committed himself. There had been a reconsideration, perhaps, but so far no change of policy. Meanwhile, he was making debating points against the opposition. He praised those who did carry the burden of battle and commended blacks who

> voluntarily came forward to make their contribution, notwithstanding the restrictions placed upon them. . . . I am very sorry to say that the attitude of the native population is in many respects more praiseworthy than that of some honorable senators opposite. There is no doubt that those sixty thousand non-Europeans who have voluntarily taken part in the struggle, even if they were only permitted to serve in a limited capacity, are an example to many of the white people who stand aside at this grave crisis.[21]

Smuts had been moved not only by a genuine appreciation of the loyal service of blacks but also by a military assessment of a threatening situation and by a political desire to silence and shame his uncooperative critics. Yet nothing was done at that time to implement his words. He did not press the debate to a clear conclusion. He merely seemed to be preparing the ground for some future substantive change.

The Nationalists took the bait. Criticism and political action picked up. In the early months of 1942 anti-Smuts propaganda reached a crescendo, only to abate as the Allied war effort stemmed the Axis thrust. On numerous occasions during the war the Nationalists attacked the government's policy regarding black forces. When Smuts sought authorization for sending forces outside Africa, the Nationalists fastened on the "imminent danger" created by the government's "policy" of arming non-Europeans (never an official policy).[22] With regard to the use of South African troops in Madagascar, the Nationalists ignored the real issues and again launched into polemics against arming blacks. The arming of blacks was, D. F. Malan argued, an invaluable aid to communist agitation among the black population still in South Africa.

One of the more awkward debates took place as a result of an ugly incident on a Cape-bound train in which some drunken

21. Quoted in Kraus, *Old Master*, p. 421.
22. Basil Kellett Long, *In Smuts's Camp* (London: Oxford University Press, 1945), pp. 71–82.

and disorderly Coloured soldiers had terrorized people on the train and at stations along the route. The Nationalists aimed to embarrass the government. Dr. Malan said that a new spirit had risen among the Coloured people, for which he blamed the policy of arming Coloured persons, the incitement of Communists, and the idea of asking Coloureds to take a role as arbiters in a conflict between white man and white man.[23] His "I told you so" tone warned again of impending bloodshed between "white and non-white in South Africa," all because there are "kaffir soldiers." Eric Louw (M. P. for Beaufort West) in support attributed the problem to the policy of using Coloured soldiers to guard white prisoners of war. He cited other incidents involving Coloured soldiers.[24] In the House Jan Hofmeyr, the Minister of Finance, tried to still the Nationalist anger, but to little avail. His plaintive plea not to blame all non-European troops satisfied no one. The arming of blacks, he insisted, was not the issue. But C. R. Swart (Winburg), juxtaposed the disarming and internment of white nationalists with the arming of the Coloured men and blamed the government for this blunder. "The old respect of the kaffir for the European you no longer get," concluded the future Minister of Justice.[25] Smuts had been in Pretoria until late in the day; when he returned that afternoon, he more deftly defused the issue and promised an investigation, and the flap calmed down with time.[26]

But it is this sort of debate that illustrates how delicate the government's position had become and why a more vigorous and open arming of blacks might have been more politically costly than militarily wise. If the prospect of a Japanese invasion of South Africa itself could not frighten whites into accepting armed blacks, it was not likely that any other combination of events would, once the Japanese threat diminished. Still, Smuts felt the manpower limits of the Union acutely, even for South Africa's limited military commitment to the north.

23. *Assembly Debates,* 23 March 1943, cols. 3867 ff.
24. Ibid., cols. 3871–73.
25. Ibid., col. 3878.
26. An account appears in Alan Paton, *Hofmeyr* (Cape Town: Oxford University Press, 1964), pp. 363–67.

Again he pressed the issue. While at the London Prime Ministers' Conference in May 1944 he wrote to his governmental colleagues to say that the time had come to arm Coloured soldiers. It is worth recalling that never before had Smuts made such a direct suggestion. In the depths of the Japanese peril he had merely said that *if* certain contingencies were to occur he would arm blacks. So far no one in his government had publicly called for arming blacks for combat assignments; all instances of weapons in the hands of blacks had resulted from specific field conditions or from the use of blacks as guards. Realizing the partisan pitfalls, the Cabinet, called into session by Deputy Prime Minister Hofmeyr despite Smuts's direct request, unanimously noted its strong feeling that Smuts's proposal "should not be proceded with."[27] Any military advantage it would bring, it was recorded, would be offset by the political damage it would do.

Thus, throughout the war the debate surged back and forth—often reflecting the military fortunes of the Allied cause. Black leaders pressed for the military roles of their people to be widened to the point of equality with Europeans. Some military leaders appreciated the need for arming blacks and for recruiting more of them. But Smuts's camp, cognizant of the visceral and emotional content of such proposals, vacillated until the time when the strategic need for armed blacks lessened. In short, the government arrived at its decision by evading a decision.

Part of the problem with the use of black forces in World War I had been the issue of control, which in turn had been a question of organization. In that war the major black units were formally under the Imperial War Council. Thus, domestic political opposition could be finessed. Since black troops were paid by Great Britain, the South African Parliament did not have to worry such controversial racial and partisan issues. But the price paid for this respite from domestic controversy was the necessity to liaise with British and other Allied commanders. Matters such as work assignments, quartering, command, social intercourse, and so forth had to be worked out in

27. Hancock, *Fields of Force*, p. 412.

liaison with others who did not necessarily share white South Africa's racial values and segregationist policies. The experiments were not, therefore, successful from the South African government's perspective. South Africans were determined to prevent a similar diffusion of authority and control in their support for the Allies in World War II.

The Mobilization of Blacks

Although the question of arming blacks was effectively answered, noncombatant black units were created early in the war. On 8 May 1940 a Cape Corps consisting of a headquarters, a Pioneer Battalion, and five motor transport companies (later expanded to seventeen companies) was formed. Some 45,015 men served with the Cape Corps. During the war the term Coloured Corps came into use, especially in its Afrikaans form, *Kleurlingkorps,* although officially Cape Corps was its title. On 26 June 1940 the Indian Service Corps, again with five motor transport companies, came into existence. Later in 1940 its name was changed to the Indian and Malay Corps, and in October 1942 it was incorporated into the Cape Corps, although it still retained its own name. Problems arose from the predominantly Muslim Malays, who protested their recruitment into the basically Hindu Indian Service Corps.[28]

The Cape Corps served largely in noncombatant services; its men were chiefly employed as drivers. Later, high ranking officers suggested that the Cape Corpsmen should be trained in the use of the rifle. The Minister of Defence, aware of possible white repercussions, did not permit the issue of rifles permanently to Corpsmen, though he did authorize essential musketry training. Later, however, some were armed and trained to use arms to serve as garrison troops and to guard prisoners of war and internees, the ultimate insult to diehard Afrikaner nationalists. Many Coloured drivers were subsequently replaced by black drivers in a progressive upgrading of assignments, all in an effort to relieve more and more whites for combat duty. Coloured units served in another important

28. Martin and Orpen, *South Africa at War,* p. 73.

capacity, in the South African Naval Service. Over eight hundred Coloured men were trained and used both ashore and afloat, principally in minesweepers and in examination vessels.[29]

In June 1940 black Africans were brought into the Union Defence Force in the form of a Native Labour Corps.[30] It soon became known as the Native Military Guards Brigade, later as the Native Military Police, and finally as the Native Military Corps (NMC). Its establishment was increased from four to eight battalions. It had been stipulated, but never really put into practice, that all officers assigned to these formations would undergo a course in a special Cadet Battalion at the Military College to ensure that the black troops were imbued with high standards of discipline. Needless to say, few officers possessed or acquired the sensitivities necessary for effective handling of culturally different peoples—they understood discipline, perhaps, but this was hardly the only effective form of leadership.

Blacks served at first as guards, batmen (army officers' assigned soldier-servants), "hygiene staff" (a euphemism for latrine diggers), cooks and waiters, and later as drivers, dispatch riders, stretcher bearers, medical aids, tailors, clerks, typists, and so forth—assignments in keeping with "South African tradition." The units of the NMC were organized by nationality and to some extent by region (Zulu, Xhosa, Northern Transvaal, and urban). In June 1940, for instance, some one thousand Zulu were recruited to guard vital military points. In that they were armed only with assegais (spears) and knobkerries and were paid but one shilling per day, one might question their military effectiveness.[31]

On 12 July 1940 all black formations were grouped together under the command of the Non-European Army Services, which assumed responsibility for recruitment, training, and

29. S. Horwitz, "The Non-European War Record in South Africa," in Ellen Hellmann, ed., *Handbook on Race Relations in South Africa* (Cape Town: Oxford University Press, 1949), pp. 542; and Martin and Orpen, *South Africa at War*, pp. 72–74, 346.

30. Martin and Orpen, *South Africa at War*, pp. 59–60, 72–74.

31. Ibid., p. 74.

Table 1.
Blacks Recruited into the Defence Force
During World War II, Cumulative Numbers

March 1940 ·	0
September 1940	9,000
March 1941	30,000
September 1941	74,000
March 1942	100,000
June 1942	106,000
February 1943	122,254

Sources: March 1940 to June 1942: "South Africa in
the Remaking," *I.c. Digest* (issued by the General
Staff, Defence Headquarters, Pretoria, August 1942),
p. 5; February 1943: *The Star* (Johannesburg, Weekly
Air Edition), 30 July 1977, p. 12 (data confirmed by
H. J. Martin and Neil Orpen, *South African Forces*, vol.
7, *South Africa at War* [Cape Town: Purnell, 1979], p.
346).

deployment. Recruitment had been relatively successful at
first, and it officially ceased after 23 February 1943. Cumulative numbers of blacks recruited into the Defence Force at
selected dates are shown in table 1. In October 1943 the combined strength of the Cape Corps and the NMC was over
92,000, all under the administrative authority of the Director
of the Non-European Army Services, whose rank was only a
colonel.[32] Recruiting statistics for the NMC by province are
shown in table 2. Thus nearly 37 percent of South African field
strength (122,254 men) were black. There were some problems, as in World War I, as some employers, especially farmers,
tried to prevent their work force from heading off to war. So
loudly did some protest that the government closed certain
areas to recruitment, especially in the Cape. Those who then
enlisted without their employer's permission found that their
employers could not be compelled to reemploy them.[33]

Although all black forces were ostensibly under the command of a single office, they did not go into action as

32. Ibid., pp. 250–51.
33. Sheila Patterson, *Colour and Culture in South Africa: A Study of the Status of
the Cape Coloured People Within the Social Structure of the Union of South Africa*
(London: Routledge and Kegan Paul, 1953), p. 219.

TABLE 2.

Recruitment into the Native Military Corps,
by Province

Transvaal	52,037
Cape	9,555
Natal	7,366
Orange Free State	4,521
South West Africa	7,000
TOTAL	80,479

SOURCE: S. Horwitz, "The Non-European War Record in South Africa," in Ellen Hellman, ed., *Handbook on Race Relations in South Africa* (Cape Town: Oxford University Press, 1949), p. 542.

NOTE: These figures exclude the large numbers rejected for various reasons. The official Defence Department figure was reported in 1975 as 77,239; *The Star* (Johannesburg, Weekly Air Edition), 30 July 1977, p. 12; and H. J. Martin and Neil Orpen, *South African Forces*, vol. 7, *South Africa at War* (Cape Town: Purnell, 1979), p. 346.

identifiable units under their own officers. In World War I the Cape Corps fought as a unit and remained an entity throughout the war. The same was largely the case with the SANLC. In World War II, however, the South African planners saw blacks strictly in terms of support. Thus some Africans and some Coloureds were attached to each unit of the Union Defence Force. For example, the composition of the Police Brigade (the Sixth South African Infantry Brigade) in June 1941 is shown in table 3. The Service Corps of the Police Brigade was, formally, never considered a part of the brigade. Stationed throughout Africa, in Madagascar, Italy, and even the U.K., every European unit had attached to it Cape Corps Coloured drivers, black stretcher bearers, and so forth. Such a policy became known as the "dilution policy," in which black formations were split into small sections and assigned to European units. They became integral yet always subordinate parts of white fighting units. The most tradition-bound white officers opposed "dilution" as too liberal, as a prelude to assimilation in direct opposition to South Africa's longstanding commitment to differentiation. Yet the dilution policy was never completely adhered to.

TABLE 3.
Racial Composition of the Police Brigade
(Sixth Infantry Brigade) in June 1941

	Europeans	Non-Europeans
Brigade Staff	42	21
Infantry Battalion	737	165
Infantry Battalion	737	165
Infantry Battalion	737	165
Regt. Field Artillery	511	35
Anti-Tank Battery	72	6
Field Company Engineers	209	70
Brigade Signal Company	203	58
Armoured Car Company	261	25
Machine Gun Company	122	20
Field Ambulance	65	213
Res. Motor Transport Co.	3	126
Brigade Workshops	84	3
TOTAL	3,783	1,072

SOURCE: F. W. Cooper, *The Police Brigade: 6th S.A. Infantry Brigade, 1939–45*
(Cape Town: Constantia Publishers, 1972), p. 32.

For example, some 44 percent of the Cape Corpsmen were in
Cape Corps units (such as prisoner-of-war and security battalions). The other 56 percent were attached to white units.[34]

There were occasionally some unusual assignments. About
four hundred blacks, for example, were assigned to the special
Mining Company of the Mines Engineering Brigade, S.A. Engineering Corps. The brigade was sent to Syria to assist in the
construction of a tunnel through a mountain. In another case,
by special arrangement with the Minister of Justice, a company
of the NMC was placed under the command of the South
African Police as special constables for duty in Cape Town and
Johannesburg. At most military airports in the Union and elsewhere where South African air forces were deployed, NMC
Maintenance Companies were on duty, cleaning, refuelling,
and loading planes.[35]

In September 1941 another experiment was launched. The

34. Martin & Orpen, *South Africa at War*, p. 250.
35. Horwitz, "The Non-European War Record," p. 543.

Twenty-first Field Regiment of the South African Artillery was formed, and about half the personnel were Zulu.[36] Drivers and signalers were European. There were two Zulu-speaking white NCOs on each gun, along with six Zulus. But before the regiment was sent to North Africa the Zulu personnel were withdrawn and replaced by whites. Apparently Zulus did not perform to the satisfaction of headquarters, although most accounts indicate that they shaped up well. Later in 1943 the Twenty-second Field Regiment tried Coloured Corps personnel, with only one white NCO to every two guns. Again, however, the Coloured men were withdrawn before the regiment left the Union. Despite ostensibly favorable reports by officers on the personnel, the experiment was discontinued before it could be fully utilized.

There was also an Anti-Aircraft Training and Reserve Depot at Robben Island where around 2,000 Coloured gunners were trained under coastal defense officers and NCOs who did make an effort to understand them. The Coloureds were carefully recruited and selected and were enthusiastically drilled; as a result, they proved to be excellent soldiers.[37] Eventually many fought in the Middle East.

But it was precisely this ad hoc, hit-and-miss approach to the use of blacks, in which they were often trained and then not used, that proved to be so inefficient. The combination of voluntarism, white racial and political prejudices, and South Africa's peculiar racial mixture and racist structure made crucial and by and large simple manpower calculations almost impossible. Invariably, excuses could be found for reversing decisions or for following unexpected or militarily illogical courses. The variety of criteria for assignment and deployment must have baffled Allied planners and commanders as well as professional South African soldiers.[38]

36. G. Tylden, *The Armed Forces of South Africa: With an Appendix on the Commandos*, Frank Connock Publication no. 2 (Johannesburg: Johannesburg Africana Museum, 1954), refers to this unit as the twenty-third Field Regiment, p. 163; and Martin and Orpen, *South Africa at War*, pp. 76, 123–24.

37. Martin and Orpen, *South Africa at War*, pp. 107–8.

38. Ibid., pp. 108–9, provides a fine illustration of such extraneous and distinctively South African complications involving South African Indian and Malay troops in the Middle East.

Morale

The dilution policy served two ends. It freed many European soldiers for "more important" combat roles, and it prevented the development of black group solidarity and unit pride. The Cape Corps and the NMC were, as a result, prevented from being listed among the units in any engagement. In addition the pick of white recruits tended to volunteer for the most prestigious fighting units. It did little for the blacks corps' morale to realize, as they certainly must have realized, that they were getting as NCOs and officers men who would have preferred to be assigned elsewhere or men who were not the best leadership material. To be sure, there were some highly motivated whites who wanted to work with black units, but their numbers were few, and they tended to be in the first wave of volunteers.

Despite being officered by men brought in from outside their units, some of whom were unsympathetic to the black forces and some of whom were incompetent, most black units served well. Still, it is doubtful that many participants shared the enthusiasm of this Basotho sergeant:

> We belong to the Eighth Army. We charged their batteries, drove their trucks, unloaded their signal stores, carried their telegraph poles, mended their wires. We were bombed with them, we enjoyed the same rations, we laughed at the same jokes, we were blown up by the same mines.[39]

Although he may have perceived a sharing of risks and experience as well as a sense of being one of the unit, in fact strict segregation prevailed whenever the South Africans could arrange it. Segregation, coupled by a lack of suitable officers and NCOs, led to a number of disciplinary problems among blacks. Discontent also stemmed from the failure to form black combat units with a pride and *esprit de corps* of their own and from the insult to the manhood and loyalty of blacks implied by the UDF refusal to arm them openly. Many blacks began to resist assignments in the north until their promised home leaves were delivered. Signs of insubordination, vandalism, passive

39. As quoted in Basil Williams, *Botha, Smuts and South Africa* (New York: Macmillan, 1948), p. 167.

resistance, and mutinous behavior grew. Many white personnel did not know how to or did not want to alleviate the underlying discontents. The fact that the commanding officers in the NMC and in the Non-European Army Services were invariably of lower rank than other commanding officers led to further problems.[40]

Many blacks emerged from the war bitterly resentful of their experiences. Segregation sometimes reached ludicrous proportions. There are accounts of Cape Corps staff sergeants in the Middle East being forced to act as cooks and batmen to white privates. When the South African army headquarters heard that South African soldiers, including a number of black stretcher bearers, killed in the battle of Sidi Rezegh had been buried in a common grave, it ordered their disinterment and reburial in separate black and white graves.[41] Thus, despite the hopes of some blacks and white liberals that a comradeship-in-arms between the races would be forged in the crucible of war in northern Africa, little positive emerged. Under the direction of E.G. Malherbe and L. Marquard, two well-known liberals, South Africa's army information and educational program provided opportunities for soldiers to broaden their racial attitudes. By and large, however, rank and file whites were not inclined to change their views.[42]

Indeed, the South African authorities to some extent sought to foist "South African tradition" upon fighting forces not under their direct control. For instance, the African Pioneer Corps was comprised of blacks from the three High Commission Territories. It was commanded by officers of the British Army.[43] These men, some 32,500, had been told that they were being recruited as fighting men. But the South African authorities in the Middle East persuaded the British to adopt a policy of not giving firearms to the citizens of the High Commission

40. On disciplinary issues, see Martin and Orpen, *South Africa at War,* pp. 245–49.

41. Roux, *Time Longer than Rope,* p. 307.

42. Ibid., p. 315; and E.G. Malherbe, *Race Attitudes and Education* (Johannesburg: South African Institute of Race Relations, 1946).

43. Tylden, *The Armed Forces,* pp. 34–35. Interestingly listed by Tylden in his "Summary of the Armed Forces in South Africa, 1659 to 1946," it consisted of nearly 20,000 Basotho, 9,000 from Bechuanaland, and 3,500 from Swaziland.

Territories. When the troops arrived in North Africa, the only arms issued them were knobkerries and assegais. The South Africans argued that if blacks from the British Protectorates were armed, those from South Africa would want the same. Back in Basutoland, those who demanded arming the Basotho soldiers were interned by the British authorities.[44] The racist virus was infectious.

By most accounts, the black forces did commendable work. The Cape Corps and the Indian and Malay Corps were the first in the field, providing transport in Ethiopia and Kenya. In many instances they were forced to make their own repairs and to improvise spare parts, but they kept the troops supplied under demanding conditions. In many cases they moved all over the region completely unarmed and at times unprotected. During operations in the forward areas every vehicle technically had to be protected by a white rifleman. Yet this made a mockery of the "dilution policy." The divisional commander therefore recommended that all drivers be armed and that each motor transport company be provided with a unit of Coloured anti-aircraft gunners. Praise for the services of these men was unstinting.[45]

Throughout the war blacks were considered as noncombatants. With the exception of the prospective Zulu and Coloured coast defense units, blacks were not employed in fighting roles. They formed no frontline units of their own even when commanded by white officers, as did Cape Corps battalions in World War I. Despite demonstrated loyalty, enthusiasm, and skill they were doomed to be subservient to whites as in South Africa itself. The Union government simply refused to treat them as real soldiers. To be sure, many men in the forward areas were armed, often with captured Italian weapons. But

44. Roux, *Time Longer than Rope*, p. 307 – 8; and Martin and Orpen, *South Africa at War*, p. 121.

45. Neil Orpen, *South African Forces, World War II*, vol. 1, *East African and Abyssinian Campaigns* (Cape Town and Johannesburg: Purnell, 1968), pp. 8, 87; Smuts, quoted in Kraus, *Old Master*, p. 421; and Gen. Sir William Platt, General Officer Commanding, East Africa, quoted in Horwitz, "The Non-European War Record," p. 540.

few received adequate training in their use, and little was done to coordinate their fighting efforts with those of the "proper" white units.

Conditions of Black Service

The conditions of service in the Non-European Army Service were not on a par with those of the white units. The highest rank to which volunteers in the Cape Corps could aspire was warrant officer I. The highest rank open to Africans was staff sergeant. But related provisions built inferiority into the arrangements. Formal relations between white and black troops were laid down in a gazetted amendment to the National Emergency Regulations. That amendment stated that non-European NCOs held their rank in the Non-European Army Service only and might not exercise any command or authority over European members of the Defence Force. In contrast, white personnel might exercise command over blacks by virtue of their superior rank or because of having been placed in command of black personnel. In the event of an emergency, and this is crucial, the senior European NCO, or even a private, must be placed in command of the black personnel, irrespective of rank.[46]

In terms of compensation the whites also went to war with financial advantages. A Select Committee on Soldiers' Pay and Allowances recommended and accepted the daily rates of pay as outlined in tables 4 and 5. In general one can see that Coloured pay rates were roughly one-half of the European rates and that Africans received about two-thirds of the Coloured rates. Annual leave time also favored whites, who received thirty days to twenty-four for the Coloureds and eighteen for black volunteers.[47]

The general rule governing pension awards was that Col-

46. As reported in the *Rand Daily Mail,* 26 January 1942, and outlined in Patterson, *Colour and Culture,* p. 219, n. 110. See "Emergency Regulation no. 34" in Union of South Africa, *Government Gazette,* no. 2988, 23 January 1944.
   47. Horwitz, "The Non-European War Record," pp. 546–47.

TABLE 4.
Daily Rates of Pay During World War II

	European		Native		
	Non-Artisan	Artisan	Coloured,[a] Malay, and Indian	Without Dependents	With Dependents
Private (first six months)	5s.	7s. 0d. to 10s. 0d.	2s. 6d.	1s. 6d.	2s. 3d.
Private (after six months)	6s.	7s. 0d. to 10s. 0d.	3s. 0d.	1s. 9d.	2s. 6d.
Lance corporal	7s.	9s. 0d. to 11s. 0d.	3s. 6d.	2s. 6d.	3s. 3d.
Corporal	8s.	10s. 0d. to 12s. 6d.	4s. 0d.	2s. 9d.	3s. 6d.
Sergeant	10s.	12s. 6d. to 15s. 0d.	4s. 9d.	3s. 3d.	4s. 0d.
Staff sergeant	11s.	15s. 0d. to 17s. 6d.	5s. 3d.	3s. 6d.	4s. 3d.
Warrant officer II	13s.	17s. 6d. to 20s. 0d.	6s. 6d.	—	—
Warrant officer I	15s.	20s. 0d. to 22s. 6d.	7s. 6d.	—	—

SOURCE: *Report of the Select Committee on Soldiers' Pay and Allowances* (1943), as reprinted in S. Horwitz, "The Non-European War Record in South Africa," in Ellen Hellman, ed., *Handbook on Race Relations in South Africa* (Cape Town: Oxford University Press, 1949), p. 546.
[a] Extra duty pay to members with trade qualifications ranged from 6d. to 2s. per day.

TABLE 5.
Supplemental Daily Married Allowances During
World War II

	Wife Only	First Child	Second Child and Each Additional Child
European (W.O. I and below)	5s. 3d.	2s.	1s.
Coloured, Malay, and Indian Native	3s. 6d.	1s.	0
	No additional allowance except as in Table 4		

SOURCE: *Report of the Select Committee on Soldiers' Pay and Allowances* (1943), as reprinted in S. Horwitz, "The Non-European War Record in South Africa," in Ellen Hellman, ed., *Handbook on Race Relations in South Africa* (Cape Town: Oxford University Press, 1949), p. 546.

oured and black pension scales amounted to three-fifths and two-fifths, respectively, of the rate applicable to Europeans. But as it was applied the black scale frequently fell below the two-fifths guideline, especially in regard to disablement pensions, widows' pensions, children's allowances, parents' and separated wives' pensions, and in other respects as well.[48]

In a variety of other ways — in the disbursement of monies from the Governor-General's National War Fund, in the demobilization process, in the unequal benefits and gratuities attending demobilization, and in the process of finding work — blacks were given a much shortened end of the stick.[49] They returned not to a hero's welcome but to the familiar racist society that before the war held them down at every turn.

Although the individual units were not eligible for ribbons, the number of personal awards gave evidence of black field effectiveness. Black members of the armed forces had earned awards as shown in table 6.

Considering that black troops had not been recruited for

48. Ibid., p. 547.
49. Ibid., pp. 547–55. See also the speech by L. G. Murray (UP), who refers to a speech by Coloured leader Sonny Leon complaining about the treatment of Coloured exservicemen, *Assembly Debates*, 9 September 1974, cols. 2523–24. See also "The Forgotten Heroes of the Last War," *The Star* (Weekly Air Edition), 30 July 1977, pp. 12–13.

Table 6.
Military Awards to Blacks in World War II

Cape Corps:	
Military Medals	12
British Empire Medals	4
Mentioned in dispatches	57
Commendations (gazetted)	2
Commendation Cards	10
Certificates for Good Service	39
Native Military Corps:	
Distinguished Conduct Medal	1
Military Medals	16
British Empire Medals	2
King's Medal for Bravery	1
Mentioned in dispatches	21
Commendations (gazetted)	6
Commendation Cards	3
Certificates for Good Service	69
S.A. Naval Force (Cape Coloured):	
British Empire Medal	1

SOURCE: S. Horwitz, "The Non-European War Record in South Africa," in Ellen Hellman, ed., *Handbook on Race Relations in South Africa* (Cape Town: Oxford University Press, 1949), p. 544. Some of the individual citations are reprinted on pp. 544–45.

combat and that they were not supposed to participate in combat assignments, they suffered numerous casualties.[50]

	Cape Corps	*NMC*
Dead & Presumed Dead	1,091	1,519
Wounded	472	770
Prisoners of War	627	1,753

Still, fewer blacks were killed in World War II than in World War I, despite a much larger contingent of black members of the military establishment in the 1940s conflict. Maj. Gen. Sir Francis De Guingand, Field Marshall Montgomery's chief of staff, once noted that South African commanders were con-

50. Horwitz, "The Non-European War Record," p. 546. A different total of non-European deaths appears in *The Star* (Weekly Air Edition), 12 November 1977, p. 6 (a total 3,153 men are listed as dead). "Notes on the Military History" (see chap. 2, n. 1) claims that 555 members of the Cape Corps lost their lives and that 1,500 were wounded (p. 14).

scious of the heavy casualties to their units and that they were aware of the domestic political repercussions of white deaths in light of rapid black population growth.[51] If this indeed were the case, black casualty figures still do not reflect a conscious policy to use blacks as surrogate cannon fodder.

The war's impact on blacks was deep but inevitably frustrating. Take, for example, the experiences of Henry Nxumalo, who later became the assistant editor of *Drum,* a popular black magazine. He had been a sergeant in the NMC.

> In Egypt we found there was no color bar. We were stationed in the desert. I'll never forget the first time I had a drink with a white officer! . . .
> Of course, I had high aims. Higher than I had ever had before. During the war I realized what I had missed. During the war I often heard how it was all going to be different after we got home. I even heard white South Africans say that when they got home they were going to see that this color-bar foolishness was done away with.[52]

On the contrary, he and thousands of others faced the daily reality of resegregation. Potlako Leballo, later to become a leader in the Pan-Africanist Congress, received his political baptism participating in a mutiny against the army's color bar regulations.[53] Herman Toivo Ja Toivo, a founder of SWAPO, was also a member of the Union's Native Military Corps. On the other hand, some white veterans tried to help their black colleagues. One of the exservicemen's associations, in 1949, even pressed government to protect the voting rights of Coloured exservicemen. It failed. More frequently, whites in South Africa were liable to talk about "cheeky" attitudes acquired by Coloured and black troops in Italy and Egypt. So they dealt with black exservicemen as they had always dealt with blacks, in strictly master-servant terms.[54]

51. Francis De Guingand, *Operation Victory* (New York: Charles Scribner's Sons, 1947), pp. 467–68.

52. Robert St. John, *Through Malan's Africa* (Garden City, N.Y.: Doubleday, 1954), pp. 224–26.

53. Gail M. Gerhart, *Black Power in South Africa: The Evolution of an Ideology* (Berkeley: University of California Press, 1978), p. 138.

54. Patterson, *Colour and Culture,* pp. 219–20.

Is it any wonder that in 1974 a veteran of the war and national vice-president of the South African Ex-Servicemen's Legion could deliver this stinging rebuke of the system, all the more biting for its sarcastic yet conscious restraint? Speaking at the annual Cape Corps service in Cape Town City Hall, he lamented:

> We who survived the war know that we fought for freedom.
> We fought for a better world, against the forces of oppression and discrimination. We fought against a country, for instance, that excluded citizens from buildings, open spaces, eating houses and jobs for ethnic reasons.
> We fought against Nazi Germany's treatment of the Jews.
> Surely, therefore, on a day like this, in a place like this, we have a right to speak out when we feel that, in our society in our own country, we experience oppression and discrimination.
> I do not want to detail all the ways in which we feel that, although we fought for freedom and although the Freedom of the City is ours, we do not live the lives of free men and women.[55]

It is not simply a matter of commitment to an abstract principle of justice, or to unfulfilled promises or expectations. The failure to measure up to black expectations, in the military service and afterward, added to the inefficiencies of South Africa. The fact is that South Africa did not use all of its manpower rationally in the war. Much of this could be laid at the door of Gen. Sir Pierre van Ryneveld, who completely dominated the administration of the South African war effort. His personalized style of command enabled him to control virtually every aspect of defense, including the most minute details. As chief of the general staff, General van Ryneveld seldom delegated authority to subordinates, seldom encouraged initiative, and seldom abided by the basic canons of military decision making. This inevitably resulted in ill-considered decisions and policies destined to be costly in terms of inefficiency and lost opportunities. There was, for instance, an extraordinary waste of black manpower, first due to the limitation of blacks officially to noncombatant roles (even against the intentions of Field Marshall Smuts and many of his line and staff

55. *Cape Times* (Cape Town), 16 September 1974.

officers) and second due to the dilution policy, which broke up the Cape Corps and the NMC units. Later in the war, in 1944, the UDF, desperately short of white volunteers, nonetheless inexplicably discharged trained and perfectly fit Coloured and black men, largely because they feared disciplinary problems and a too fast, massive demobilization at war's end.

Moreover, the pattern soon became established of drafting to black units white officers and NCOs either who were unwanted or who had been failures in their own units or who completely lacked understanding of or even sympathy for the conditions of blacks either in the service or in civilian life. Many officers were unhappy at being arbitrarily posted to the NMC or to the Cape Corps. In some cases the Non-European Army Services had become a dumping group for misfits from white units. These difficulties led to problems of discipline in various black formations. When efforts were made to correct these deficiencies, General van Ryneveld did little to support those who sought to upgrade the quality of the white officers commanding black forces.[56] For blacks it was fortunate that the chief of the general staff's influence declined as units moved further from the Union and closer to the theater of war. Yet, though General van Ryneveld may have complicated their lives, for blacks it was more important that South Africa's commitment to racial segregation and discrimination was to prevail over practical manpower and military issues. So deeply rooted was the racist mentality that even the rational recruitment of black manpower into the armed forces, which in the long run was designed to defend the exploitative economic order, could not be applied in a rational and efficient fashion.

56. Martin and Orpen, *South Africa at War,* pp. 245–53.

4

The Nationalists Take Power

NEAR WAR'S END Smuts had come to the position that armed blacks might be a useful part of the Defence Force. He no longer campaigned against the training and arming of black men as he had in 1917. But Smuts in 1945 was no longer the political force he was in 1917. Even his colleagues in the Cabinet had overruled his proposal of 1944. A different day in race relations was just around the corner, and Smuts and his partners must have realized it. The Smuts government accepted the principles of perpetuating the Non-European Army Service, but before they could draft the precise conditions for postwar black service, they were defeated in the celebrated 1948 Nationalist election.

By June 1948 the new Minister of Defence declared that the Cape Coloured Corps and the NMC would be disbanded. They were allowed to retain their title as a noncombatant corps until, in April 1949, the *Government Gazette* announced their disbanding as units of the Permanent Force. A modest number of Coloureds were retained as the Cape Corps Auxiliary Service. As with minority hiring policies in industry elsewhere, blacks in the Union Defence Force were the "last" hired and the first fired. The "ethnic formula," as Cynthia Enloe calls it, has as its military analogue "the last mobilized, first demobilized."[1] Thus, demobilization becomes a state strategy for "normalizing" ethnic stratification: there is a hurried return to prewar patterns of ethnic exclusion from the security forces. The groups least trusted are relegated to positions on the outside, far from access to the control mechanisms of state.[2]

George Golding, a member and exchairman of the Coloured Advisory Council, voiced the stinging disappointment of the Coloured community. "I have no doubt that if the present Government is ever faced with war, it will find it impossible to do without the combatant services of the Coloured people, who if called upon, will respond loyally and readily."[3] Golding's message needed almost fifteen years to be tested, but for the moment it meant little to the National Party government. Coloured and black exservicemen were particularly hurt by these decisions. When the former director of the Non-European Army Service offered to raise 100,000 black troops in South Africa for service in Korea, an offer which was forwarded to Washington, no enthusiasm was aroused in South Africa.[4] The black units had been a symbol to Nationalist politicians of everything that they had been fighting against for decades. They had to be discontinued if for no other reason than to demonstrate Nationalist predominance and independence. Later, when the white nation became more united in the face of external pressures, the Nationalists might reconsider their ideological posture. But during their first flush of victory they would not.

Malan's Efforts to Delay Decolonization

The matter of "arming the natives," as it was called, continued to surface even after the war. It was a favorite Nationalist issue.

1. Cynthia H. Enloe, *Ethnic Soldiers: State Security in Divided Societies* (Athens: University of Georgia Press, 1980), p. 53.
2. Ibid., p. 72.
3. *Cape Times* (Cape Town), 19 April 1949; as quoted in Sheila Patterson, *Colour and Culture: A Study of the Status of the Cape Coloured People Within the Social Structure of the Union of South Africa* (London: Routledge and Kegan Paul, 1953), p. 220.
4. Ibid.

In the 1940s and 50s the issue emerged in a new form as a matter of foreign policy. In 1945 Nationalist leader D. F. Malan advanced the idea that South Africa might have to cooperate with the colonial powers in Africa to prevent the "militarization" of the natives. In order to preserve Africa for Western European Christian civilization it would be necessary that:

> The powers that have interests in Africa can agree that the native population should no longer be used in the battlefields of the world, and that they will not be given military training or be armed, so that they will not constitute a danger to each other and to other nations in Africa.[5]

But collaboration with imperialists had not been the Nationalists' strong suit.[6] Smuts might have been more comfortable persuading the Colonial Office or Whitehall to share this view, for the idea was not that remote from Smuts's 1917 warning about black armies in Central Africa or from his plea to arrive at some convention to prevent the training of blacks. Now, almost thirty years later, Malan had taken up the call that Smuts had only recently abandoned. In fact the hiatus between proposals was not that great. In the 1930s the South African ambassador in London expressed a willingness to lift sanctions against Italy and to agree to give Rome a mandate over Ethiopia if that mandate stipulated that the "natives" should not be armed.[7] According to the British Secretary of State for Dominion Affairs, the most important part of this proposal in the ambassador's eyes concerned not arming the blacks.

Throughout his term as prime minister Malan repeated his call for an agreement to disarm the blacks in Africa.[8] In the

5. Union of South Africa, *House of Assembly Debates* (Hansard), 19 March 1945, col. 3956.

6. See Kenneth W. Grundy, "Anti-Neo-Colonialism in South Africa's Foreign Policy Rhetoric," in Timothy M. Shaw and Kenneth A. Heard, eds., *Cooperation and Conflict in Southern Africa: Papers on a Regional Subsystem* (Washington, D.C.: University Press of America, 1976), pp. 351–64.

7. Sam C. Nolutshungu, *South Africa in Africa: A Study in Ideology and Foreign Policy* (Manchester: Manchester University Press, 1975), p. 47. Reported by Malcolm MacDonald, British Secretary of State for Dominion Affairs, D.O. [Dominions Office] 114/68/9, 22 May 1936.

8. E.g., D. F. Malan, *Foreign Policy of the Union of South Africa* (Pretoria: State Information Department, 1948).

summer of 1949 the Minister of Defence, F.C. Erasmus, was able to secure from the Attlee government in the U.K. an assurance that blacks in the High Commission Territories would not be armed.[9] This was essentially a continuation of the wartime policy of Great Britain. This campaign culminated in Malan's proposal in 1954 to execute with the colonial powers an African Charter in which four points were to be mutually developed:

1. The protection of the indigenous peoples of Africa against penetration by the peoples of Asia;
2. the guidance of Africa along the road of European civilization;
3. the suppression of Communist activities; and
4. the prevention of the militarization of Africa.

Naturally, Malan was concerned about the defense of South Africa in the face of what he saw as the unacceptably rushed pace of decolonization to the north. So he proposed that such an agreement be arrived at not by means of a conference but by a less formal form of communication and cooperation.[10] These proposals had little hope of approval. All the colonial powers in Africa used black troops. It was too late to prevent arming blacks. Nonmilitarization in this case would be demilitarization. In Parliament Malan was closely questioned along these lines. Was this possible? Would South Africa also agree to demilitarize? Malan hoped that the British would unilaterally agree not to arm the natives.[11] But who else in the colonies was there to arm? How could the colonial powers be persuaded to establish an African Defence Force, especially one that South Africa wanted to dominate, without using black troops? There was no way the Nationalists could inveigle the colonial governments to return to open white supremacy. Despite great talk in

9. Henry Gibbs, *Twilight in South Africa* (New York: Philosophical Library, 1950), pp. 192–93; critical comment on this effort appears in *The Forum* (Johannesburg), 30 July 1949.

10. *Assembly Debates*, 4 May 1954, cols. 4491–97.

11. Ibid., cols. 4500–4501; Nolutshungu, *South Africa in Africa*, pp. 64–68; Amry Vandenbosch, *South Africa and the World: The Foreign Policy of Apartheid* (Lexington: The University Press of Kentucky, 1970), p. 161.

government and in Parliament, little came of the African Charter idea. By 1955 the Nationalists had to begin to admit the inevitability of independent black states.[12]

The Defence Act of 1957

The focus of Nationalist attention in their first few years in power had been domestic policy, particularly the articulation and rationalization of the entire apartheid system with its accompanying array of security laws designed to maintain the segregationist order. It was not until 1956 that an omnibus defense bill was drafted to replace the 1912 Defence Act, with its numerous amendments and regulations that had been appended through the years. The Defence Act of 1957, as it emerged, was designed to update the old legislation and to clarify and restructure the maze of past defense measures. To that end a Select Committee was constituted and the bill was laid before Parliament in February 1957.

It was clear at this point that the Nationalists had still not come to terms with the need to employ blacks in any but the most menial "auxiliary" positions in the Defence Force. The Defence Act of 1957 was parsimonious on the matter of blacks. In fact it virtually repeated the words of the 1912 Act on these matters. It indicated that the Act should not apply to certain groups of persons (including females and "persons who are not white") and then provided that:

> The Governor-General [later to read the State President] may with the approval by resolution of both Houses of Parliament by proclamation in the *Gazette,* apply any provision of this Act . . . to such persons who are not white persons, as so defined, or any class of such persons: Provided further that nothing in this section shall be construed as preventing any female or any person who is not a white person as so defined from engaging voluntarily and in accordance with regulations for service in the South

12. Nolutshungu, *South Africa in Africa,* passim, especially pp. 60– 129; and Kenneth W. Grundy, *Confrontation and Accommodation in Southern Africa: The Limits of Independence* (Berkeley: University of California Press, 1973), pp. 228– 41.

African Defence Force in such capacity and subject to such conditions as may be prescribed.[13]

So, although by terms of the bill nonwhites were to be excluded
from military service, under certain conditions the governor-
general and later the state president might (with the approval
of Parliament) engage them voluntarily and in keeping with
already prevailing military regulations.

The opposition United Party, or at least some members of it,
focused their criticism on three features of the bill: (1) its territorial limitations on the compulsory use of the Defence Force
outside "South Africa"; (2) the absence from the bill of a Council
of Defence; and (3) the upgrading of the commando formations for frontline service.[14] The racial issue was not central to
the United Party (UP) position, although it did emerge later in
the debate when the party spokesman on defense, L. C. Gay
(South Peninsula), raised the "very delicate question" of the use
of the non-European population.[15] He indicated that his party
was "with the Government and we are against the arming of
the Native population of this country." But, as a sort of harbin-
ger of later years, he added that the situation was approaching
in which the government of the day might have to reexamine
this position. In this future South Africa's small white population might have to fight side-by-side with the black communities further north. What should South Africa do? he asked. He
was aware that South Africa did have millions of blacks prepared to fight. But quickly he added that he was not advocating
any departure from the "traditional attitude of the country."
But if South Africans were talking about "survival," maybe
they had better consider noncombatant assignments for
blacks. This position really did not differ much from that of the

13. Defence Act, no. 44 of 1957, sec. 2, in *Statutes of the Republic of South
Africa*. This provision was to be quietly altered by the state president in February 1978 when he promulgated a change in the General Regulations for the
South African Defence Force and the Reserve. By a simple and subtle reword-
ing in reference to voluntary service to refer merely to "persons," discrimination in the armed forces was no longer legal. See "R. 341," in Republic of South
Africa, *Government Gazette*, no. 5888, 24 February 1978, p. 29.
    14. L. C. Gay, in *Assembly Debates*, 18 February 1957, col. 1288.
    15. Ibid., col. 1301.

Nationalists, except that the government's bill reflected an even more limited perception of threat. In its view military service in South Africa was still voluntary, exclusively white, and geographically bounded. The government's only policy concession to the manpower constraints of a small white population was that for the first time foreigners who were white would be permitted to volunteer for service in the Permanent Force.[16]

Representatives for the natives pursued this opening far more vigorously. Walter P. Stanford (Liberal Party, Transkei) even offered an amendment which included a provision insisting that government agree "to train members of all sections of the adult male population for service in any capacity, including combatant service, for use in defence of the country."[17] In defending his amendment he developed essentially five arguments. First, in relation to manpower, he said, "It seems very difficult to see how it is logical to place the burden of defence of the whole country, with our multiracial population, entirely on the shoulders of the white man alone." Second, he noted that exclusion of blacks was not consistent with the government's "new Africa approach" to foreign policy. Third, he noted that the police force included all races and that blacks there had demonstrated efficiency and discipline. Fourth, since the primary defense task of the military was in Africa itself, blacks could not be sensibly excluded. Not only would South Africa's image in the north be improved by black soldiers, but among South Africa's blacks a pro-South African attitude would be promoted. Finally, he put the case for the social benefits of this step. It would, he submitted, give South African blacks discipline, pride in their unit, and pride in their country — in short it would make loyal South Africans out of them.[18] Nationalist J. H. Abraham (Groblersdal) snapped back rhetorically: "Is it not a fact that most Mau Mau leaders in Kenya were ex-members of the King's African Rifles?"[19] In his initial rebuttal the Minister of Defence, F. C. Erasmus, took note of Stanford's

16. Ibid., cols. 1281 ff., and especially cols. 1284–85.
17. Ibid., 20 February 1957, col. 1509.
18. Ibid., cols. 1514–16.   19. Ibid., col. 1515.

amendment and then disdainfully opined that that position "represents such an extremely small proportion of the European population of South Africa that he will forgive me if as in the past I advance no arguments against it."[20]

Few Nationalists spoke directly to Stanford's amendment. The most prominent was A. H. Vosloo (Somerset East), who reiterated the government's position that in case of hostilities "we shall make use of the Natives and Coloured people in the auxiliary services of our Defence Force. . . . But they will not be used in the armed forces." Vosloo's singular argument in opposition was that he felt that in case of conflict with a "Coloured race" South Africa's blacks would likely side with their black brothers.

> Whenever these people have had the opportunity of establishing friendly relations with other Coloured races they have consistently made it clear that they do not stand on the side of their good friends, the Europeans, but rather on the side of the Coloured races. . . .[21]

Frank Waring (Caledon) addressed himself to the police argument. He noted the difference between unarmed police and soldiers with firearms. Otherwise, his statements were just more repetition — "I am completely against the arming of Natives," and "I am not prepared to agree that the Coloured man should be used to carry arms, or should be trained in modern warfare." Not only would "95% of the people of this country" [a characteristic form of subspeciation in which whites and people are equated] not agree with arming blacks, but further, he maintained, it could be a "considerable time, if ever" before there will be any change in "the principle" of not arming "the Bantu."[22] H. T. van G. Bekker (Kimberley District) used a more ominous terminology when he spoke of "training . . . Natives in the art of warfare." Harkening to the past, he declared that "this country is suffering today because of the policy followed in the past when non-Whites were armed."[23]

20. Ibid., 25 February 1957, col. 1642.
21. Ibid., 20 February 1957, cols. 1517–18.
22. Ibid., 21 February 1957, cols. 1543–44.   23. Ibid., col. 1568.

Actually, the Nationalists argued both ways—that arming blacks in the past had produced negative results and that it was a "tradition" in South Africa not to arm blacks. On these issues Stanford countered by marshalling historical examples that demonstrated that men of color could be reliable allies of whites and that they did not necessarily side with darkly pigmented enemies of whites—his examples were the uses of the Cape Corps against Turks in Palestine and of the Gurkhas and the West African Frontier Force (blacks) against Japanese in Burma.[24] Moreover, he argued that blacks had fought in virtually every war involving South Africa. Even under the old Boer republics blacks were liable to be called up on commando. So, contrary to Nationalist arguments, the use of blacks for military and even combat duty was "not a new principle." Rather, it was new to exclude them as this bill did. Stanford was ably seconded by Liberal Native Representative Margaret Ballinger (Cape Eastern Circle). She got Stanford out of the difficult spot to which he had been led earlier by Nationalist questioners when he had insisted that blacks ought to be subject to call-up and should be trained for combat. She, in turn, interpreted the bill to show that, in fact, blacks could volunteer for service if the government was prepared to accept them and that government would be entitled, without a Parliamentary resolution, to give them training and prepare them for service in the Defence Force. She maneuvered the Minister of Defence to agree with that interpretation and added her own clarification:

> What we were really concerned about is that non-Europeans should not be excluded from combatant service in defence of their country. . . . [We are] not proposing that compulsory service should be imposed upon our African population. . . . We feel the Africans should have the right to volunteer for service, and that in volunteering for service, they should be trained for defence.[25]

Thus, she and the Nationalists neatly sidestepped the issue by agreeing, in a way, that there was no issue. Clause 7 of the 1912 Act had been substantially preserved forty-five years later. But

24. Ibid., 26 February 1957, col. 1760.
25. Ibid., col. 1770.

although the voluntary use of blacks was legally possible, government policy clearly opposed such a step. During this debate and early into the 1960s numerous Nationalist declarations that blacks would never be armed made the government's position clear and consistent.

"Tradition" and Reality

Yet we have seen that contrary to Nationalist ideology it has not been a South African "tradition" to exclude blacks from military or combatant service. Through decades, indeed through almost two centuries of South African life, blacks have been employed — selectively, cautiously, and usually reluctantly — to help assert and later to defend white dominance. By and large blacks, and especially Coloureds, proudly and effectively served in whatever capacity was demanded of them. Coloured troops had been in the pay of various Cape governments steadily from 1793 until 1870.

However, it has been a longstanding part of that tradition to have blacks serve in subordinate and usually menial capacities. Both English speakers and Afrikaners, those in power and those out, shared the same attitude and projected it into policy when they could. It cannot be gainsaid that the predominant white concern, especially since the mid-nineteenth century, was the fear of armed blacks. Although many blacks may have excelled in battle and may have demonstrated unswerving loyalty to their white commanders, there remained a "strong prejudice . . . against the organisation and arming of the coloured classes."[26]

But these prejudices varied in intensity with time and with the situation. They depended mainly on the government's most recent or most vivid experiences with black forces and on the perceived gravity of the security situation. In addition, the use of blacks was contingent upon the opportunities to exploit

26. From a paper published by the Cape government in 1897, quoted in J.S. Marais, *The Cape Coloured People 1652–1937* (Johannesburg: Witwatersrand University Press, 1959), p. 134.

extant political and military divisions between groups and within them. Nonetheless, as the years passed and as the white communities grew larger and stronger, the necessity to arm blacks or to use them as combatants, and the likelihood that they would be used, declined, and a reputed "South African tradition" against their use took root and grew which was only remotely related to historical practice, although it was very much in keeping with historical preference.

5

The South African Defence Force

To UNDERSTAND BETTER the contemporary place and role of black forces within the SADF one must first understand the organization and composition of the SADF itself. The rather unique and complex structural milieu of the SADF has, itself, provided a useful point of entry for the employment of blacks and for their increasing deployment in combat roles. By locating blacks at first outside the regular white formations, in the interstices so to speak, the SADF was first able to deflect expected white criticism and to soften the white electorate to subsequent, perhaps less digestible changes. Organizational diversity also provides a helpful means for experimentation with the use of blacks. Hence, it becomes imperative that we make sense of this crazy quilt of formations, services, and units.

The Organization of the SADF

The defense establishment of South Africa can be divided into a regular force of full-time career Defence Force employees and a part-time force made up of non-career personnel. The regular force consists principally of the Permanent Force (PF) of professional soldiers (army), airmen (air force), and seamen (navy). These elements provide the cadres for the administration of all SADF units, the professional and instructional core of the SADF, and the personnel for manning sophisticated weapons systems. In 1977 the Permanent Force constituted only 7 percent of the SADF strength, although the military authorities would have desired that figure to be 13.5 percent.[1] At that time the Permanent Force was manned to 80 percent of approved strength.[2] Although the PF was expanded by 28.6 percent from 1977 to 1979, there was no marked increase in the ratio of PF to total SADF.[3] The Department of Defence claimed that it intended to double the PF by 1981.[4] Yet it has proved difficult to retain PF personnel, especially those who acquire skills in high demand in industry. The average manpower turnover for the period 1965 to 1975 was 15.5 percent annually, in other words an average period of service of only 6.45 years, hardly adequate for a career military service.[5] Yet since 1976 a vigorous recruitment program has apparently increased applications and recruitment intakes to the PF.

Since the inception of the National Party government English speaking South Africans have been less inclined to regard the Defence Force as a career. Indeed, there is considerable evidence in the early years of Nationalist government that SADF was to be politicized at higher ranks and that "untrustworthy" elements, that is, English speakers and those associated with the country's World War II effort, were encouraged to seek premature retirement.[6] So markedly Afrikanerized has

1. Republic of South Africa, Department of Defence, *White Paper on Defence and Armaments Supply, 1979* (Simonstown: S.A. Navy Printing Unit, 1979), p. 3.

2. Ibid., p. 5.

3. Ibid., p. 3.

4. Statement by Deputy Minister of Defence Kobie Coetsee in Republic of South Africa, *House of Assembly Debates* (Hansard), 23 April 1979, col. 4758.

5. Republic of South Africa, Department of Defence, *White Paper on Defence, 1977* (Simonstown: S.A. Navy, 1977), p. 15.

6. The political struggle during and after World War II between Nationalists and those with a less exclusive sense of nation, the English speakers, for control of the SADF is covered in Kenneth W. Grundy, *Defense Legislation and Communal Politics: The Evolution of a White South African Nation as Reflected in the Controversy over the Assignment of Armed Forces Abroad, 1912–1976*, Papers in International Studies, Africa Series, no. 33 (Athens: Ohio University Center

TABLE 7.
SADF Force Levels

	Army		Navy		Air Force		
	PF	CF	Commandos	PF	CF	PF	CF
1980–81	71,000 (60,000)	120,000	110,000	4,750 (1,250)	10,000	10,300 (4,000)	25,000
1979–80	48,500 (40,000)	100,000	90,000	4,750 (1,250)	10,000	10,000 (4,000)	25,000
1978–79	50,000 (43,000)	138,000	110,000	5,500 (1,400)	10,500	10,000 (4,500)	25,000
1977–78	41,000 (34,000)	130,000	90,000	5,500 (1,400)	10,500	8,500 (3,000)	25,000
1976–77	38,000 (31,000)	138,000	90,000	5,000 (1,400)	10,500	8,500 (3,000)	25,000
1975–76	38,000 (31,000)	138,000	75,000	4,000 (1,400)	10,400	8,500 (3,000)	3,000
1974–75	34,500 (27,500)	60,000	75,000	4,450 (>1,250)	9,000	8,500 (3,000)	3,000
1973–74	10,000	80,000	75,000	2,500	9,000	5,500	3,000
1972–73	10,000	80,000	75,000	2,300	9,000	5,500	3,000
1971–72	10,000	> 23,000	78,000	3,000	6,000	5,000	3,000
1970–71	10,000	22,300	58,000	2,250	1,250	5,000	3,000
1969–70	5,700	≅ 60,000	58,000	2,500	1,200	5,000	3,000
1968–69	5,700	≅ 45,000	58,000	1,500	1,000	4,700	3,000
1967–68	......	......	......	......	......	......	......
1966–67	5,700	≅ 55,000	51,500	3,000	......	3,000	......
1965–66	5,500	13,500	51,500	3,500	......	4,000	......

SOURCE: It is government policy not to disclose SADF force levels; see Republic of South Africa, *House of Assembly Debates* (Hansard), 5 May 1980, Q col. 701. These data were drawn from an annual published by the International Institute for Strategic Studies (formerly the Institute for Strategic Studies), *The Military Balance* (London: International Institute for Strategic Studies, 1965–81). Here we begin with the 1965–66 volume, published in 1965, and end with the 1980–81 volume, published in 1981. The information can be found in the sixteen consecutive volumes beginning with the 1965–66 volume, at pp. 35, 38–39, (no reference), 51, 53–54, 52, 38, 39–40, 41–42, 44, 44–45, 47, 49–50, 53–54, and 54–55, respectively. No figures are available for 1967–68 as South Africa was not included in the volume for that year. Figures in parentheses in PF columns refer to conscripts (national servicemen) in those services.

the SADF become that the government today is reversing itself and is making efforts to attract more English speakers to the Permanent Force. In 1974 a military spokesman noted that 85 percent of the army's Permanent Force, 75 percent of the air force, and 50 percent of the navy were Afrikaans speaking at home. Special recruiting drives have been launched to broaden the white ethnic balance in the PF.[7] Moreover, there is a serious problem not only in attracting qualified applicants but in keeping them in the Defence Force.

Perhaps an unexpected source of PF recruits may be found in the effects of the Zimbabwean settlement and the establishment of the Mugabe nationalist government in Harare. In April 1980 reports began to be heard of white Rhodesian security force officers resigning to take up posts elsewhere — particularly in South Africa. Many reportedly came from the Rhodesian Light Infantry, the Grey's Scouts, and the army's elite unit, the controversial Selous Scouts.[8] In fact, Radio Mozambique even reported that large numbers of the Selous Scouts were to be transferred to the SADF as "a complete military unit." Radio Mozambique, quoting the Soviet news agency (TASS) and the French agency (AFP), said the unit would be used operationally in both Namibia and in South Africa. The SADF immediately denied the story. Large numbers of the Selous Scouts (perhaps 80 percent) were black. Therefore, it is questionable whether the black Scouts would move south and, if so, whether the SADF would structurally accommodate a "mixed" formation.[9] In fact, even before the Selous Scouts was disbanded in July 1980 many of its black troops rejoined its parent organization, the Rhodesian African Rifles, to become a part of the new

for International Studies, 1978). See also Brian Bunting, *The Rise of the South African Reich* (Harmondsworth: Penguin, 1964), pp. 137–38. An English speaker hounded out of the service in 1961 tells his story in *The Star* (Johannesburg, Daily Edition), 30 December 1979, p. 1. There is some evidence that this policy still exists in a less overt form.

7. *The Star* (Daily Edition), 13 December 1974.

8. *Rand Daily Mail* (Johannesburg), 11 April 1980, p. 2; and *New York Times*, 27 May 1981.

9. *The Star* (Daily Edition), 11 April 1980, p. 1; and *The Sun* (Baltimore), 27 July 1980.

and integrated Zimbabwe Defence Force. Several hundred
white members quietly slipped south to take up one year contracts with an option to extend. They are to function on a
counterinsurgency and tracking unit for northern Namibia. A
good part of the Rhodesian Special Air Services also went over
to the SADF.

It is not easy to determine exactly how many foreigners are
involved in either the SADF or its Permanent Force. When
asked how many persons who are not South African nationals
are employed in the Permanent Force, government officials
repeatedly insist that "it is not in the public interest to divulge
this figure."[10] Yet reports continue to circulate, especially in the
foreign press, that indicate that these numbers are not
insignificant. The SADF has employed soldiers who had previously served with Portuguese armed forces in Angola and in
Mozambique, with various anti-MPLA and anti-Frelimo black
movements, and with various Rhodesian security force units.
This fact, plus the 1978 legislation requiring all white male
immigrants under the age of twenty-five to take out South
African citizenship after two years of residence (thereby making them liable for military service), has swelled the ranks of
foreigners in the SADF.

Officially the SADF does not recruit mercenaries. Rather,
such individuals are moved right into regular SADF structures
(with some exceptions, for example, the 32 battalion in Namibia; see chapter 11). Many of these non-South Africans are
blacks who are recruited for special assignments such as cross-
border operations (into Angola), intelligence, and "dirty
tricks." The raids into Angola and Mozambique have involved
foreigners, as has a good deal of the heavy fighting in Namibia.
Journalists visiting the Caprivi Strip base of the Portuguese-
speaking 32 Battalion in 1981 had been told that the 32 Battalion had killed 807 guerrillas in two years and had lost 40 of
their own men. The SADF has acknowledged the loss of only
around 150 troopers in that period. If these figures are accurate (and there is reason to challenge them) it would indicate

10. E.g., *Assembly Debates,* 13 February 1981, Q col. 133.

that foreigners bear an inordinate burden of casualties and undertake the most dangerous missions. The 32 Battalion consists of around 1,000 troops. There are an estimated 50,000 SADF and Namibian Army soldiers in Namibia. With 2 percent of the fighting force, the 32 Battalion presumably suffered almost 27 percent of the combat deaths.[11] According to unconfirmed reports the two "South Africans" killed in the January 1981 raid on ANC installations outside of Maputo were foreigners, and the units undertaking this raid were composed mostly of Rhodesians. South Africa's affection for the concept of a citizen army may well have been revised in its search for battle-hardened soldiers.

In addition to the Permanent Force, the regular forces are also composed of a number of auxiliary services as well as the regular civilian employees of the SADF. All are regarded as career personnel, as distinct from part-timers.

In a society with a tradition of a part-time citizens' armed force, it is easy to understand the central role of the part-time defense establishment. If the Permanent Force provides administration and organization, the professional spine of the defense establishment, the part-time forces provide the bulk and the body and, just as importantly, the political links with the citizenry. Prior to 1967 white males between the ages of eighteen and twenty-five were subject to a ballot or lottery system by which they were required, if selected, to do nine months military training. Throughout the 1960s intakes were enlarged. Then in 1967 a Defence Amendment Act (No. 85 of 1967) abolished the ballot system and made military service compulsory for all medically fit young white men. The act also extended the initial period of service from nine months to twelve months. Today all white males between the ages of eighteen and twenty-five are conscripted for two years of compulsory service. The extended obligation was raised in 1977 (effective January 1978) in the face of considerable popular and partisan opposition. Yet of the 59,052 (63,104) men called for National Service in 1977, for example, 32,659 (37,518) ap-

11. *New York Times,* 27 May 1981.

plied for deferment or exemption. Of these requests, only 564 (1,070) were refused.[12] Thus, there are approximately 50,000 National Servicemen at any one time. Of the 30,000 youths entering the National Service in 1973, 62 percent declared Afrikaans their home language and 38 percent English. So even where the defense burden is by law supposed to fall evenly among all white language groups, the English speakers presumably secure a disproportionate share of the exemptions.[13]

In 1977 white male National Servicemen constituted only 6.6 percent of the total SADF strength, although they were a much higher proportion of the ready force at any one time.[14] These National Servicemen, on completion of their two years' service, are fed into either a Citizen Force unit, where they must serve 360 days' service or training and 360 days' operational service during a period of twelve years, divided in cycles of 120 days.

Able-bodied individuals who have not been National Servicemen, either because they were too old when conscription was instituted or because they have been exempted for one reason or other, may volunteer for either the Citizen Force or the Commandos, and if they have not previously been a member of the PF or the CF or the reserve units of either, they must serve in a Commando for four consecutive years. The CF and the Commandos represent the part-time establishment, subject to some degree of regular training each year and ready for rapid mobilization in an emergency.[15] Each branch of SADF — the army, navy and air force — consist of PF, National Servicemen, and Citizen Force. The army alone has Commando formations, although increasingly commando-type organization is being used in civil defense capacities, most particularly to

12. *Assembly Debates,* 13 April 1978, Q col. 614; the 1976 data in parentheses is from ibid., 25 April 1977, Q col. 931.

13. *The Star* (Weekly Air Edition), 29 September 1973, p. 6.

14. Department of Defence, *White Paper, 1977,* pp. 15–16.

15. It is characteristic of the confidence of SADF leadership in CF units that most of the troops involved in the 1978 Cassinga raid into Angola were CF members. See *Rand Daily Mail,* 13 July 1982, p. 1.

protect key industrial and mining facilities.[16] As of 1977 the part-time manpower component constituted 83 percent of the SADF strength. Of the part-time force, 55 percent of total strength was in the Citizen Force and 28 percent in the Commandos.[17]

Finally, there are the Reserves, consisting of exmembers of the Permanent Force, Citizen Force, and Commandos who have fulfilled their service obligations and who are maintained on the reserve lists until they reach the age of sixty-five. They are merely a source of manpower supplementation only and cannot be regarded as part of the defense establishment proper.

Since the early 1960s structural and command changes have served to bring about greater integration of SADF components and formations and greater rationalization of functions. This trend has been, of course, a worldwide one, and the SADF has merely conformed to organizational patterns developed elsewhere. But in a society as disparate and heterogeneous as South Africa, faced with crucial defense shortages (manpower, skills, funds, materials due to arms embargoes) and political problems, improved coordination at the top becomes absolutely necessary for efficient military operation.

The Militarization of White Society

Particularly noteworthy has been the increasing militarization of the educational system. This process has involved the conscious creation of a social atmosphere that makes military service seem attractive, military responses to policy issues sensible, and greater military strength and expenditures seem acceptable — one which in general prepares the population for conditions of siege and war. Cadet detachments have been set up in the white boys' secondary schools. There some 150,000 to 200,000 boys are given paramilitary drill and training and are

16. See the debate on the National Key Points Bill in *Assembly Debates*, 12 June 1980, cols. 9120–53; and 6 June 1980, Q cols. 844–45.

17. Department of Defence, *White Paper, 1977*, p. 16.

prepared for national service or are encouraged to join the Permanent Force upon graduation. Many of the Cadet detachments are being affiliated to Permanent Force and Citizen Force regiments. Even before high school, youngsters are urged to attend voluntary veld schools where, inter alia, political indoctrination to the "South African way" softens resistance to the next level of training.[18] In addition the news and entertainment media, particularly the state-owned and operated radio and television networks and the Publications Control Board, have contributed to a one-sided atmosphere that tends to glorify if not to romanticize the military service.[19] Part is attributable to outright intimidation. Part is conscious public relations. In 1980 the SADF employed ten persons in press liaison and forty-eight in public relations work.[20]

On 23 March 1980 the *Sunday Times* of Johannesburg published a story about a SADF document headed "Psychological Action Plan: Defence Budget Debate" and dated 12 February 1980. That document detailed secret steps to manipulate the news media in order to nullify the opposition's criticisms of the prime minister. The document was signed on behalf of the chief of the SADF, General Malan, by Maj. Gen. Phil Pretorius, director general of Civic Action. Such direct dabbling in partisan politics and in the affairs of Parliament shocked many observers, who had regarded the SADF as a professional fighting force, nonpartisan in structure and behavior. It is also strange in light of the support which both opposition parties regularly provided the SADF. The prime minister, clearly em-

18. "The March of Militarism," *Financial Mail* (Johannesburg), 23 June 1978, pp. 97–98; and *Financial Times* (London), 5 July 1978.

19. The press can be intimidated, for example, by the establishment of a commission of inquiry into all aspects of news reporting on defense; see *Cape Times* (Cape Town), 6 December 1979, p. 2. In a recent instance SABC production personnel refused to be associated with a saber-rattling and blatantly propagandistic "documentary" on the SADF, and a private company had to be hired to film the show; see *Sunday Express* (Johannesburg); 30 March 1980, pp. 1–2. See also the agreement between the Newspaper Press Union and the Deputy Minister of Defence of March 1979, described in South African Institute of Race Relations, *A Survey of Race Relations in South Africa, 1979* (Johannesburg: South African Institute of Race Relations, 1980), p. 77.

20. *Assembly Debates*, 26 May 1980, Q cols. 802–3.

barrassed by the disclosure, nonetheless characteristically attacked the press and the opposition. He passed the matter off as a minor error of judgment by certain junior officers. Opposition leader Dr. Frederick Van Zyl Slabbert argued that "if an image is created that the Defence Force is simply the National Party in uniform, this country will split from top to bottom."[21] The next week, Revelation Ntoula of *Voice* tartly jibed Dr. Slabbert: "You see," he wrote, "we Blackies fully perceive the role of the army, but without sounding too nasty, to most Black members of the army, it is indeed synonymous with the Nationalist Party." In short, if apartheid were eliminated, then the need to spend millions on defense would not be there.[22]

Interestingly, Target One of the Psychological Action Plan is the black Africans, Indians, and Coloureds in the Defence Force, "in particular the fact that recruiting is not as successful as it could be. . . ." Black attitudes toward the SADF had to be improved. A media campaign to enhance this image was to be launched, and thereby more and better black applicants would be attracted to the armed forces. We shall deal with this issue later. Suffice at this point to indicate that this element of the Action Plan drew little criticism from the press or from parliamentarians.[23] By their silence, leading white spokesmen implied that such manipulation was perfectly acceptable. To seek to channel public opinion and to create a positive image for the SADF is understandable to most politicians. But to turn that propaganda covertly on opposition politicians themselves aroused a howl that the very basis of "democracy" was tottering.[24]

The prime minister rejected the opposition's call for a parliamentary Select Committee to investigate the SADF's covert

21. Ibid., 25 March 1980, cols. 3502–15 (prime minister) and 3477–82 (Dr. Slabbert).

22. *Voice* 4, no. 13 (April 1980): 2. See also student criticism of Dr. Slabbert's naiveté in the pamphlet *Army News* (Johannesburg: Milcom, Students Representative Council, Witwatersrand University, 1980), p. 2.

23. Percy Qoboza, then editor of *The Post* (Johannesburg), commented on these issues; see *Rand Daily Mail*, 26 March 1980, p. 2. H. H. Schwarz raised the issue in *Assembly Debates*, 25 March 1980, cols. 3499–500.

24. For details of this episode, see *Sunday Times* (Johannesburg), 23 March 1980, p. 1; and 30 March 1980, p. 20; *Rand Daily Mail*, 24 March 1980, pp. 1–

plan to "nullify" the opposition during the budget debate on the Defence Vote. Instead, the prime minister appointed a SADF board of inquiry headed by the former chief of the Defence Force, Adm. Hugo Biermann. This in-house investigation, as expected, exonerated the SADF and found no willfulness or negligence by anyone concerned in drawing up, authorizing, handling, or distributing the document. The farthest the report would go was to admit that "serious errors of judgement" had been made. No disciplinary steps were recommended. The Biermann report was never published.

Yet within months another SADF pamphlet entitled *The Reason Why* was printed, propagating the policies of the National Party and attacking the opposition. The chief of the Defence Force, General Malan, repudiated this document and promised action against those responsible. They had violated a SADF directive requiring all documents affecting party politics to be cleared by the chief of the Defence Force.[25] Again the internal mechanisms of the SADF, at the highest levels, were able to whitewash the embarrassing yet expected partisan meddling of the SADF in the country's political life.

Recruitment and the Evasion of Military Service

Despite this pro-SADF environment, South African discos are not in danger of going out of business for want of white male clientele. We have already mentioned the difficulties of the Permanent Force in maintaining itself at approved strengths. Improved pay scales and benefits, vigorous recruitment campaigns, and a sluggish economy contributed to an increase of 80 percent in applications to join between 1975 and 1978.[26] Yet the Defence White Paper for 1979 refers to "an onerous brain drain" from the Permanent Force and to the burdens of train-

2; 25 March 1980, p. 12; 26 March 1980, pp. 1–2, 4; and 31 March 1980, p. 7; *Sunday Express*, 30 March 1980, pp. 1–2, 8–9; and *Assembly Debates*, 24 March 1980, col. 3325, and 25 March 1980, cols. 3477–515.

25. South African Institute of Race Relations, *Survey of Race Relations in South Africa, 1980* (Johannesburg: South African Institute of Race Relations, 1981), p. 201.

26. *Financial Mail*, 23 June 1978, p. 97.

ing replacements.[27] It is the "leadership element," senior non-commissioned officers and junior officers, and the instructors that are in short supply. The SADF increasingly has had to rely upon junior leaders and instructors from the National Service Force. The Permanent Force has also introduced a short-service system by which already qualified members of the Citizen Force and Commandos have been recruited into the Permanent Force on a voluntary basis for short periods (one year and more) to supplement the leader corps. This, it is claimed, is a stopgap measure to carry through the heavier period of enlarged National Service intakes and extended (from twelve to twenty-four months) initial continuous service. SADF authorities have been willing to entertain diverse suggestions to enable them to fulfill their training functions. Still, attracting and retaining "qualified" — meaning skilled, educated, and white — careerists continues to bedevil the Defence Ministry as it has for years.

The situation in the National Service is somewhat different. In addition to efforts to secure exemption, mostly by continuing one's education, there is some measure of evasion of conscription. Occasionally students go abroad either to prolong their university training or to assure an unbroken degree course. Others simply leave the country on extended "vacations." Since 1975 an estimated 3,000 conscripts per year fail to report for service. According to a defector from the regime's National Intelligence Service, the Directorate of Military Intelligence predicted that over 5,200 conscripts would evade service during 1980.[28] Not only are such actions illegal and subject to stiff penalties, but the Defence Further Amendment Act of 1974 provides for a fine of R10,000 or ten years imprisonment or both for anyone convicted of advising or encouraging any other person against giving military service. Under these terms many a clergyman or parent risks prosecution for merely discussing alternatives or for providing draft counseling. The bill

27. *Department of Defence, White Paper, 1979,* pp. 3–6.
28. *Observer* (London), 6 July 1980, p. 10; and Committee on South African War Resistance, "No to Conscription in South Africa's Armed Forces," in United Nations, Department of Political and Security Council Affairs, Centre Against Apartheid, *Notes and Documents,* no. 16 (April 1981): 4.

TABLE 8.
Evasion of Compulsory Military Service

	Failure to Report		Failure to Serve After Having Reported	
	Charged	Convicted	Charged	Convicted
1975	3,314	595	10	10
1976	3,566	898	18	18
1977	3,814	507	25	25
1978	3,123	284	6	6

SOURCES: For 1975 to 1977, Republic of South Africa, *House of Asssembly Debates* (Hansard), 17 February 1978, Q cols. 181–82; for 1978, *Assembly Debates,* 22 February 1979, Q cols. 157–58.

had been a reaction to the debate inside the South African Council of Churches regarding "just wars" and the use of violence as it relates to the justice of the cause for which it is being employed.[29] Still, the Defence Minister's bill was fully supported by the opposition United Party, although not by the Progressive Party.

This sort of irascibility to criticism of government and of the need to defend government policy by force of arms if necessary seems particularly acute regarding compulsory military service. *National Student,* the official journal of the National Union of South African Students (NUSAS), never a popular organization in government circles, was permanently banned in July 1979 because the Publications Control Board found its May issue undesirable. The offending issue dealt mainly with the question of military service. In the board's view the articles

29. See the London publication of the Africa Bureau, *X-Ray* 5 (December 1974): 4. An effort to counter such questioning attitudes can be found in the Pretoria publication *Uniform,* no. 54 (November 1979): 4, where the black chaplain of the 21 Battalion, of all people, argues that biblical study dictates that all parents are duty-bound to teach their sons to defend their country. See also the pamphlet *Conscientious Objection or Conscientious Obligation?* published by the conservative South African Catholic Defence League, an organization opposing political activism among church leaders. This pamphlet directly challenges the 1977 declaration by the Southern African Bishops Conference defending the right to conscientious objection to military service and the reiteration of that declaration at the Pastoral Consultation in 1980. Large parts of the pamphlet are reproduced in *The Citizen* (Johannesburg), 20 May 1981.

were "calculated to discourage South Africans from doing military service and demoralise the South African Defence Force, . . . to cast doubt on the cause for which South African soldiers are fighting and harm South African morale, . . . undermining the South African defence effort."[30] Other publications on the subject have been banned, especially those of MILCOM, a subcommittee of NUSAS that deals with military matters. Occasionally the bans are lifted on appeal to the Publications Appeal Board.[31]

Alan Paton, the novelist, must have been courting legal action when he asked the fiftieth anniversary conference of the South African Institute of Race Relations:

> Is South Africa worth fighting for? Can young white men go in good conscience to the border, to fight against men who almost without exception are black, and who believe that they have a duty to liberate this country from its present rulers, and in particular from the oppression of its racial laws? . . . When we go to the border, what do we in fact fight for?[32]

He went on to ask why an Indian South African would become an officer in the navy or why a young Coloured soldier would fight on the border. Could his statement have been a technical violation of the Defence Further Amendment Act? His answer left the question still open—the only reason one would go to the border would be "to fight for the chance to make this a more just society."[33] Never mind the counter-argument that there must be far more direct and efficient ways to improve or change South Africa than by fighting on the border on behalf of a regime whose commitment to greater social justice is subject to doubt. Never mind the fact that his "answer" begs the question, as it should, and that it places responsibility for an answer squarely on the shoulders of each eligible conscript and

30. *Sunday Times,* 8 July 1979, p. 11. Nonetheless, NUSAS continued to press this line after the banning; see *The Star* (Daily Edition), 26 July 1979, p. 3.
31. *Army News,* p. 6.
32. Alan Paton, *Towards Racial Justice: Will There be a Change of Heart?,* delivered at the Fiftieth Anniversary Conference of the South African Institute of Race Relations, 3 July 1979 (Johannesburg: South African Institute of Race Relations, 1979), p. 12. See editorial comment on this speech in *Rand Daily Mail,* 5 July 1979, p. 10.
33. Ibid., p. 14.

volunteer. By failing to provide unambiguous guidance to his audience, he might be accused of "casting doubt on the cause for which South African soldiers are fighting."

Despite these profound moral issues, the extent of draft dodging would appear to be, if one can believe official reports, rather limited. If, indeed, young South Africans are in compliance with the compulsory military service provisions of the Defence Act, it need not be because they have thought through the vexing moral issues and found the government's position sound. More likely, it is the absence of legitimate alternatives, the oppressive effectiveness of the government's enforcement machinery, or the high social and economic costs of noncompliance that assure obedience to the law.

There is, for example, no provision in the law for exemption based on conscientious objection. The most the authorities will permit is to allow members of recognized church groups which *forbid* their members to wage war to render national service in noncombatant capacities.[34] Those who refuse to register or to report, for any reason, are liable to prosecution. Of those convicted for failing to report or for refusing to serve after having reported, 150, 95, 86, and 55 (in 1975, 1976, 1977, and 1978 respectively) claimed conscientious objection. In 1978 all 55 indicated that they were Jehovah's Witnesses. The problem is that other denominations historically with a pacifist testimony do not "forbid" their members from engaging in armed service to the state. Rather, they tend to see pacifism as a matter of individual conscience. The result is that conscientious objectors are repeatedly charged and punished for their persistent refusal throughout their period of service eligibility. It is technically possible to prosecute and punish a recalcitrant conscientious objector until he reaches the age of sixty-five. Over the years church groups, often led by the Society of Friends

34. The argument for a change of the law is fully developed in James Moulder, "Conscientious Objectors: The Argument for a Non-Military Alternative," *New Nation* (January 1980), pp. 13–16; although this still involves cooperation with the compulsory service provisions of the Defence Act. The recognized denominations for purposes of sec. 97(3) of the Defence Act are Jehovah's Witnesses, Plymouth Brethren, Christadelphians, Suppliant Faithists, and Seventh Day Adventists; see *Assembly Debates,* 14 May 1980, Q col. 764.

(Quakers), have pressed for a nonmilitary alternative (as opposed to a noncombat assignment within the SADF as presently constituted), but so far they have been rebuffed by the
authorities.[35]

In May 1978 it was revealed by the security police that a
group called SALSCOM (South African Liberation Support
Committee) had distributed a publication entitled *Omkeer*
("About Face"). The publication gave advice and offered assistance to deserters and draft evaders and, alternatively, encouraged some to infiltrate the army and to attempt to undermine it
from within. SALSCOM sought to assist resisters in leaving
South Africa, to provide them with an overseas support base,
and to lobby for their political asylum.[36] Other groups, the
Committee on South African War Resistance (COSAWR) and
the South African Military Refugees' Aid Fund (SAMRAF),
based in New York, launched similar campaigns in 1979 and
1980.[37]

These groups have had relatively little impact in fostering
desertion, although there has been some. In 1977 government
denied reports of between ten and one hundred black and

35. A memorandum compiled by the Commission on Violence and Non-Vi-
olence of the South African Council of Churches was submitted to members of
government in November 1980 but has presumably not moved government to
change policy; see *The Star* (Daily Edition), 17 February 1981, and *The Times*,
16 May 1981. Government's anxieties over conscientious objection led to an
alarmist secret report, "Resistance to Military Service," circulated by the intelligence service; see *Observer*, 13 January 1980; and *Sunday Post* (Johannesburg),
13 January 1980. See also the extended account of one conscientious objector's
trial and a clerical reaction in *Cape Times*, 5 December 1979, p. 7; and coverage
of this issue in South African Institute of Race Relations, *Survey, 1979*, pp. 81–
82; and *Army News*, pp. 3 and 5.

36. South African Institute of Race Relations, *Survey of Race Relations in
South Africa, 1978* (Johannesburg: South African Institute of Race Relations,
1979), p. 54. Critical background on SALSCOM and its predecessor organizations appears in "Salscom: Trying to Seduce South African Defence Force
Abroad," *To the Point* (Johannesburg), 17 March 1978, pp. 14–17, in which
SALSCOM publications are quoted at length. See also South African Liberation Support Committee, *Towards an Understanding of the Role of Whites in the
South African Struggle* (London: South African Liberation Support Committee
[1977?]).

37. *Observer*, 29 October 1979; and *Die Vaderland* (Johannesburg), 25 March
1980.

white deserters from the SADF while assigned in Namibia.[38] The actual number well may exceed one hundred. The government naturally wants to downplay the realities for fear of contributing to an ever larger problem. In his statement the Minister of Defence referred to thirty-one convictions under the Military Discipline Code for absence without leave, but he did not regard these as desertions. The testimony of deserter Bill Anderson before the United Nations Council on Namibia and in various speaking engagements in the United States and Great Britain, however, would seem to indicate considerable questioning by National Servicemen of SADF brutality in Namibia and some willingness to consider desertion.[39]

In this discussion, so far, we have not mentioned a number of ancillary defense and defense-related establishments, including the "homelands" armies and national guards, the military formations for Namibians, the South African Police, the Railway Police, the Prisons Service, and other security and civil defense agencies. Many will be covered subsequently.

What has been developed in South Africa is an increasingly tight military organization, capable of far more efficient operation than existed when the Nationalists first came to power. The integration of diverse formations, more uniformly trained at the lower levels and more effectively managed and commanded at higher echelons, means that the SADF is a more professional enterprise than at any time in the past. High proportions of the white male citizenry are involved. The ideological setting among white South Africans is dominated by a sympathetic but by no means unquestioning acceptance of the need for a strong military establishment. Into this overall atmosphere is being injected the fact of small but growing numbers of black male and white female volunteers. This vital question bears study — what impact will these so far cautious and almost experimental changes have on the defense establishment itself and on the wider South African society?

38. Statement by the Minister of Defence as quoted in *Assembly Debates,* 1 February 1977, Q col. 67.
39. See, for example, *Philadelphia Inquirer,* 3 April 1977, p. 8–B.

6

The White Establishment Debates
the Military Use of Blacks

BY THE 1970s there was hardly a white politician of
national stature who had not fallen in with the prevailing view-
point that the defense of South Africa should involve all population groups and that larger numbers of blacks would have to
be brought into the armed forces in a variety of roles. The
transformation was much like that of the back-seat driver who,
having neither control of the vehicle nor the perspective of the
driver, perceives himself to be in continual danger. Now, having learned to drive and charged with piloting the vehicle, he is
not so frightened. The prospect of armed black soldiers, indeed, looks reassuring considering the alternatives.

To be sure, widespread white anxieties can and do find expression in the Herstigte National Party (Reformed National
Party; HNP) and among the more implacable and unbending
members of the Broederbond and the South African Bureau
of Racial Affairs (SABRA). In these quarters it is the view that
whites should beware of black soldiers in the SADF as a threat
from within. Black soldiers can never be loyal to "white civilization" and to the *volk*. To think that blacks can be brought to do

the regime's military bidding is self-delusion. But even within the National Party, reservations find a voice.[1]

Granted, the HNP and its followers currently pose only a minor electoral threat to the heretofore unified and well-organized National Party. Nonetheless, the Nationalist leadership chooses to fear the HNP as a wedge that could divide the *volk*. In the 1981 parliamentary elections the Nationalists sought to isolate and silence the HNP. They managed, despite the HNP securing 13 percent of the vote, to prevent the HNP from gaining any seats in the House. Yet there is still reason to fear those to the right of the Nationalists precisely because they are powerful in some Afrikaner circles. And they are gaining in popularity. In past elections the Nationalists drew between 83 and 85 percent of the Afrikaner vote. In 1981 its support from Afrikaners slumped to 63 percent, with 33 percent voting for the far right parties. Naturally, the Nationalists will take steps to win back these voters.[2]

Although there are signs that in selected constituencies the HNP can force the governing party to reconsider important positions, it would appear that the ruling party and its principal white opposition parties do agree on this—defense of the Republic necessitates a deeper involvement from all population groups. During the 1981 campaign, for example, the prime minister was challenged at Nationalist rallies on integration in the SADF. He used these occasions to defend his policies.[3]

In large measure, white resistance to this proposition has been broken down largely because of the government's cautious phasing in of black fighting forces in the South African Cape Corps (SACC) and its Special Service Battalion (SSB), in

1. See the editorial commenting on the debate on this issue in the Transvaal Congress of the National Party in *Beeld* (Johannesburg), 14 September 1978. Illustrative is the comment by the leader of the Afrikaner women's organization, the Kappiekommando: "We cannot have blacks and whites fighting side by side when they fought against each other at the Battle of Blood River"; *The Star* (Johannesburg, Weekly Air Edition), 31 January 1981, p. 8.

2. Hermann Giliomee, "The parting of the ways for Botha," *Cape Times* (Cape Town), 6 May 1981.

3. E.g., *The Star* (Weekly Air Edition), 21 March 1981, p. 2.

the South African Police, among the various indigenous military formations in Namibia, and with the 21 Battalion (black)
within the SADF. The lessons of the Zimbabwe-Rhodesian Security Forces, in which upwards of 85 percent of the manpower was black, might have been decisive. The considerable
arguments in favor of the government's proposed course
weigh heavily in the debate, and it might be helpful to review
them here.

The Manpower Issues

Of first importance has been a battery of manpower considerations, both in terms of the economy and the defense establishment but also in terms of evolving domestic race relations.
According to population estimates for mid-1977 (which include Transkeians among the total South Africans) black Africans accounted for 71.9 percent of the total population; whites
were 16.2; Coloureds were 9 percent; and Asians were 2.8
percent.[4] Assuming no expulsion of large numbers of blacks
into truly independent and viable homelands and given both
patterns of immigration and emigration similar to those in the
past and likely changes in birth and death rates, it would appear that by the year 2000 the black African proportion will
rise to around 74.1 percent; the whites will slip to 13.7 percent;
and the Coloureds and Asians will stand at 9.7 and 2.4 percent,
respectively.[5] If unrest and insecurity were to continue, that
white figure would most likely drop lower due to a reduction in
immigration and an increase in emigration, especially among
younger whites. Many analysts, therefore, conclude that there
is no way the current regime or even some liberalized deriva-
tive of it can survive the inexorable logic of these numbers
without change.

But this is only one facet of the demographic chamber of
horrors of white supremacists. A supply of inexpensive labor is

4. Calculated from data presented in South African Institute of Race Relations, *Survey of Race Relations in South Africa, 1978* (Johannesburg: South African Institute of Race Relations, 1979), p. 49.
5. From data reported in Cynthia H. Enloe, "Ethnic Factors in the Evolution of the South African Military," *Issue* 5 (Winter 1975): 22.

of paramount importance. Racial separation held in place by force is the best mechanism to achieve this goal. Because of shortages in skilled and experienced personnel, it has become increasingly necessary for the particular structure of apartheid envisioned by the leaders of the National Party at the time when they consolidated their hold on government in the 1950s to be revised, added to, and generally modernized. There has been not so much a relaxation of the highly segregated structure as there has been a modification seeking, in large measure, the same ends as before — a cheap labor supply assuring the retention of white wealth, privileges, and political domination. Thus, although the past decade has seen the grant of "independence" to four superficially primed homelands, the government and many others have had to rethink the homelands policy at the same time that they are going forward with it. In addition, alterations in roles played by blacks in the South African economy have necessitated scrapping some features of job reservation, limitation on black worker representation, apprenticeship practices, and even some elements of the pass laws and the Group Areas Act; these have been necessary to tamp down smoldering discontent and to regenerate the economy. Neither end has been achieved. The basic fact is that there are not enough economically active whites to enable the regime to continue blindly with its segregationist policies in the form in which they operated at the beginning of the 1970s.

When one adds to this the threat of external invasion and internal unrest, the manpower bow is drawn all the more taut, coming dangerously close to the breaking point. The Defence Force is not unaware of this issue. Where some countries express their defense problems in terms of "guns and butter," the South African establishment is more likely to see them foremost as questions of economic mobilization or military mobilization. There has not yet been a problem of adequate capital for both priorities, although such a difficulty may yet surface. Rather, the question is one of obtaining sufficient skilled manpower in the "right" racial mix. For every white called up for military service and thereby removed from the economy, often from a supervisory position over blacks, the economy takes one more step closer to stagnation — unless blacks are significantly upgraded economically, and for South Africa this has seemed to be such a sensitive issue, or unless they are employed in larger numbers for defense, or both.

In a fashion, the issue is reduced to an ultimate manpower dilemma. On the one hand, there is the need for greater numbers to defend the regime against the independence movement in Namibia (SWAPO), against the expression of general discontent among blacks domestically (and various foreign-based expressions of that discontent), and against the external threat posed by hostile or potentially hostile regimes on South Africa's borders, determined to assist revolutionary movements both within and without. On the other hand, there is the need to keep the economy operating in order to continue to make life comfortable for the white populace and to allow some rewards to trickle down in order to qualify black perceptions of deprivation by improving black material standards (again with the effect of making life secure for the dominant white group). At the time of the Angolan invasion, the increase of violence in Namibia, and the Soweto demonstrations and killings, the manpower issue may have been of paramount importance. Still, the military situation of the white regime is far from desperate. To be sure, demands on young white males have grown steadily, especially in recent years, but mobilization is hardly on a wartime footing. Today some 1.2 percent of South Africa's males between eighteen and forty-five years are serving in the armed forces; this figure includes 7 percent of white males.[6] The impact is more economic than strategic, although the trends are clear.

The solution to the manpower problem is not nearly so simple as some would have it. As long as blacks continued to serve in "traditional" military roles — as laborers, drivers, administrative personnel, cooks, orderlies, and so forth — the question of control was easily answered. But there is a substantive difference between blacks performing essentially quasi-economic roles in the defense establishment and blacks performing combat roles. Once a person is armed and trained to fight,

6. Chester Crocker, personal communication (November 1980), p. 41.

equipped with the latest skills in counterinsurgency methods, riot control, naval and parachute skills, for example, and once he is enabled to assume supervisory and even, within limits, command responsibilities, a psychological and practical meta-morphosis occurs — a new persona is unlocked.

Control may still be possible, depending on structure, de-ployment, and dozens of other variables, but it is not auto-matic. Important tactical and combat proficiencies that hereto-fore have been the legal monopoly of the dominant group are being transmitted on a small scale to individual members of the repressed groups. It takes a leap of faith, a calculated risk, an act of desperation, or an exercise in arrogance for the South African power structure to move in these directions.

Clearly, manpower concerns alone did not carry the debate on the use of blacks in the armed forces. In regard to the government's position on the expanded recruitment of blacks into the civil service, traditionally looked upon as a form of patronage for Afrikaner partisans, the manpower questions are secondary to the political concerns. Despite some 17,000 vacant positions in state departments, the Public Service Asso-ciation and government officials resist employing blacks in larger numbers. To them, this is a political, not a technical matter.[7] Although the supply of cheap labor is important, the necessity for political control comes first. Without political dominance the application of coercion becomes fitful and un-reliable.

So far the blacks in defense have been more symbolic than numerically significant. There are important signs that this may be changing, but so far black soldiers have not been used in sufficient numbers to be able to say that they have provided more than temporary relief of the manpower pressures. Other arguments for their use must also be explored.

Civic Action and Domestic Politics

Perhaps as popular as the manpower argument has been what might be labeled the domestic political concern. In short, the

7. *The Star* (Weekly Air Edition), 18 July 1981, p. 3.

argument is that maintaining order in a racially heterogeneous society demands that all groups must stand together. Defence Minister Botha combined race and class in his arguments when he told his party congress in Durban that the military capability of South Africa depends on South Africa succeeding "in establishing a strong middle class — not only among Whites, but the Black and Brown people as well."[8] W.M. Sutton (UP, Mooi River) said that blacks are the "Conservatives of the countryside." They want to help, and "we have to inspan and use them."[9] Conceptions of defense against insurgency and civil unrest revolve around a frequently quoted arithmetical maxim that the struggle demands 80 percent political and 20 percent military action.[10] This ratio is taken as axiomatic, as if it had a mystical quality to it.

To the end of political action, the government and the SADF refer to a "Winning Hearts and Minds" (WHAM) philosophy. As part of the practical and propaganda efforts undergirding WHAM, the SADF in January 1978 established a subsection of *Burgersake,* or Civic Action, in the Staff Division Operations. It also created an ethnology unit. Prior to 1978 similar assignments were performed by an organization operating in Namibia, which since 1974 has been a part of the S. A. Army. In time the activities of the Civic Action program expanded and the functions were divided, the subsection Civic Action concentrating on policy and coordination and the executive functions remaining with the branches of the service, mainly the army. *Burgersake* was headed by the former commander of the Transkeian Defence Force and Secretary of Defence to the Transkeian government, Maj. Gen. Phil Pretorius. Pretorius is also a top graduate of a special course in psychological warfare at Fort Bragg, North Carolina.[11]

Civic Action consists of around eight hundred national servicemen who serve mostly as teachers, agricultural specialists, administrators, medical doctors, and engineers. They work in

8. Ibid., 14 August 1976, p.1.

9. Republic of South Africa, *House of Assembly Debates* (Hansard), 22 April 1977, col. 5889.

10. See, e.g., W. Vause Raw in *Assembly Debates,* 17 April 1978, col. 4835.

11. For a biographical sketch of Pretorius, see *Paratus* 29 (March 1978): 6.

the "border areas" to improve relations with the black residents.[12] Some are even employed in schools in urban townships, in which case the propaganda message becomes heavy-handed. National servicemen serve in full uniform, which includes holstered revolvers. On at least one occasion the SADF teachers distributed copies of a SADF magazine, *The Warrior,* in which it is claimed that there is freedom in South Africa and that the true leaders of black people are not "convicts" like Nelson Mandela but Community Council leaders such as David Thebehali. In protest against this "gun toting battalion" students boycotted classes.[13] When, in 1979, the Regional Director of Education and Training suggested using national servicemen teachers to relieve teacher shortages in secondary schools in Soweto, prominent black community leaders condemned the idea.[14] Chief Gatsha Buthelezi of Kwa-Zulu also complained about the tone of the Civic Action program in his homeland. He indicated that, although he favored SADF Civic Action presence, he opposed the insistence on wearing military uniforms. It added, he maintained, to the appearance that "the propaganda value of the exercise was a priority to the military authorities, rather than a genuine wish to help, for humanitarian considerations."[15] His analysis was on the mark.

The fact is that Civic Action, when first launched, was regarded as very much the professional, modern way to combat civil unrest. The psychological weapon was to be a most powerful arrow in the SADF quiver. And Maj. Gen. Pretorius seemed to be the bright young officer to lead the program. Gen. Mag-

12. From interviews conducted in Johannesburg, 25 June 1979; and Pretoria, 16 July 1979; and also from Republic of South Africa, Department of Defence, *White Paper on Defence and Armaments Supply, 1979* (Simonstown: S. A. Navy Printing Unit, 1979), p.16; and numerous articles in *Paratus.* The Deputy Minister of Defence, in a reply to a question in Parliament, indicated that the personnel strength of the subsection Civic Action averaged 184 persons plus those attached to the army; see *Assembly Debates,* 25 April 1980, Q col. 653.

13. *The Post* (Johannesburg), 31 January 1980; *Sunday Post* (Johannesburg), 2 September 1979.

14. *Sunday Post,* 10 February 1980.

15. *Rand Daily Mail* (Johannesburg), 21 February 1980. The program in KwaZulu began in February 1980. See also *Financial Mail,* (Johannesburg), 17 August 1979.

nus Malan stressed time and again the need to gain the "trust and faith" of the local population in order to combat insurgency.[16]

On paper Civic Action seems to make sense. Some departments of government have had difficulty persuading young, urbanized civil servants to take up assignments in the embryonic homelands and in rural areas. Under the guise of military discipline such services can be supplied. The idea of the social welfare services being provided by compulsory service formations is akin to the suggestion by Ray Swart (Progressive Federal Party [PFP], Musgrave) that a multiracial, volunteer "peace corps"-type organization be established, linked to the military apparatus (perhaps as a form of alternative service).[17] Thus: "If the lessons of Viet Nam, the Far East and other trouble spots in the world are taken into account, it is essential that the Defence Force should be seen by the peoples of Southern Africa as their guardians of security and not as a symbol of oppression."[18]

But psychological operations and Civic Action fool few blacks. In early March 1980 the subsection Civic Action was officially ended (though civic action activities still are conducted by the army). And two weeks later Maj. Gen. Pretorius and his unsubtle approach to psychological operations ran afoul of the South African press (see chapter 5 above). Pretorius, an "expert" on psychological warfare, had become too rigid, too manipulative, too heavy-handed. His Civic Action had failed to achieve what it set out to do; his covert operations had become public information; and he and the programs associated with him had become expendable.

The problem is not so much the personality or methods of those leading Civic Action but the fact that the program is, in essence, a part of the government's "total strategy" designed to control the majority populace and perpetuate apartheid. Civic Action involves the deployment of national servicemen doing

16. *Rand Daily Mail,* 13 June 1979.
17. *Assembly Debates,* 17 April 1978, cols. 4919–23; *The Star* (Weekly Air Edition), 22 April 1978, p. 8.
18. D.J. Dalling (PFP, Sandton) in *Assembly Debates,* 9 September 1974, col. 2475. See also James Moulder, "Conscientious Objectors: The Argument for a Non-Military Alternative," *New Nation* (January 1980), pp. 13–16.

their obligatory military service. Although they may be furnishing a "nonmilitary" form of service, their activities have a basic military purpose. They wear military uniforms and carry weapons, and the disciplinary machinery of the SADF is in force at all times. Defence Headquarters clearly sees Civic Action in its military context. In short, although Civic Action may have positive ramifications in the lives of some of the inhabitants in terms of the social services provided, it is at heart an instrument of control. It has involved virtually no black input in deciding which programs to undertake or how to manage them in the interests of the people.

The Public Relations Dimension

Yet the concept of Civic Action links up nicely with another theme — that of the need for South Africa to erase the image of a "white regime" resisting black claims for equality. Quite some time ago, long before it was stylish to do so, Harry Oppenheimer, the financier and industrialist, proposed that Africans should be allowed to take a greater part in the defense of South Africa. Otherwise, the rest of the world would interpret South Africa's arms buildup as a means of oppression of racial groups within South Africa.[19] The rest of the world must be brought to see that the southern African struggle is not a race war but rather a battle between communism, on the one hand, and South African nationalism and western civilization, on the other.[20] To this end, what must be created, said some, is a defense force that is "truly representative of the whole population."[21] In Harry Schwarz's words, "We believe it [defense] is not merely a 'White's only' function. We believe that the defence of the borders is in fact a function involving the community as a whole and that South Africa needs an Army of all its people, all its races."[22] The fact that the black personnel are all volunteers adds to the propaganda effect, or as Cmdt. Hendrik Swanepoel of the 21 Battalion put it, "the external political

19. *The Star,* (Weekly Air Edition), 19 February 1963.
20. Harry Schwarz in *Assembly Debates,* 21 April 1977, cols. 5783, 5801.
21. Editorial in *The Star* (Weekly Air Edition), 22 April 1978, p.11.
22. *Assembly Debates,* 9 May 1977, col. 7088.

value."[23] "With Blacks in South African Army uniforms, you can say, 'Heck, this proves that this is not a White man's struggle anymore.'"

What is particularly naive in this type of thinking is that South African officials assume that the West, and the United States in particular, will applaud the greater use of blacks without looking deeper into the underlying purposes for which these steps are being taken. South Africa's blacks are not so credulous. Insofar as the enlistment of blacks is designed to deflect Western criticism and thereby reduce pressures for genuine shifts in the power structure, the West should not be fooled. There are plenty of politicians and some military men in South Africa itself who regard the SACC and the 21 Battalion chiefly as public relations gestures rather than as ways to improve the fighting capacities of the SADF. "The main field application of black soldiers," one high ranking officer said, "is in influencing the local population." Government spokesmen themselves have begun to use the incongruous terms "people's army" and "true people's defence force," creating a strange sound in the ears of those who had been listening to that same government all these years.[24] So, for both domestic and foreign policy purposes, a multiracial armed force is favored *not* as a first choice, and this should be emphasized, but because it is seen to have become a political and economic necessity.

Other Social Considerations

Other politicians speak of the inequities of having whites bearing the burden of defense alone.[25] Many a white citizen has complained about being cannon fodder and about having his career disrupted.[26] Less admissible by Nationalists, but none-

23. *New York Times*, 16 September 1979, p.16.
24. G. de V. Morrison (Craddock), R. F. van Heerden (De Aar), and A. J. Vlok (Verwoerdburg) in *Assembly Debates*, 2 March 1979, cols. 1720, 1730, and 1752. See also Maj. Gen. E. A. C. Pienaar, inspector general of the air force, in *Rand Daily Mail*, 28 January 1979; and the report of the Steyn Commission cited approvingly by the prime minister in *Assembly Debates*, 1 May 1980, col. 5300.
25. E.g., W. Vause Raw, in *Assembly Debates*, 6 May 1976, col. 6167; and *The Star* (Weekly Air Edition), 16 February 1974, p. 9.
26. See, e.g., the letter to editor in *The Star* (Weekly Air Edition), 26 February 1977, p. 9; and the replies on 12 March 1977, p. 9.

theless effective, is the point that blacks have, historically, made good fighters. "Can one imagine a better advantage than an African who was born and who had grown up in the bush, who is used to the heat and the conditions, fighting for South Africa in the conditions which he knows best."[27] Black people make "very doughty warriors." Although this argument is intended to win converts, it hardly helps to remind South Africa's whites that blacks "certainly had a very fine military tradition, as our forefathers found out."[28] This very point can lead to some hesitation. Some Nationalists are still wary of expanding the use of blacks and of giving blacks extensive combat roles and greater authority. The idea that people of color can go and fight the war for whites and that whites can merely occupy command positions should be guarded against, Thomas Langley (NP, Waterkloof) told his colleagues. "We should learn from history that he who defends his country physically, is the man who inherits the country."[29] In his discourse Langley went on to cite Alexander the Great, the Roman Empire, and the Britons, arguing that when slaves, mercenaries, and others were used these practices eventually led to the collapse of the empires. Perhaps this is particularly revealing of a train of Nationalist thought — that South African blacks are comparable in position and status to slaves or, in their fighting capacity, to mercenaries. There is no hint here that blacks could become full-fledged citizens or that a totally nonracist South African nation might be possible.

Other economic and social considerations (besides manpower) also are injected in the debate. Some have contended that the formation of special service battalions (not all to be used militarily) can take up the slack of unemployed blacks.[30] Despite the facts that military service is a most expensive and ineffective way of dealing with unemployment, that those most

27. Raw, in *The Star* (Weekly Air Edition), 16 February 1974, p. 9; see also journalist Al J. Venter, quoted in *The Star*, 30 October 1971, p. 6.

28. G. W. Mills (UP, Pietermaritzburg North) in *Assembly Debates,* 21 April 1977, col. 5806.

29. *Assembly Debates,* 9 May 1977, col. 7098.

30. W. H. D. Deacon (Independent United Party [IUP], Albany) and J. W. E. Wiley (IUP, Simonstown) in *Assembly Debates,* 20 and 21 April 1977, cols. 5737, 5795.

likely to be unemployed are also least likely to make good
recruits, and that the unemployment problem is so endemic
and extensive among black South Africans that such a solution
would barely scratch the surface, the argument was broached.
Why not use defense expenditures to stimulate economic activity in the black community? As more blacks are hired into the
SADF new jobs are created. By training black artisans in the
Defence Force and the armaments industry skills are provided
to enable blacks to upgrade themselves. Thus, so we are told,
defense, rather than diverting capital from needed social pro-
jects, serves a double purpose.[31] It would be, however, unwise
to require a defense force to resolve the social problems that
surround it. Admittedly, the SADF cannot be isolated from
wider society, but the SADF is not a social welfare agency — it is
a professional military force. The possibility of a social welfare
function for the SADF is precisely the line the Nationalist government does not want to adopt publicly. To be sure, citizen
military service may generate a commitment to the fatherland.
But although the Nationalists are willing to sit back and allow
their opponents to push them in directions they are heading
anyway, under no circumstances can they acquiesce to the position that greater and more equitable use of blacks in the SADF
will lead to social rewards in terms of changes in race relations
in civilian life. The Nationalists perceive that their own constituents will not subscribe to such reasoning. Langley, for example, has accused the Progressive Reform Party (PRP) and the
UP (the predecessors of the present PFP and New Republic
Party [NRP] respectively) of trying to bring their "integration
ideals" in "via the back door."[32]

Opinion in the SADF Hierarchy

There is a body of opinion, entrenched at higher levels at
Defence headquarters, that perceives the SADF as the van-
guard of social reform in South Africa. It is not unusual to hear
opinions expressed such as those of Adm. Ronald A. Edwards,
chief of Staff Personnel. He sees the Defence Force as a catalyst

31. H. Schwarz in ibid., 21 April 1977, col. 5782.
32. Ibid., 9 May 1977, cols. 7097 – 98.

for South African society as a whole, encouraging the regime to abandon rigid racist patterns and to make the transition to institutions predicated on the principle of merit. "In some ways we're spearheading the thing," he said. "We're chipping away at things that have encrusted themselves onto our national life over the years."[33]

Even more openly corrosive to the trappings of petty apartheid are the views of Maj. Gen. G. J. J. Boshoff, chief of Army Logistics. To gain the flavor of this view, apparently strongly felt since it was made public in an address to youth leaders, it is helpful to quote at length.

> We will never be able to withstand modern threats unless all the nations of South Africa strive for solidarity and form a solid communal front against outside attack. . . . It is pathetic to see how some individuals stand around passively and rely on the Defence Force to protect their country. We humiliate each other with words . . . kick each other out of the way, without knowing that we are busy undermining our own particular [white] nation and are handing our communal fatherland to the enemy on a plate . . . . We must recognize that today there is no basic apparent difference in the lifestyle of the Black and White man. We must realize that these Blacks I have just referred to are no longer pleased with the traditional social segregation regulations. They revolt against our hardnecked refusal to make new concessions about social intercourse with them. They accuse us of discrimination on grounds of colour and that we are denying their humanity.[34]

He calls on whites to overcome the two "sicknesses" which are stumbling blocks to better race relations: first, the fear of losing white identity if there is "socialisation" with blacks and, second, the apologetic attitude regarding white privilege.

These messages are designed for public consumption by the defense hierarchy and in tone these plans for an approach to meritocracy are self-assured. Make no mistake, SADF leaders are committed to maintaining the status quo, the fundamental political order of things. They know full well that the instruments of education remain firmly in white hands. The transition even to a meritocracy of sorts would be slow, and advantage would continue to be with those who establish the

33. *New York Times*, 16 September 1979, p. 16.
34. *The Star* (Daily Edition), 26 April 1977.

standards and who judge performance. The government, of course, must distance itself from such statements, for the social and political repercussions frighten them. Nonetheless statements of this sort continue to appear, largely, one suspects, to impress foreign interests.

Conclusions

By and large, throughout the dozens of debates on the use of blacks, little real controversy has arisen. Nationalists and their government stand firm and watch the opposition, keen on demonstrating its unquestioned loyalty to the state on this defense issue, call for a more complete and rapid implementation of a policy government has already launched and carefully nurtured. And as each new step is taken to deepen and broaden black military roles, government has the enviable task of observing opposition politicians and the press grudgingly praising government, calling for more action but fundamentally approving of government's policy on this one issue.

What resistance there is in Parliament comes largely from the Nationalist right wing. It is not so much a challenge or a confrontation that these spokesmen offer, but more a restraining hand — a counsel of prudence based on fear and an inherent conservatism. Thus a Langley lectures Parliament on the history of empires using slaves and mercenaries to guard against outside threats. There are the implied warnings in code or via buzzwords — J. W. Greef's (NP, Aliwal) references to "Non-Whites" doing "certain work" so that more white national servicemen will be available for "essential operational duties."[35] To this can be added Langley's fear of "swamping the Defence Force with non-Whites" and even the Defence Minister's assurances that training of black commandos would take place only "in specific directions" and for "specific purposes."[36] In Parliament the issues joined deal with the pace of black recruitment, responsibilities and roles, degrees of equality and segregation, and, by implication, modes of control. Many of the opponents of a wider use of blacks for defense have been

35. *Assembly Debates,* 22 April 1977, col. 5851.
36. Ibid., 22 April 1977, col. 5904.

won over or silenced by the carefully modulated policies P. W. Botha has devised during his tenure at Defence. Botha, as prime minister, is careful to insert cautionary signals in his speeches to disarm his critics on the right. At the same time that he endorses a "representative Defence Force," he hedges. Phrases like "as far as the economy allows" and "cannot be built on numbers only" signal his awareness of whites' misgivings. "The manpower problem cannot be solved overnight, as people think, simply by adding elements from the people to the defence force."[37] Even opposition within the SADF itself seems to have been muted in the public debate, as would generally be expected, but hardly to the degree that it has. Commandant Swanepoel, commander of the black 21 Battalion, had earlier in his military career been opposed to arming blacks. "But now that I've worked with these people, I'm absolutely convinced of their loyalty and their willingness to fight for the cause." What else could he be expected to say? Yet this view is illustrative of a more widely held set of attitudes within the middle level of the Permanent Force. It is also significant that Cmdt. Swanepoel served four years as a military aide to Botha at the Department of Defence.[38] But it is not that the commandant has been totally won over. He is quite *verkrampte* on some race issues and is perhaps less optimistic and romantic about the prospects of genuine integration in the forces.[39] But, nonetheless, here is a hardened professional military man singing the virtues of a black military unit, carried along by the momentum of a ministry and a defense establishment pragmatically altering the character of the force, although not its purposes.

For the moment white opposition to blacks in the SADF has been eclipsed. It still seethes beneath the surface. Within the Defence Force it creates awkward moments, delaying and resisting change and questioning why. And always there are the gnawing doubts that this course may undermine the "nation" the whites have come to worship and defend.

37. Ibid., 1 May 1980, col. 5300.
38. *New York Times*, 16 September 1979, pp. 1, 16.
39. Interview, Lenz, 25 July 1979.

7

Blacks in the
South African Police

THE MOVEMENT TOWARD the use of blacks in the
Defence Force began, perhaps unwittingly, with the employment of blacks in the South African Police (SAP) — unwittingly
in the sense that blacks in the SAP were not intended, at first,
for traditional military or defense purposes. Rather, in order
to secure compliance with and enforcement of the domestic
laws of South Africa, it had been deemed important to utilize
members of the various racial groups to police their own peoples. In fact large numbers of blacks were employed by the
SAP—they functioned in a paramilitary, hierarchical setting;
they were eventually armed and assigned for duties on the
borders; indeed, they were even deployed outside of the territory of the Republic of South Africa. So black involvement in
the SAP, although not strictly a SADF matter, contributed to a
willingness to train blacks for military purposes and, eventually, for combat roles.

This chapter cannot be a full-scale treatment of the political
and security aspects of the SAP.[1] Rather, we shall attempt to

1. Scholarly literature on the SAP is thin. The treatments closest to this
perspective are Albie Sachs, "The Instruments of Domination in South Af-

touch upon those aspects of the police which affected and affect the eventual employment of blacks in the SADF itself — the recruitment and use of black members and their quasi-military development. In other words we shall look briefly at the SAP as an armed force in the total defense posture of the Republic and at the growing involvement of the SADF in maintaining domestic order in collaboration with the SAP.

The SAP as a Paramilitary Organization

All police forces are to a large extent political organizations. Their principal function is to enforce the laws, and, as a coercive instrument of the state, they are designed ostensibly to maintain a particular constitutional order. F. W. Maitland almost a century ago referred to the obvious similarity between the words "police, policy, polity, politics, politic, political and politician."[2]

Yet as political organizations police institutions have increasingly assumed quasi-military and paramilitary functions. Cynthia Enloe writes of the worldwide pattern of militarization of the police, that is, of the acquisition by police institutions of military characteristics.[3] This has generally been prompted by the particular character of contemporary insurgencies. As the military phase of the struggle for power takes shape and as its bases of operation widen to include sanctuaries and assistance from abroad, the police counter by escalating, so to speak, their own responses.

The South Africa case, however, is somewhat different, although here too there has been considerable progression along the lines mentioned above. The SAP's strong paramili-

rica," in Leonard Thompson and Jeffrey Butler, eds., *Change in Contemporary South Africa* (Berkeley: University of California Press, 1975), pp. 223 – 49; and Phillip Frankel, "South Africa: The Politics of Police Control," *Comparative Politics* 12 (July 1980): 481 – 99.

2. In F. W. Maitland, *Justice and Police* (London, 1885); and quoted in Séamus Breathnach, *The Irish Police: From Earliest Times to the Present Day* (Dublin: Anvil Books, 1974), p. 27.

3. Cynthia H. Enloe, "Ethnicity and Militarization: Factors Shaping the Roles of Police in Third World Nations," *Studies in Comparative International Development* 11 (Fall 1976), especially pp. 27 – 33.

tary features evolved from the exigencies of its colonial situation. What emerged were crossbred institutions of white social control which blended the characteristics of both police and military organizations.[4] The pre-Union provincial police forces were structured along military lines, as was the South African Mounted Rifles (SAMR), established in 1912, a "third force" between the regular SAP (established in 1913) and the Union Defence Force. The SAMR came to be absorbed into the SAP in the 1920s.

The longstanding practice of policeman-cum-soldier has been continued to this day in the fuzzy and overlapping division of labor between police and the defense forces. To be sure, there is no "proper" model in a formal sense. The challenge confronting the Pretoria regime cannot easily be divided into discrete issues of domestic order and territorial integrity. An appreciation by the authorities of this reality of modern revolutionary struggle has contributed to a blurring of distinctions between the police and the military. A desire for organizational clarity prompts separation. The urgency of effective counterrevolutionary tactics necessitates coordination and overlapping.

The SAP today is more closely identified with the executive branch of government, especially during the last three decades of National Party rule, while the SADF, with its greater emphasis on technology and professionalism, is more likely to see itself as a support for the regime, though not necessarily as an arm of the National Party per se. Granted, diverse policies and events through the years would seem to demonstrate a success on the part of the National Party government in "capturing" the SADF. But, at least, more distance exists between the SADF and the party than between the SAP and the party, if only in relative terms.

In what ways can the police be regarded as a paramilitary organization? To begin with, the official purposes of the two organizations, the SAP and the SADF, are complementary. Defence Department white papers repeatedly make reference to collaboration between the two. For example, under "De-

4. Frankel, "Politics of Police," p. 482.

partmental Strategic Policy" in the 1973 white paper is, first, "The Defence Force must at all times be able to assist the SA Police in preserving internal order." In that same white paper it is stated that the army's "aim" is to be prepared at all times "to provide effective support to the SA Police in preserving internal order and to counter insurgency and conventional threats." Still later, one can read that each territorial command of the army must be able "to give immediate local assistance to the SA Police from sources other than the Commandos and without mobilizing troops for the purpose."[5] Various statements by officials and politicians reiterate this commitment.[6]

To implement their aims diverse planning and coordinating bodies have been instituted. The 1961 Defence Amendment Act provides for the establishment of an interdepartmental committee to coordinate internal security operations between the SADF and the SAP. A further amendment in 1963 provides for Citizen Force members and members of Commandos to act as policemen in times of emergency.[7] In addition, the device of compulsory military service has been used to channel young national servicemen into the SAP to offset manpower shortages and for counterinsurgency purposes.[8] In 1975 the first batch of five hundred conscripts were diverted from the SADF to undertake national service in the SAP. This system continues, with around one thousand conscripts now being diverted into the SAP each year.[9] Joint staff courses at the S.A. Defence College have, since 1977, included officers of the SAP among their participants, and the curriculum includes a phase

5. Republic of South Africa, Department of Defence, *White Paper on Defence and Armament Production, 1973* (Pretoria: Government Printer, 1973), pp. 5, 8 – 9. See also *White Paper on Defence, 1977* (Simonstown: S.A. Navy, 1977), p. 9; and *White Paper on Defence and Armaments Supply, 1979* (Simonstown: S. A. Navy Printing Unit, 1979), p. 19.

6. E.g., those of the Minister of Defence in Union of South Africa, *Senate Debates* (Hansard), 26 April 1961, cols. 3669 – 70; and in Republic of South Africa, *House of Assembly Debates* (Hansard), 24 June 1967, col. 8267.

7. Irving Kaplan, et al., *Area Handbook for the Republic of South Africa* (Washington: Government Printing Office,1971), p. 743.

8. *The Star* (Johannesburg, Weekly Air Edition), 26 October 1974, p. 2.

9. International Defence and Aid Fund, *The Apartheid War Machine: The Strength and Deployment of the South African Armed Forces*, Fact Paper on Southern Africa, no. 8 (London: International Defence and Aid Fund, 1980), p. 46.

dealing with "The Defence Family and Police Forces."[10] These are just a few examples of the nature of the liaison.

In like measure the SAP is prepared to support, and has supported, the SADF in defending the territory from external incursion, both in South Africa proper and in Namibia and Zimbabwe. The SAP is regarded as "the first line of defence in the event of internal unrest." Its members are trained in infantry drill, combat, and riot control, as well as in the conventional police skills. Before the extensive unrest of the late 1960s government authorities were under the impression that the SAP, if expanded in size, would be able to contain the smoldering political and military unrest facing the regime. By deploying the SAP on the borders and later outside the republic the government could characterize the insurgents as criminal elements rather than as guerrillas seeking political ends. The introduction of universal white male conscription in 1967 and the subsequent fourfold increase in SADF operational forces demonstrates a realization that the SAP is organizationally and militarily unequal to the task. This major shift of emphasis in security thinking, in addition to the functional overlaps between the SAP and the SADF, contributes to the SADF ascendency in the South African political scene.

Since the late 1960s, when the escalating Namibian conflict drew attention to deficiencies in police training in combating guerrilla tactics, greater stress has been given to the formation of special counterinsurgency (COIN) units.[11] The number of policemen completing COIN courses has grown since 1967–68, when 618 were passed. In 1971–72, 2,202 finished such courses.[12] The first blacks (294 trainees) to take part in this training started in 1972. In 1977–78, 1,322 policemen of all races completed riot control and COIN courses, including refresher courses.[13]

10. Department of Defence, *White Paper, 1979*, p. 20; Republic of South Africa, South Africa Defence College, *Joint Staff Course: 1978, Course Review* (n.p., n.d.).
11. *The Star* (Weekly Air Edition), 13 April 1974, p. 3; and 20 April 1974, pp. 12 – 13; and Frankel, "Politics of Police," p. 489 – 93.
12. Frankel, "Politics of Police," p. 497. These courses are described in "Learning to survive in a life-or-death situation," *Paratus* 32, (May 1981): 30 – 31.
13. Republic of South Africa, *Annual Report of the Commissioner of the South*

Every policeman under the age of fifty is liable for service on the border, which involves trying both to combat infiltration and to stem the flow of black youths leaving the country for training abroad as guerrilla fighters. Each policeman must serve two three- to six-month stints. Tours of duty in these "operational areas" have become the rule, so most policemen have on-the-job experience as well as formal COIN training. It has not been revealed how many police are on the "borders," but their numbers are understood to be a considerable drain on normal law enforcement sections of the SAP.[14]

Units of the SAP have operated in the Zambezi Valley, in support of the Rhodesian security forces, between 1967 and 1975, when they were withdrawn with great fanfare. Service there was not popular, and bonuses (R1,200 for whites and R900 for blacks) were offered to men who served for a continuous period of twelve months.[15] Although it is not easy to learn details about post-1975 South African involvement in Zimbabwe, there had been some military and police collaboration with the Smith and Muzorewa regimes. South African combat police were deployed in southern Zimbabwe, ostensibly to protect Beit Bridge. In the process there continued to be high-level coordination between the SADF and the SAP. An even greater measure of chiefly military planning and cooperation between Salisbury and Pretoria marked the period of the "internal settlement" (1978 to 1980).[16] When SAP units were withdrawn from Zimbabwe they were immediately transferred to Namibia rather than reintegrated into the domestic police network.[17]

African Police for the Period 1 July 1977 to 30 June 1978 (Pretoria: Government Printer, 1979), p. 3.

14. According to the Minister of Police in 1969 the "northern border" was patrolled by eight hundred white and three hundred nonwhite policemen at any one time; *Rand Daily Mail* (Johannesburg), 3 June 1969, quoted in South African Institute of Race Relations, *A Survey of Race Relations in South Africa, 1969* (Johannesburg: South African Institute of Race Relations, 1970), p. 33.

15. *X-Ray* 5 (December 1974): 3.

16. For a more complete coverage of this period see Anti-Apartheid Movement, *Fire Force Exposed: The Rhodesian Security Forces and Their Role in Defending White Supremacy* (London: Anti-Apartheid Movement, 1979), pp. 36 – 37.

17. South African Institute of Race Relations, *A Survey of Race Relations in South Africa, 1973* (Johannesburg: South African Institute of Race Relations, 1974), p. 312.

Likewise, SAP units have been assigned to the "northern border" since the 1960s, especially in South West Africa in the early period of the insurrection. After a steady increase in police numbers on the borders it became evident that the task was becoming more military in nature. The government then reduced the numbers of policemen and replaced SAP units with army units.[18] Yet SAP units continued to patrol in Namibia and South Africa (as well as in Rhodesia). These units were racially mixed from the beginning, and since 1972 they have been trained and armed for anti-guerrilla combat. They have been engaged in battle and have suffered casualties.

In early 1974 the army began to take over border defense responsibilities in Namibia, and the army's first border fatality occurred shortly thereafter. Even so the SAP continues to select men for border duty. Indeed, coordination between the two institutions marks the transition. Combined SADF-SAP operations in Namibia have been common.[19]

Since the Zimbabwean transition to independent black government, in addition to the independence of Angola and Mozambique, intensified SAP border patrols are being manned by ordinary policemen transferred to border posts for a routine tour of duty as well as by heavily armed members of the SAP Task Force. Nonetheless, infiltration grows; the flight of potential guerrilla trainees continues, and discoveries of arms caches and reports of guerrilla incidents make the border areas increasingly less secure. Large numbers of white-owned farms in border areas have been abandoned or are unoccupied, and this adds to a feeling of apprehension on the parts of the remaining white residents and of the authorities.

Recent changes brought about by the Police Amendment Act of 1979 have further confused the already blurred distinction between the police and the SADF. Two provisions in the act further contribute to the militarization of the SAP. First, members of the police force may conduct searches without warrant and seize materials at any point within the Republic

18. Nicasio G. Valderrama, "Recent Developments in the Build-up of South African Military Forces," in United Nations, Department of Political and Security Council Affairs, Unit on Apartheid, *Notes and Documents*, no. 31 (September 1975): 2.

19. E.g., *Cape Times* (Cape Town), 29 June 1976, p. 1.

within a distance of ten kilometers of any border. Given the proliferation of parcels of land belonging to "independent" homelands, the range of police activity is widened immensely. The old act permitted such action for only one mile. Secondly, the state president may, in the event of war or other emergency, employ the police to assist in the defense of the Republic, "whether within or outside the Republic" (the previous act added an indefinable proviso "but in South Africa"). He may also place the police or any part thereof "under the orders and directions of such person as the State President may for that purpose appoint."[20]

The latter clause is not unlike sections 1 and 6 of the Defence Amendment Act of 1976, by which all geographic bounds are removed on the external deployment of members of the SADF without their prior written consent. The opposition in Parliament resisted both the geographical carte blanche given the SADF and the same features of the Police Amendment Bill. To what extent were the police becoming, legally, an adjunct of the army, a second arm of the military? Is that not the effect of a clause by which the state president can place the police under such persons as he appoints? In reply the Minister of Police sought to reverse the opposition's argument, noting examples of army personnel serving under the Police Department, but by so doing he reconfirmed the intimate links between the two forces:

> At the present moment the SA Police are entitled to use certain units of the Army under given circumstances in any internal crisis in order to control riots. Certain parts of the Army become part of the police for a certain period and are also under police command . . . . In the same way the police are now also granted the right to act in any capacity in or outside the Republic . . . .[21]

In order to facilitate overseas assignment and to remove doubts about the legality of earlier assignments of SAP units to Rhodesia, the government sought to amend the Police Act again in 1980. The 1979 act had authorized the president "in the event of war or other emergency" to employ force members outside of South Africa. Regulation 4(5) of the SAP regu-

20. "Police Amendment Act, 1979: no. 64 of 1979," secs. 2 and 3, in Republic of South Africa, *Government Gazette* 168, no. 6500, 13 June 1979.

21. *Assembly Debates,* 27 March 1979, col. 3362.

lations, by which the SAP was deployed in Rhodesia, had been used, but questionably. The new act gives power to the Commissioner of Police with ministerial approval to authorize SAP service outside the Republic in the exercise of police functions.[22]

In short, the past decades have seen the security forces of the South African state become even more coordinated and, if not a seamless web, sufficiently seamless to assure no safety for regime opponents by virtue of lack of coordination between or unexpected lacunae in the laws and duties of the two branches — the SADF and the SAP. As a S.A. Police report indicated regarding the SAP in Rhodesia, "The argument as to whether they are police or army is quite academic. In Rhodesia at least they have exactly the same function as the Rhodesian Army."[23] Admittedly there has been some friction between the SADF and the SAP, especially during the years when Gen. Hendrik van den Bergh was close to Prime Minister Vorster and headed the Bureau of State Security (BOSS) and when P. W. Botha was Minister of Defence. There were regular contests over jurisdiction (e.g., which group would have principal responsibility for intelligence gathering and evaluation) and policy (e.g., how to deal with the Frelimo Government in Mozambique and with the civil war in Angola). With General Malan at the right hand of the prime minister and BOSS, later called the Department of National Security (DONS) and now known as the National Intelligence Service, largely discredited and weakened thanks to Vorster's demise and to the "Muldergate" scandal in the Department of Information, the old competition has abated. Within each organization, as well, there are internal tensions, as one would expect in large bureaucracies. These have, so far, proved to be manageable.

Blacks in the SAP

As the SAP became increasingly involved in military functions, so too did large numbers of blacks, as members of the SAP,

22. Ibid., 28 March 1980, cols. 3824–31.
23. As quoted in International Defence and Aid Fund, *Apartheid War Machine*, p. 46.

become involved in the sorts of combat roles traditionally associated with the defense of the state. Blacks have long constituted a large proportion of the SAP establishment. For the last
decade and a half roughly half (or slightly less) of the members
of the police force have been black. The SAP has become a
multiracial institution, if not in command structure, at least in
composition. The latest official figures, from 31 December
1979, placed black membership in the SAP at 49 percent of the
total.[24] The SAP has had little difficulty recruiting from black
groups, although Coloureds and Indians have historically been
less enthusiastic about enlistment compared to African blacks;
the Police Reserve, on the other hand, has had little success
appealing to the black communities for volunteers. On 31 December 1978 the breakdown by group was: 877 Indians, 1,795
Coloureds, and 12,990 black African members of the SAP.[25]
Many blacks look upon the police as an alternative channel for
employment and upward mobility especially since unemployment has become an endemic feature of black subsistence
through the 1970s. Larger numbers of black applicants are
matriculants. In contrast, the authorities have had difficulties
attracting qualified white applicants who wish to regard the
police as a career. Despite this situation, the SAP has rejected
large numbers of applicants, especially since 1970.[26] Many of
the applicants are educationally ill-prepared. Most are drawn
from the lower-middle and working classes of the white (especially Afrikaner) social structure. More resignations from the
service, officially referred to as wastage (mostly by the purchas-
ing of discharges), also occurs among whites than among
blacks. With regard to the Reserve Police Force, a lower proportion—as of the end of 1979 only 16 percent of the reserves—is black.[27]

The imbalance is even more pronounced, however, when
one considers the racial distribution by rank. According to the
annual report of the Commissioner of Police, as of 31 Decem-

24. 16,275 white and 15,613 black members; see *Assembly Debates*, 19 February 1980, Q cols. 114–16.
25. *Assembly Debates*, 14 February 1979, Q cols. 63–64.
26. Frankel, "Politics of Police," p. 497.
27. *Assembly Debates*, 6 June 1980, Q col. 848.

TABLE 9.
Members of the Police, by Rank and Race, 1976

	White	Black
Major and above	725	0
Captain	670	11
Lieutenant	793	61
Warrant officer	2,072	27
Sergeant	4,473	2,751
Constable	9,076	13,189
TOTAL	17,809	16,039

SOURCE: South African Institute of Race Relations, *Survey of Race Relations in South Africa, 1977* (Johannesburg: South African Institute of Race Relations, 1978), p. 105; and Republic of South Africa, *Annual Report of the Commissioner of the South African Police for the Period 1 July 1977 to 30 June 1978* (Pretoria: Government Printer, 1979), p. 2.

ber 1976 rank distributions were as shown in table 9. Despite some slight improvement since 1976 the basic racial hierarchy is undisturbed. By the end of 1980 there were 21 Indian, 33 Coloured, and 85 African commissioned officers in the SAP. Considerably better progress has been made at lower ranks, where there is a total of 940 black warrant officers.[28] The improvement has partly grown out of a response to the 1976 rioting in the consideration that members of subject peoples may best be able to contain incipient violence. Also in keeping with post-riot analyses has been an accelerated effort to give black officers greater responsibility for police work in the townships. Today, police stations in Soweto are staffed mainly by blacks (although division headquarters is still under white command). A few other stations, mostly in rural areas, are independently administered by black officers. By August 1981 there were 50 stations under "nonwhite" command (35 under Africans, 14 under Coloureds, and 1 under an Indian officer).[29]

Black police have participated in most of the "border" oper-

28. As of 31 December 1980; see *Assembly Debates,* 30 January 1981, Q cols. 16 – 18.

29. Frankel, "Politics of Police," pp. 494 – 95, 499; and *Assembly Debates,* 28 August 1981, Q cols. 233 – 34. This represents a reduction of nineteen African stations since 1978. Most represented stations in recently "independent" homelands.

ations since the late 1960s, in the Zambezi Valley of Zimbabwe, on the Republic's borders, and in Namibia (Caprivi, Ovambo, and elsewhere). These men have been armed and, since 1972, trained and equipped with automatic and semiautomatic weapons. Their officers have been almost exclusively white, with black sergeants in support. The units assigned are usually mixed racially and generally they spend a tour of three months on the border. This policy could be justified by white politicians and their constituents because of the remoteness of the combat areas from "white" South Africa.

The police in South Africa have carried guns as a matter of course since the early 1950s, although mounted police in rural areas have been armed since 1913. As a rule, however, few black policemen carried revolvers until recently, at least not before the late 1960s. Today, every recruit, white or black, passing through police college (Pretoria for whites, Hammanskraal [Transvaal] for black Africans, Bishop Lavis [Cape] for Coloureds, and Wentworth [Natal] for Indians) is issued with a side arm and an R1 rifle by the Department of Police.[30] The R1s are always kept in the strongrooms of the police stations—they are never taken home. The side arms are usually handed in at the police station, unless a detective is likely to be called out during the night. Murder and Robbery Squad members and senior officers might qualify for this; few blacks would. In special circumstances, rioting, and border duty the SAP uses submachine guns, sneeze machines (for riots), and shotguns. These are drawn from police arsenals as needed.

Chances are, therefore, that few white South Africans are likely to encounter an armed black policeman, certainly not one equipped for combat. The recent creation of black counterinsurgency formations to function in urban areas may render armed black police more visible to the white citizenry.[31] Nonetheless, the knowledge that black men are serving in an armed force, if in the eyes of white South Africans for no reason other than to keep their own black people in line, does contribute to a willingness to accept black people in the De-

30. *Rand Daily Mail*, 17 January 1979.
31. *The Star* (Weekly Air Edition), 13 September 1969, p. 7; and *Assembly Debates*, 22 June 1976, col. 1279.

TABLE 10.
Base Salaries of the Police, by Rank and Race, 1980

	White	Coloured, Indian	African
Major	R8640 – 11580	R7200 – 9900	R6300 – 8200
Captain	7200 – 10320	6300 – 8640	5160 – 7200
Warrant officer	4350 – 7200	3720 – 6300	3000 – 5160
Sergeant	3540 – 6600	3000 – 5790	2200 – 4740
Constable	2100 – 5160	1842 – 4320	1272 – 3540

SOURCE: Republic of South Africa, *House of Assembly Debates* (Hansard), 11 May 1979, Q cols. 852 – 56; and 3 March 1980, Q cols. 281 – 84. In 1981 the Minister of Police refused to publish particulars of police salaries and other service conditions when the information was requested by an opposition member of Parliament. *Assembly Debates*, 7 October 1981, Q col. 659.

fence Force itself. It certainly breaks down the hollow postulate that no weapons should be allowed in the hands of blacks and encourages a more flexible and selective approach to this facet of public policy. In many respects the functional line between SAP and SADF has become indiscernible.[32]

We have already made reference to the racially segregated character of police units in terms of the command structure and of the variable access to weapons and other facilities within the SAP. Financial benefits for members of the SAP are also allocated according to race. From basic pay to other inducements, one's color determines one's rewards. As of March 1980 basic compensation ranges in selected ranks were as shown in table 10. Despite wage increases, compensation is still inadequate to attract sufficient qualified applicants. In May 1979 the number of vacancies in the force was considerable: 2,176 white and 1,769 black openings.[33] In addition, differential bonuses for voluntary service in Zimbabwe prevailed, and levels of subsistence allowances on border duty differed according to race.[34] Other fringe benefits are based on race rather than on

32. This very line was developed by the leader of the opposition, Sir de Villiers Graaff (UP, Groote Schuur) in 1974; see *Assembly Debates,* 4 February 1974, col. 23; and the Defence Minister's rejection of the parallel, 7 February 1974, col. 305.

33. South African Institute of Race Relations, *A Survey of Race Relations in South Africa, 1979* (Johannesburg: South African Institute of Race Relations, 1980), p. 250.

34. South African Institute of Race Relations, *A Survey of Race Relations in*

rank alone or on seniority. Of course, promotion and other job prospects have been, for years, a function of race.

Popular Attitudes Toward the Black Police

Today the police force has far closer daily contact with the black population than does the SADF. The police are widely regarded as the coercive political instrument of the central government. They are responsible for enforcing the formal rules of the system, rules which to the blacks are substantively and procedurally unjust and racist. The force is designed not only to fight crime — in the sense of "protecting" potential and actual victims of crime — but also to destroy certain black resistance movements and other forms of political opposition to the regime. As far as black people are concerned, black policemen are as responsible for their oppression as the whites — perhaps more so, since black police are vigorous and frequently violent accomplices to the dominant system. That many black policemen may perceive of police work as a bona fide route for upward mobility, and that they may be performing a useful public service, is small consolation to black citizens who must adapt to repressive laws. Moreover, black police have undergone rigorous indoctrination and have been screened carefully to weed out those less psychologically inclined to favor the existing order. This contributes to the low image of the black police, especially since the Soweto uprising in 1976.

The police leadership has consciously sought to employ other blacks against their racial kin. In the 1976 and 1977 unrest the police, including black police, were responsible for recruiting insecure and politically conservative migrant workers to attack those dissidents seeking to prolong the protest in the townships.[35] These "black specials" were armed dur-

---

South Africa, 1972 (Johannesburg: South African Institute of Race Relations, 1973), p. 312.

35. South African Institute of Race Relations, *South Africa in Travail: The Disturbances of 1976/77, Evidence Presented by the South African Institute of Race Relations to Cillié Commission of Inquiry into the Riots at Soweto and Other Places During June 1976* (Johannesburg: South African Institute of Race Relations, 1978), p. 114.

ing the rioting and went into "battle" against student protesters and boycott organizers.[36] In other ways the police sought to manipulate tribal tensions. They brought into Soweto rural black policemen unfamiliar with local peoples, thereby securing dutiful hoplites more willing to use brutal force against fellow blacks. The result is that, by and large, township residents fear and resent black police perhaps more than they do their white colleagues.[37]

Despite the deserved reputation for brutality of the black police, much of which is brought on by a professional desire to demonstrate organizational loyalty and to please white superiors and thereby assure acceptance and perhaps promotion, there is some evidence that all black policemen do not conform to this image of a bloodthirsty "Black Jack." Reports abound of a reluctance by some black policemen to enforce certain race laws, including the pass laws (although this may be a function of police corruption as much as of sympathy for the victims of the laws). In rare instances a few black police have been supportive of the resistance fighters. One of the charges against one of those accused in the Bethel Pan-Africanist Congress (PAC) Trial was that in September 1975 he "aided a group of 15 Black municipal policemen to undergo military training abroad," an act which allegedly took place in Soweto.[38] By and large, disloyalty is minimal among black policemen, and for this they are hated in the townships. Black policemen, their families, and their property were and are conscious targets of the dissidents in Soweto.[39] So effective has the social ostracization been that the SAP depends increasingly on rural black recruits rather than on urban blacks.

The violence that marked the unrest of 1976 did add to

36. See Counter Information Service, *Black South Africa Explodes* (Washington: The Transnational Institute, 1977), p. 36; *The World* (Johannesburg), 24 August 1976; and *Sunday Times* (Johannesburg), 28 August 1976.

37. *Post* (Johannesburg), 15 January 1979; Frankel, "Politics of Police," pp. 493–95.

38. Glenn Moss, *Political Trials, South Africa: 1976–1979*, Development Studies Group Information Publication 2 (Johannesburg: Development Studies Group, University of the Witwatersrand, 1979), p. 63.

39. South African Institute of Race Relations, *South Africa in Travail*, p.115; *Rand Daily Mail*, 9 April 1980, p. 2.

existing pressure for change within the SAP. Efforts have begun to improve police-community (i.e., urban black) relations.
This has led, among other things, to accelerated black promotions into higher ranks, devolution of greater responsibility to
black officers, application of "softer" forms of riot control technology (e.g., water cannon, rubber bullets, "sneeze machines"),
and, in January 1979, the creation of a Public Relations Division of the SAP.[40] It would appear from statements made by
police officials that this unit cannot be regarded as a bona fide
attempt to improve relations between the black community
and the police but rather an attempt to improve the "press"
received by SAP and thereby to assure better police control of
the community. As Phillip Frankel carefully points out, the
socialization process in South Africa is very much geared to
acceptance of coercion as an integral feature of race relations.[41]
To the SAP relations ipso facto mean control — not the adop-
tion of structural alterations in police institutions that might
reorder the basis of black relations with the cutting edge of the
regime, the police. They do not see "community relations" as a
noncoercive response to the threat of civil violence except insofar as manipulation of information can render more effective
control. Many white South Africans pay lip service to the necessity of improving the police image in the townships. So far,
at least, substantive initiatives have not dealt with the essence of
the issues. Black hostility continues to mount toward the regime and toward its most obvious agent in the townships, the
police — black as well as white. Continuing reports of raids on
township police stations, which have come to be armed camps,
forces of occupation in every sense, and harrassment of black
policemen are only the tip of an iceberg of discontent and
hatred for the racist regime. Not much can rescue the image of
the police at this point.

Given black South Africa's domestic experience with the
SAP, the roles of blacks within that organization, and the evolving but by no means unique militarization of the SAP, it is
perfectly understandable that the police seem to have a more

40. South African Institute of Race Relations, *Survey, 1979,* pp.106 – 7.
41. Frankel, "Politics of Police," pp. 493 – 95.

negative image than does the SADF. In like measure blacks in
the SAP are less highly regarded than blacks in the SADF,
although there is no systematic data on which to base this statement. Yet there does seem to be a distinction made in the
popular mind between SAP and SADF. The more citizens interact with the domestic coercive arm of the state, the less they
seem prepared to cooperate. In other words they see it for
what it is, the engine of their own repression. There is a lesson
here for the SADF. People simply will not accept those, especially from their own people, who are seen to be used to keep
them subjugated. Police are, so far, the most direct manifestation of that subjugation. The SADF is more remote, less obvious, and hence less loathed and distrusted. But as the struggle becomes more violent and more domestic and as the police
experience greater difficulties containing the unrest, a pattern
of SADF deployment in the townships could, as in Zimbabwe,
lead to a transference of rejection, something the SADF wishes
to avoid.

Military personnel have participated in joint actions with the
police in Soweto and in Coloured townships. They try to keep
to the background, but the evidence is clear — either the situation in urban areas is so serious that it is necessary to call in the
SADF or the Defence Force has begun to assume a new civilian
political role. The SADF was involved in the 1976 and subsequent disturbances, but it was deployed to defend white resi-
dential areas and business districts rather than to play an active
combat role in the townships. In 1976 the government wanted
to portray the events as a disturbance involving criminals and
police. To involve the SADF directly would give the appearance of a civil war or uprising. Apparently government is less
able to deny the obvious these days.

8

Coloured Soldiers and Sailors:
A Tradition in Transition

WE HAVE SEEN how the Coloured population historically has been intimately associated with white South Africa in
security and military affairs. So close has been that contact and
so deep that military tradition that one Nationalist M.P.
boasted that "with a few years' interruption, the Cape Corps
can certainly lay claim to seniority as the oldest South African
regiment."[1] The general point might be made with regard to
all social relations between whites and Coloureds in that society. The Coloured population has customarily identified more
closely with the whites than with other black peoples. And
conversely, whites more readily identify and associate with Coloureds than with darker South Africans. Certainly this should
not be construed to mean that the two groups accept one another, nor more particularly that whites regard Coloureds as
part of the white community — far from it. But in relative and
historic terms the links are unmistakable.

1. P. J. Badenhorst in Republic of South Africa, *House of Assembly Debates*
(Hansard), 9 September 1974, col. 2531. The same view was expressed by
Adm. H. H. Biermann, former chief of the SADF; see *Cape Times* (Cape Town),
19 September 1977.

Racial Attitudes

Skin color alone, however, does not sufficiently explain the nexus between whites and Coloureds. The Coloured population is, by and large, westernized. Various components of culture—language, religion, family structure, geographical distribution, housing patterns, heritage, values, and mores—all point up the fact that Coloureds differ from whites chiefly in skin color and in the ways they are treated by the dominant white society in which they are dispersed. But if Coloureds and whites have been drawn together it has been out of a common fear and not out of a common respect or admiration. It is *swart gewaar,* the black menace, carefully played upon by white politicians, and an appreciation of their own marginality that has prevented middle-class Coloureds from identifying with black consciousness and an inclusive black nationalism. For many Coloureds the desire to maintain and enhance social position relative to the dominant whites can best be fulfilled by associating with groups considered to be of high prestige and by disassociating with those low in the prestige hierarchy.[2]

It is the ambiguous status of the Coloured people—their westernized, almost Afrikaner, culture and their physical proximity to the surrounding white community (at least in comparison with blacker South Africans)—that South Africa's whites and some Coloureds have subtly manipulated.[3] To be sure, Boer nationalists are not about to renounce generations of ingrained racial prejudice. Despite the official rhetoric that nation and not race is the *raison d'être* of separate development, governmental policy does not accept a view commonly mouthed by some liberal whites—that the Coloureds arrived just nine months after the Dutch, and because of centuries of cooperation, cohabitation, and interaction Coloureds are really brown Afrikaners. As one *verligte* Afrikaner sociologist put it: "Shorn of all its niceties, the insistence on the retention of

2. For examples of such prejudicial, anti-black views, see Marianne Brindley, *Western Coloured Township: Problems of an Urban Slum* (Johannesburg: Ravan Press, 1976), pp. 75–77.

3. E.g., see Graham Watson, *Passing for White: A Study of Racial Assimilation in a South African School* (London: Tavistock, 1970).

this racial basis, the insistence on the protection of the identity of the Whites, *reveals a naked racism at the basis of the Nationalist ideology.*"[4] Few would openly repeat the view of M. W. Holland, a white representing Coloured interests in the House of Assembly, when he asserted: "Our Coloured fellow citizens are westerners by background, westerners by origin and are also potential westerners. They must be set alongside the Whites. Potentially the Coloureds are brown Whites."[5] Similarly, when a 1975 survey put the question: "Do you regard an Afrikaans-speaking Coloured person who is a member of the Neder-duitse Gereformeerde Kerk as an Afrikaner?" the reaction among all white language groups was that 67.2 percent said "yes," 29.3 percent said "no," and 3.5 percent did not answer. Nearly 80 percent of white Afrikaners in the Cape answered "yes," compared with 59.5 percent in the Transvaal.[6] It is this kind of thinking that, to *verkrampte* Afrikaners, represents the Achilles heel of the *volk*. One highly placed member of the Broederbond put it: "The Coloureds are not just brown Afrikaners. In the beginning we were not racially prejudiced. If you were Christian you were welcome. But their culture drifted away. They did not share our values . . . . If we let them in [the *volk*] they will so weaken our culture as to destroy us."[7]

The government's position is more subtle. Indeed, with a bit of minor modification a government spokesman might be able to subscribe to Holland's view, the key imprecise words of which are "alongside of." The government does not deny the cultural similarities between Coloureds and whites. Nonetheless it emphasizes the distinctions between the two groups. The Coloureds are an identifiable group, and the identifying characteristics must be recognized and perpetuated. This can be done, the government would argue, not by the application of the Bantustans or homelands policy but by another mode of

4. S. P. Cilliers, "The Concept of Citizenship and the Future of the Coloured Community," in Michael G. Whisson and Hendrik W. van der Merwe, eds., *Coloured Citizenship in South Africa* (Rondebosch: Abe Bailey Institute of Interracial Studies, University of Cape Town, 1972), p. 144; the italics are his.

5. *Assembly Debates*, 5 May 1969, col. 5308.

6. *The Star* (Johannesburg), 11 October 1975, p. 7.

7. Interview, 28 June 1979, Pretoria.

segregation euphemistically called "parallel development." In many respects this policy is an ad hoc, somewhat flexible set of responses to diverse and dynamic pressures. But first a separation of institutions and societal processes that both groups share would be necessitated before new, "parallel" structures could be fashioned. Not only did the Nationalist government set out systematically to dismantle institutions whites and Coloureds had in common and to deny numerous civil and political rights to Coloureds but it has resisted the more recent efforts to "bring Coloureds into the *laager.*" Inclusion into the citizenry of the country does not necessarily mean assimilation, but the National Party behaves as if one would automatically lead to the other. Yet citizenship is fundamentally useless if it effectively subordinates one before the law. Citizenship for Coloureds has borne with it a connotation of being second class that appears to be tolerable only in the sense that there are third and fourth class citizens below. The Theron Commission to study Coloured affairs made several important recommendations in 1976 that would make symbolic gestures and real concessions to Coloureds.[8] Despite the fact that such recommendations, even if completely implemented, would not bring Coloureds full equality, the government rejected most of them out of hand.

In this sort of environment it is small wonder that the idea of black consciousness and solidarity should fall on fertile soil. Black consciousness is an inclusive concept, embracing black Africans, Coloureds, and Indians. Although there have been mergers and alliances involving political groups and spokespersons representing these three racial groups in the past, the recent manifestations of black unity appear to have a greater chance of taking root largely because white rejection is nearly complete. After over three decades of Nationalist rule the displacement of whites from power by anything less than revolu-

8. S. T. van der Horst, ed., *The Theron Commission Report: A Summary of the Findings and Recommendations of the Commission of Enquiry into Matters Relating to the Coloured Population Group* (Johannesburg: South African Institute of Race Relations, December 1976). The Government Printer issued only the Afrikaans version of the report. An English translation of the summaries at the end of the chapters was provided to members of Parliament.

tionary upheaval seems unlikely. The black peoples have
learned of the apportionment of force the hard way. Years of
rejection have taken their toll. Attitudes are changing, at first
imperceptively, but still they are changing. The change shows
first among younger and lower-class Coloureds. No matter
how loudly the theme of *swart gewaar* is played, the whites' fear
of black African nationalism has not convinced young Coloureds to deny their African brothers. In the process their
parents and the more established Coloureds are coming to
regard their class interests and their color as complementary.
Although many have viewed their situation in this way in the
past, most Coloureds adopted the view that the interests of
their class and color might best be furthered by trying to identify with whites. Yet whites have repeatedly rejected such an
identification. But now class and color can coalesce into a solidarity among blacks which is increasingly proletarian. It would
be foolish to assume that the time has arrived for this process to
blossom. But it would be equally blind not to see its first signs.

So far, at least, it has been difficult to breathe institutional life
into the various calls for black solidarity. Organizations do not
thrive in an atmosphere of governmental repression. Sponta-
neously, however, as at Cape Town in 1976, Coloureds and
black Africans have been able to supply their own fluid political
leadership and structure, and in the process some Coloureds
have lined up with other blacks. But formal linkages have
proved impossible to forge. For many Coloureds, perhaps for
still a majority of them, it has proved difficult to bridge the
cultural and linguistic gaps between themselves and black Africans. The reverse relationship has likewise obtained. In a survey of middle-class Africans in the Transvaal in the early 1960s
Coloureds were found to be less popular among black Africans
than foreign Europeans or even English-speaking South African whites. The Coloureds were disliked because of their alleged refusal to accept black Africans or to associate themselves with them. Coloureds were accused of trying to place
themselves in positions above Africans by exploiting their relative advantages and privileges *vis-à-vis* Africans. Over half of
the black Africans surveyed took that position. Others accused

Coloureds of what has been called "false consciousness" or self-delusion. Only 10 percent accepted Coloureds openly as "brothers."[9] Melville Edelstein's 1973 survey of young black African students in Soweto seems to indicate changes in attitudes regarding social distance and stereotypes.[10] Whereas urban African matriculants naturally associate more readily with other African blacks of diverse ethnic groups, their second preference went equally to Coloureds and English-speaking South Africans, followed by Indians, Jews, and Afrikaners in that order. Although practically all groups were more favorably seen by pupils born in the city, black African acceptance of Coloureds seemed particularly high among city-born Africans. Among such people tolerance and the greater proclivity for association grows with the urbanization process.

This is not nearly so apparent when dealing with racial stereotypes held by Coloureds. Edelstein's work in the Coloured community of Johannesburg indicates that Coloureds associate most easily with other Coloureds, followed by Indians, English-speaking South Africans, Chinese, Jews, Afrikaners, and finally "Bantus," or black Africans.[11] In other words, as late as 1973 Coloureds in Johannesburg would seem to have preferred to associate even with Afrikaners before they would associate with black Africans. Expressed differently, most Coloureds are proud to be Coloured but would like to be called South African (53 percent). Only 2 percent would prefer to be called "blacks," and in between this range of preference appear names such as Coloured (24 percent), Coloured South African (10 percent), Malay (6 percent), and Cape Coloured (4 per-

9. E. A. Brett, *African Attitudes: A Study of the Social, Racial and Political Attitudes of Some Middle Class Africans,* Fact Paper no. 14–1963 (Johannesburg: South African Institute of Race Relations, 1963), pp. 48–55.

10. Melville Leonard Edelstein, *What Do Young Africans Think? An Attitude Survey of Urban African Matriculating Pupils in Soweto with Special Reference to Stereotyping and Social Distance: A Sociological Study* (Johannesburg: Labour and Community Consultants, 1974), pp. 106–7.

11. Melville Leonard Edelstein, *What Do the Coloureds Think? An Attitude Study of the Coloured Community of Johannesburg* (Johannesburg: Labour and Community Consultants, 1974), p. 83.

cent).[12] Among those who favor a separate Coloured nation, most would not exclude other racial and ethnic groups. Even so 22 percent would exclude black Africans from their nation.[13] The Edelstein surveys, then, paint a picture of black Africans increasingly receptive to closer relations with the Coloureds and Coloureds still largely anxious to keep their distance. Much, however, has happened in South Africa since 1973.

David Curry, then deputy leader of the (Coloured) Labour Party, told a 1971 Cape Town conference that the Coloured people were moving away from white society toward their fellow oppressed, the Africans.[14] But this process has just begun and is by no means far advanced. The survey data would suggest that so far, at least, widescale sympathy and collaboration between Coloureds and black Africans are a thing of the future. However, recent experience indicates that white government policy may have reached a point of no return for the Coloured community. Repeated rejection and rebuff have taken their toll, and larger numbers of Coloureds, especially among the young, are prepared to identify with black Africans. The government, despite efforts to manipulate the Coloured leaders and institutions, have pursued policies that bring about the very outcome they least desire, black solidarity.

Institutional Structures

Despite these underlying currents it was to the Coloured community, or more particularly to selected elements of that community, that the National Party government first turned to satisfy the manpower requirements of the Defence Force. Unlike their predecessors in the First and Second World Wars Coloured leaders, even those involved with agencies and institutions set up by the white government to deflect Coloured political activism, had not appealed to government for a more

12. Ibid., p. 77.
13. Ibid., pp. 77, 91.
14. *The Star* (Daily Edition), 1 May 1971.

active role for their people in the defense of the state. Surely some older Coloureds longed for the nostalgia of the Cape Corps and for the reflected glory that that unit had brought the community. But experience had demonstrated that few concessions would attend military service.

The Cape Corps was disbanded in 1949, to be replaced by a new Cape Corps Auxiliary Service, instituted in 1950. But the latter was designed to provide little more than menial services. Early in 1963 the government decided, and the Minister of Defence announced in Parliament, that the Coloured Corps should be revived as an integral part of the Permanent Force.[15] It was to be a cautious beginning, taking effect in September 1963; training was to begin in January 1964. The old Cape Corps was thus reformed under a new name, the South African Coloured Corps. Its headquarters were at the training center at Eersterivier near Cape Town. The first year's intake was limited to one hundred and forty, with some men especially selected as potential instructors.

Legally these new developments posed few problems. The 1957 Defence Act in effect at the time had merely continued the policy on blacks first developed in the 1912 act. The use of black volunteers has been legally possible all along, and the establishment of the SACC thus was relatively easy since no act of Parliament was necessary. Nonetheless, there had been some National Party embarrassment since the government had again and again and unequivocally maintained that it would never arm blacks in defense of South Africa. Although the Defence Act had been amended in May 1963, minor changes contained therein did not apply to the issue of Coloured volunteers.

Yet even in 1963, with neither a commitment in Rhodesia nor a hot war in Namibia to trouble it, the government was beginning to fear eventual manpower shortages. In the early 1960s a series of statutory changes and governmental statements reflected the tenor of that concern. The Defence Amendment Act of 1961 increased the period of training for Citizen Force trainees. The 1963 Defence Amendment Act

15. *Assembly Debates*, 19 February 1963, cols. 1576– 77.

gave greater flexibility in the deployment of Citizen Force and Commando forces for police duties.[16] The Minister of Defence, J. J. Fouché, stated that: "Our aim is to train every young [white] man for military service whether he is flat footed or not."[17] The Transvaal Congress of the National Party voted overwhelmingly to extend military training to white women (although it was not until 1970 that government announced plans for military training of women), and there the minister reported that by 1963 62 percent of South Africa's white men would have received military training.[18] This was a period, 1960–64, of a steady growth of the Permanent Force from approximately 9,000 to around 16,000. Looked at in this context it is hard to accept the view of one high ranking SADF officer who maintained that it was not really a manpower issue that brought about greater use of blacks. Rather, he argued, whites had been bearing a disproportionate share of South Africa's defense, and, out of "fairness" to whites and to blacks, blacks should be brought in to help defend the country.[19]

In this atmosphere of expansion the Coloured Corps was reborn, a reluctant junior partner created only because the government could think of no better substitute. As originally conceived the Coloured Corps was to be entirely a noncombatant formation. The SACC volunteers were to be treated as career members of the Permanent Force. Once the first Coloured instructors qualified in 1964, SACC men were given opportunities to serve as instructors, musicians, storemen, clerks, drivers, cooks, stretcher bearers, or medical orderlies in the army and seamen, storesmen, clerks, stewards, cooks, engineroom mechanics, riggers, shipwrights, electricians, shops carpenters, and surveyor-recorders in the navy.

To assuage anticipated white reluctance the minister

16. United Nations Security Council, *Report of the Special Committee on the Policies of Apartheid of the Government of the Republic of South Africa,* S/5426, 16 September 1963, pp. 121–22.

17. *Assembly Debates,* 28 May 1963, col. 6784; *South Africa Digest,* 13 June 1963.

18. U.N. Security Council, *Apartheid,* pp. 131–32.

19. Interview, Vice Adm. Ronald Edwards, chief of Staff Personnel, SADF, 16 July 1979, Pretoria.

specified that Corps members would neither be trained in nor used for combat. Indeed, they would be employed in "traditional" musterings, some of which he specified. The first intake was indeed trained in drill and ceremonial duties, first aid and hygiene, and driving and maintenance of vehicles. Yet despite efforts to downplay it, Coloured recruits also received firearms instruction, though it was confined to single-shot small arms for self-defense and for the protection of government property. This emphasis on the SACC as an auxiliary noncombat labor force seemed to lessen white opposition, especially after the 1957 Defence Act was amended in 1963 to preclude a nonwhite officer from arresting a white solider or from exercising any authority over a white soldier.[20] In fact there was little to fear, since no black officers existed at the time, and few, if any, were contemplated. According to the Military Discipline Code then in force a Coloured soldier would always be junior to a white soldier, even if he should outrank his white colleague.[21]

By and large a version of the "dilution policy" applied by which SACC members, trained in a specific support skill, would be assigned to standing units of the Permanent Force. Thus the SACC was principally a training unit designed to provide men for noncombat administrative, artisan, and menial services in white units.

A significant shift in structure came in 1972. Although recruitment issues will be covered later, it had become apparent that young Coloured men with requisite educational standards were not being attracted in sufficient numbers to the Coloured Corps. Two changes sought to rectify this problem. The name of the corps was changed to the S.A. Cape Corps, the respected name of the Coloured units serving in the world wars. It was hoped that the tradition and distinction of these earlier units would rub off on the new Cape Corps. Government tried mightily to transfer that reputation. In 1974 the Minister of Defence authorized the present Cape Corps to assume its predecessor's battle honors, all of which had been gained in World War I. In 1978 State President Dr. Nico Diederichs

20. U.N. Security Council, *Apartheid*, p. 123.
21. *Argus* (Cape Town), 3 April 1972, p. 1.

finally awarded the unit its regimental colors, which bore the SACC's eight battle honors.[22] Continuity had been officially sanctioned.

The second structural change was more clearly designed to attract more volunteers. In July 1972 Minister of Defence P. W. Botha announced the formation of a Special Service Battalion for Coloureds, associated with the Cape Corps.[23] Like other Coloured formations the SSB is also voluntary, but with a difference. The SSB was established as a form of national service for Coloureds. Instead of immediately being attached to the Permanent Force, as had been the case with the pre-1973 SACC, young men volunteered for military training in the SSB as a form of national service. The training was to be identical with that provided young white National Servicemen who had been called up. The first sixteen weeks of basic training is devoted to drill, saluting, military law and discipline, gunnery, fieldcraft and signals, hygiene and first aid, "citizenship and leadership," and map reading. After that the men undergo eight weeks of vocational training, and this is followed by six months honing these military and vocational skills, a part of which is usually spent in the operational areas of Namibia.[24]

At the end of a year's training members of the SSB are given the choice of reentering civilian life (government maintains that demands for their services are high) without any further military obligations or of alternatively joining the Permanent Force, either in the army, the navy, or today in the air force. The SACC, then, would itself consist of first year volunteers in the SSB and infantry and maintenance companies as part of the Permanent Force. Other PF members of SACC might find themselves in various white units removed from SACC command if their specific skills were required. Even Coloured parabats or paratroopers have been trained. Although attached to the SACC for administrative reasons, they are deployed as part of the airborne forces.[25]

22. *Cape Times*, 28 February 1977, 8 April 1978, and 10 April 1978.

23. *The Star* (Weekly Air Edition), 15 July 1972, p. 2.

24. *Cape Times*, 12 August 1972.

25. *Assembly Debates*, 17 April 1978, col. 4817 (Minister of Defence); *Cape Times*, 19 April 1978; *South Africa Digest*, 28 April 1978, p. 4; *Rand Daily Mail* (Johannesburg), 18 April 1978; and *Paratus* 29 (December 1978): 11.

Early in 1979 it was announced that in January 1980 a twenty-four month voluntary service in the SSB would be possible, presumably as an alternative to the twelve-month service.[26] The following year, effective 1 January 1980, the SSB was enlarged and reorganized, split into three separate units, an infantry battalion (First SACC Battalion), a logistics unit (SACC Maintenance Unit), and the Cape Corps School.[27] The latter unit represents the first officer training facility for blacks.

In 1978 it became possible for Coloureds who had opted to leave the SSB or had earlier resigned from the SACC in order to reenter civilian life to become members of Citizen Force regiments. Some of the established "white" CF regiments (e.g., Kimberley) opened their doors. In other cases all-Coloured CF units were formed.[28] As it presently stands, practically all the institutional alternatives open to white National Servicemen are ostensibly available to Coloured volunteers — civilian life without military obligation (not open to whites, who must do further part-time service), the Citizen Force (strictly on a voluntary basis), and the Permanent Force in a variety of branches of the service. Even the historical bastion and symbol of Afrikaner civil soldiery, the commando, is being pried open. Early in 1978 the chief of the Defence Force, Gen. Magnus Malan, urged commandos "to consider" accepting blacks. P. W. Botha, in 1978, stated that blacks who did join commandos would be used for guard duty and for other auxiliary duties — as part of a support service corps.[29] Apparently some commando units were resisting these instructions. A few months later the SADF went even further. In September 1978 SADF headquarters authorized commandos throughout the country to recruit blacks into the army to be trained to serve in combat units and to be required to do border duty.[30] The number of Coloured

26. *Cape Times*, 24 April 1979.

27. *Cape Times*, 24 December 1979, p. 2; *Eastern Province Herald* (Port Elizabeth), 28 January 1980.

28. *Cape Times*, 11 October 1978.

29. *Rand Daily Mail*, 25 January 1978. For editorial comment, see *South Africa Digest*, 27 January 1978, pp. 7 and 26–28.

30. South African Institute of Race Relations, *Survey of Race Relations in South Africa, 1978* (Johannesburg: South Africa Institute of Race Relations,

individuals these decisions have effected is miniscule. Where all-Coloured commandos have been formed, however, the transition has been easier.[31]

Overall, however, the 1972 changes had marked effects on Coloured military service. As options opened recruitment picked up, and the SACC began a series of policies that served as examples for other black units in combat as well as noncombat roles.

Force Levels

The Coloured Corps was not an immediate success. In fact, during its first decade of reincarnation it was an apparent failure. This is particularly the case if it is looked at in terms of force levels and recruitment problems.

The SACC began in an atmosphere of some optimism. In 1964 the training center at Eersterivier could accommodate one hundred and forty men. Defence Force spokesmen circulated expansion plans for eventually six to seven hundred men.[32] But growth came slowly. Initially the standards were set too high. Maximum age was at first raised from thirty to thirty-five years, and the minimum educational levels were lowered from Standard 8 to Standard 6 for all but candidate instructors, where levels of Standard 8 still applied.[33] The approved establishment of the SACC as of 1 April 1965 was to be 527. At that time fewer than one hundred were attached to the unit. There is little reason whatsoever to believe the chief of the general staff of the army when he claimed early in 1965: "At the beginning, recruiting was not so good as we had hoped but now we can get as many men as we want."[34] That same figure of

1979), p. 55; *The Star* (Weekly Air Edition), 23 September 1978, p. 2; and "Ladybrand se kleurlinge is Uitstekende Soldate," *Paratus* 32 (July 1981): 38.

31. E.g., the Bloemfontein City Commando made up of Coloured employees of the Musgrave weapons factory. It was formed in 1978 and by 1980 had thirty men led by a white lieutenant. "Bloemfontein is Trots op sy Kleurling-Peloton," *Paratus* 31 (March 1980): 26–27.

32. *Cape Times*, 18 June 1964.

33. *Cape Times*, 20 June 1964. According to a 1975 recruitment leaflet Standard 7 was the minimum, but the corps' commandant has said that Standard 6 is the minimum (interview, 9 July 1979, Eersterivier).

34. Gen. P.J. Jacobs in *Argus*, 6 February 1965; Republic of South Africa,

527 applied at the end of 1966 too, and yet by January 1967 only 414 applicants had been accepted by the selection boards.[35] In the words of Camp Commandant M. J. B. Bredenkamp, there were "still a lot of vacancies." The recruitment figures alone are revealing, though we should be careful since announced force levels and recruitment figures are not always comparable and seldom add up to the levels announced by different offices. In 1967 Commandant Bredenkamp disclosed that in the first almost four years since the corps had been established in April 1963, over 2,000 inquiries had been received.[36] Of these 414 were at the time accepted. The breakdown he presented did not add up, though the data are useful. The 2,000 inquiries yielded 998 actual applications to join the corps. Of these, 455 were rejected for the following reasons:

Medical problems	112
Criminal records	54
Educational deficiencies	98
Age criteria	18
Inadequate documentation	105
Other reasons	68

Another 65 applications were still pending, and 63 more had been accepted but had not replied to the notification. Of the 414 accepted, not all completed their two years training, and fewer still went on to continue in the Permanent Force. Hence, quite a small corps existed. In 1968 Defence Minister Botha published even lower figures.[37] He stated that in 1964 65 men joined SACC, in 1965 80 men, in 1966 70 men, and in 1967 100 men. These 315 are some 175 fewer than the figure which was published in the *Cape Times* almost a year earlier.[38] Botha also

---

Department of Defence, *White Paper on Defence, 1965–67* (Pretoria: Government Printer, 1967), p. 5.

35. According to Camp Commandant Bredenkamp, *Cape Times*, 20 February 1967. An even lower number of 215 had actually joined the corps by this time. Data supplied in 1968 by Minister of Defence Botha, *Cape Times*, 31 May 1968.

36. *Cape Times*, 20 February 1967.

37. *Cape Times*, 31 May 1968.

38. 24 June 1967. According to this article there were 280 men at Eersterivier, 220 short of maximum capacity.

indicated declines during this period in the number of uniformed Coloured corpsmen assigned to the navy (from 50 in 1965 to 41 in 1967). This amounted to 125 Coloured vacancies in the navy and 108 in the army in 1967. Despite computational and reportorial discrepancies one fact remains clear — the Coloured Corps had been unable to maintain itself at approved force levels, and it had considerable difficulty securing qualified applicants. When looked at critically, the data presented by Commandant Bredenkamp seem to imply that the SACC would have accepted practically any applicant who met the minimum announced standards. All that was asked was that they be between the ages of eighteen and thirty-five, that they produce a birth certificate, evidence of completion of Standard 6, and two testimonials, that they have no criminal record, and that they pass the physical examination. Otherwise, little selectivity was exercised.

Young, educated Coloured men had been scorning the Defence Force. They were reluctant to make a career-long commitment, that is, one to the Permanent Force. The economic inducements were not sufficiently appealing. The status attending SACC membership was marginal. The result was, and still is, that local men from the Peninsula and Western Province show little interest in the corps. Rather, "up-country people" from places like Upington, Oudtshoorn, the Northern Cape, and the Karoo enroll. The officer commanding the battalion of 1981 recruits indicated that only 20 percent of them came from cities.[39] Likewise a disproportionately low number of Malay and Muslim Coloureds join. And this general pattern has continued as men from the Western Cape have other, more attractive economic opportunities. Moreover, there is further evidence that the more worldly-wise Kaapenaars do not always approve of their Coloured brothers serving in the SADF in defense of a hated status quo. During the first few years corpsmen were not permitted off base in their uniforms. They were labeled "Vorster's Dogs" by local youths, who set upon corpsmen they could identify. Apparently this has changed since the

39. *Cape Times*, 20 February 1967; and interview, Pretoria, 16 July 1979; and *Paratus* 32 (April 1981): 35.

early 1970s, although in 1977 the commandant, in reporting "the outstanding reception" SACC recruiters received in all parts of the country, indicated that in "one town" there was a hostile reception.[40]

Recruiting techniques have been fairly straightforward. Advertisements in the press, pamphlets, and recruitment tours by teams from the unit (now featuring Coloured officers) are employed. Particularly the latter have been successful. They usually involve mass physical-training displays, retreat ceremonies, and band concerts. The principal targets are secondary schools, especially in the Cape hinterland. After the performance an officer explains conditions of service and distributes application forms and literature. Finally, would-be recruits are encouraged to write directly to the corps' commanding officer, or applicants are urged to present themselves at police stations, where they will be interviewed and will undergo psychological testing.[41] Toward the end of the 1960s recruitment began to pick up, but not significantly. By 1971 only 430 of the 627 posts in the SACC were filled (68 percent), and only 50 percent of the 248 Permanent Force posts for the SACC in the navy were filled.

The inauguration of the Service Battalion, with its first year akin to voluntary national service and with no initial obligation to the Permanent Force, seems to have solved the problem. After 1972, apparently, recruitment became easier, and larger and larger intakes were enlisted. The corps advanced from a 32 percent vacancy rate in April 1972[42] to a waiting list of several hundreds in the late 1970s. Early in 1974 the complement of the SACC was stated to be 678 men.[43] From intakes numbering 150 in January 1975 to a 1981 intake of 1,456 (for two years of national service) there has been marked expansion — considering SADF's reputation for caution in the use of

40. Interview with Cmdt. Ben Cronjé, Eersterivier, 9 July 1979; and *Cape Times*, 23 August 1977.

41. See, e.g., *Cape Times*, 31 December 1965; 14 July 1973; and 7 August 1973.

42. *Cape Times*, 27 April 1972.

43. *Assembly Debates*, 29 April 1975, Q col. 852–54.

blacks. What is more, with recruitment much easier than in the past, "well above expectations" according to the commandant, it has been possible to continue to refer to the SACC as an "elite" organization.[44] Greater selectivity is now possible. The 1978 intake (intakes are now just once a year) almost "doubled" the size of the regiment, and the infantry component expanded to full battalion size.[45] Between February 1977 and February 1978 there had been an increase of 40.6 percent in the number of Coloured people in the Defence Force.[46] One mid-1978 estimate put the figure at 2,100 ("plus") Coloureds in the army, 450 in the navy, and 75 in the air force.[47] If one adds the 1979 intake of 900 (33 percent greater than in 1978) and the 1980 to 1982 intakes of 1,500 each, less a normal number of resignations and noncontinuations, the current (1982) estimated size of the Cape Corps would be around 4,900 in all services (including around 1,200 in the army Permanent Force, 800 in the navy PF, and 25 in the air force PF). This figure, of course, includes three intakes of SSB (now called the South African Cape Corps Battalion [SACCB]) recruits. Coloureds constitute around 6 percent of the total Permanent Force.

Further evidence of SACC expansion appears in the desire of the government and the Defence Force to augment training and quartering facilities for the formation. Sometime in 1977 government began to examine the possibilities of taking over the Cadet Training Scheme's property at Fauré, not far from the current SACC base. That institution had been under the direction of the Coloured Representative Council (CRC), yet officials of the CRC had never been approached for consultation or agreement about the proposed changes. The result was

44. Interview with Maj. Johan Beyers, regional public relations officer, Cape Town, 9 July 1979. See also the statement by Cmdt. Leon Martins in *Cape Times*, 23 August 1977; *Cape Herald* (Cape Town), 5 January 1980; and *Eastern Province Herald*, 28 December 1979. Of the 2,737 volunteers for the 1982 intake, 1,456 were accepted; see *Assembly Debates*, 8 March 1982, Q col. 317.

45. *Cape Times*, 23 August 1977.

46. Minister of Defence reporting in *Assembly Debates*, 17 April 1978, col. 6848; and *Cape Times*, 18 April 1978.

47. Personal correspondence, 25 September 1978 and 12 October 1978.

an added issue of contention when, in November 1979, P. W. Botha met with Coloured leaders. At that time, and in the midst of a rancorous discussion, Norman Middleton (Labour) appealed to the Defence Force not to take over the Fauré camp until a report had been produced and discussed. He agreed that the SACC needed extension of its camp, but why not at its present base? The Fauré camp, he argued, is ideal for detention of juvenile offenders.[48] His wishes went unheeded. The 1981 intake of the First S.A. Cape Corps Battalion moved into the Fauré camp to begin its training.

Precise and reliable force level figures, however, are difficult to secure. One has to piece together data carefully. Invariably conflicting reports appear. One Defence Force spokesman referred to the "high number" that sign on for the Permanent Force at the end of the year's training. Another said that "approximately ten percent" want to go into the Permanent Force and that "almost all are accepted."[49] And a 1977 report claimed that "about one quarter" of the 1977 intake applied to join the Permanent Force.[50] Who is one to believe? Actually, the 10 percent figure might be regarded as respectably "high," considering that only 3 percent of white national servicemen want to join the Permanent Force. Yet when one considers that the Coloured Service Battalion men are all volunteers to begin with, while white national servicemen are conscripts, the discrepancy is understandable. Given the marked growth of the SACC of late, it would appear that the actual continuation figure leans toward the higher estimates.

In the process of training larger and larger intakes a cadre of trained soldiers, many of whom are attached to Citizen Force regiments, are expanding the potential Coloured role in defense, even if large numbers do not make the Permanent Force a career. Likewise, the provision of the 1979 Act that introduced twenty-four-month volunteer service for Coloureds will also expand the Cape Corps.[51]

48. *Cape Times,* 22 November 1979; pp. 4 and 6 contain the transcript of this discussion.
49. Interviews, Eersterivier, 9 July 1979; Pretoria, 16 July 1979.
50. *Paratus,* Supplement (February 1978), p. iii.
51. *Cape Times,* 24 April 1979.

Other Defense Force Formations of Coloureds and Indians

To complete the picture, it is necessary to point to a number of formations outside the SADF Army. In proportional terms the greatest concentration of blacks in the SADF can be found in the S.A. Navy (SAN). Some 16.8 percent of the SAN members are Coloured, and 7.6 percent are Indians. Nearly one-quarter of the navy's full-time manpower is black, some 1,160 men. This proportion has been increasing steadily through the 1970s, from 17.4 percent in 1977 to 20 percent in 1978.[52] If one were to omit national servicemen from the total these figures would climb to 22.9 percent (Coloured) and 10.3 percent (Indian) respectively.[53]

The use of Coloureds in the SAN goes back to 1963, when recruiting first began. In April 1965 Coloured recruits were enrolled on a permanent basis. They first received basic training at the SACC Training Centre at Eersterivier. Later they were assigned to the naval base at Simonstown for further training. At present Coloured seamen serve on a hydrographic ship, a boom defense vessel, and on a minesweeper. Most South African warships include Coloured crewmen in a wide range of postings. Coloured civilians are employed widely in the shipyards themselves.

Initially Coloured seamen could rise to the rank of warrant officer I, or chief petty officer. In fact white and Coloured ratings do not share the same facilities, nor are pay and all fringe benefits the same between races.

It was announced in 1977 that Indians and Coloureds would be eligible to receive training as naval officers at Gordon's Bay Naval College.[54] Several officer candidates were enrolled. By 1980 seven Coloured officers had been commissioned, and the first Indian midshipman qualified for commission in 1978.

---

52. South African Institute of Race Relations, *Survey of Race Relations in South Africa, 1979* (Johannesburg: South African Institute of Race Relations, 1980), p. 83.

53. These figures are derived from extrapolations based on data from diverse sources, including International Institute of Strategic Studies, *Military Balance, 1979–1980* (London: International Institute of Strategic Studies, 1980); and interview data.

54. South African Institute of Race Relations, *Survey, 1978*, p. 55.

In January 1977 a small contingent of Coloureds were transferred from the SACC to the air force (approximately twenty-
five men). Indians may also be assigned to that branch.[55] These
men function purely in an administrative labor capacity as
ground personnel, storemen, equipment assistants, chefs,
painters, and firemen.[56] The Coloureds have already undergone basic training with the Cape Corps at Eersterivier. They
are quartered at Eersterivier and are transported to Ysterplaat
Air Base daily.

Once again, as with the SACC, the Coloureds in the SAN
were regarded by SADF headquarters as guinea pigs. Their
successful incorporation into the navy led to the establishment
in January 1975 of an Indian Corps Training Battalion, based
at Salisbury Island, Durban. In fact thirty-three men under-
went special training from October to December 1974 in preparation for the volunteer intake in January 1975.[57] This new
formation represented another about-face by P. W. Botha, who
in 1968 had said that Indians would not be used in the SADF.
Instead his 1973 white paper on defense announced plans for
the service battalion, to be fashioned along lines "similar to that
for Coloureds . . . ."[58]

To implement these plans the commandant general of the
Defence Force, Adm. H. H. Biermann, met members of the
S.A. Indian Council (SAIC), a government appointed body.[59]
A month after this closed-door session the new corps was offi-
cially announced.[60] The fact is that the Indian Council and the
Natal Indian Ex-Servicemen's Legion had earlier asked the
government to form such a corps, and they regarded the Cape
Corps as the appropriate model.[61]

55. *The Star* (Weekly Air Edition), 24 June 1978, p. 3.

56. *South Africa Digest,* 25 February 1977, p. 12.

57. *Rand Daily Mail,* 4 December 1974.

58. Republic of South Africa, Department of Defence, *White Paper on Defence and Armament Production, 1978* (Pretoria: Government Printer, 1973),
p. 11.

59. *Natal Mercury* (Durban), 6 June 1974.

60. South African Institute of Race Relations, *A Survey of Race Relations in
South Africa, 1974* (Johannesburg: South African Institute of Race Relations,
1975), p. 56; *Sunday Express* (Johannesburg), 14 July 1974.

61. *The Star* (Daily Edition), 14 May 1975. And further the government had
effectively made its views known in the white paper of April 1973.

Yet all was not smooth sailing. The Salisbury Island base was to have opened in January 1975 with two-hundred volunteers. By that time only thirty-four men had signed on, despite an intensive recruitment campaign in Natal and Transvaal.[62]

An opening eleven-month training period, with theoretical and practical curriculum, is supposed to provide the volunteer with the basis for a decision regarding his career in the Permanent Force. Later the training period was increased to twenty-two months. If a volunteer decides to return to civilian life, he is issued a certificate of competence and, it is claimed, assisted in finding work. According to a 1979 report 95 percent of each intake (so far around one hundred and fifty per year) apply to join the Permanent Force on completion of basic training.[63] Clearly, if this is accurate, the navy does not accept all who wish to continue. In March 1979 it was reported that 832 men had enrolled in the Indian Corps since its inception. Altogether the current PF complement numbers around three hundred and sixty. Obviously, 95 percent would not be accommodated.[64] After completion of basic training those who wish to continue in the navy are sent for specialized training as gunners, stewards, chefs, clerks, and administrative staff.

The Indian Corps Training Battalion was later converted into a Permanent Force naval unit and renamed S.A.S. *Jalsena,* ostensibly because Indian spokesmen claimed that thousands of Indian youths were eager to volunteer for service provided it could be made professionally secure.[65] According to the Minister of Indian Affairs the executive of the S.A. Indian Representative Council called on the Minister of Defence to arm the Indian Corps so that they might contribute "their share to the defence of South Africa."[66] In many ways the Training Battalion has been a pet project of SAIC chairman, Dr. A. M. Moola. The Indian Reform Party, also represented on the SAIC, is less enthusiastic. Council member Abu Ebrahim stated in mid-

62. *Natal Mercury,* 11 January 1975.
63. *Paratus,* 30 (March 1979): 4.
64. *South Africa Digest,* 2 March 1979, p. 13.
65. Maj. C. J. Nöthling, *Blacks in the South Africa Defence Force,* South Africa Foundation Briefing Papers, no. 21 (Johannesburg: South Africa Foundation, 1980), p. 3.
66. *Assembly Debates,* 26 January 1976, col. 87.

1978 that he opposed Indian involvement in the Defence Force until Indians are afforded equal rights.

There is little evidence that Indians are particularly keen on joining,[67] even though the small intakes nowadays are oversubscribed (191 of 509 volunteers were accepted in January 1982). Intakes were not oversubscribed in the first few years. Patriotism does not explain the decision to join. Rather, unemployment figures prominently in the Indian community, and the SADF is regarded as a reasonable option. Sandwiched in an otherwise optimistic newspaper account of the signing of the first two Indian recruits to the air force, an account in which Defence Force spokesmen were quoted positively and uncritically at length, it was noted, however, that both recruits said "a big motivation was that they were unemployed."[68]

In March 1977 it was reported that P. W. Botha was considering establishing an operational volunteer infantry corps for Indians.[69] Again the SACC was said to be the model. But when questioned in Parliament on this a week later the minister denied that he had considered this, although he did admit that consideration was given to the employment of Indians in the army, presumably not as a distinguishable infantry corps.[70]

Finally, facilities to train black Africans in the S.A. Navy are not yet available. More than eighty black members of the Auxiliary Service (called Pioneers) perform menial tasks at Simonstown, but they are not part of the Permanent Force. Most of these men are Xhosa. This practice dates back to the years of the British Admiralty, and some of the present serving members of the SADF Auxiliary Service have themselves been transferred from the Admiralty.[71]

Compulsory Service?

With current annual intakes expanding and the ranks of the SACC keeping pace with government's perceived needs it

67. Ibid., 5 May 1980, Q col. 701; and 4 March 1982, Q cols. 257 – 58.
68. *The Star* (Weekly Air Edition), 24 June 1978, p. 3.
69. *The Star* (Weekly Air Edition), 19 March 1977, p. 5.
70. *Assembly Debates*, 25 March 1977, Q col. 717.
71. "The South African Navy's Prize Pioneers," *Paratus* 31 (February 1980): 22.

would seem, for the moment at least, that the issue of compulsory military service for Coloured males has been temporarily deferred. Both the Defence Act of 1912 and the debate on the 1957 Act addressed the issue of compulsory service for blacks, dismissing that possibility summarily. If blacks were to be used, it was to be only voluntarily, chiefly when the government wanted them, and not vice versa.

In the last few years the idea of compulsory military service for blacks has been increasingly mooted, and by elements closer and closer to government. It was hardly novel to hear members of the Progressive Party or of the Progressive Federal Party urging government to move on the idea.[72] Nor were many eyebrows raised when the Theron Commission unanimously (that is notable) recommended the introduction "in stages" of compulsory military service and a school cadet system for Coloureds.[73] But the resolution introduced at the Transvaal Congress of the National Party calling upon government to institute compulsory military training for Coloureds and Indians and an extension of military training for blacks is worth noting.[74] And when the Minister of Defence indicated, as he did in 1977, that there was a possibility of national service being introduced for Coloured and Indian youths, then the idea must be considered seriously. One could infer from P. W. Botha's speech to students at Port Elizabeth that the only reason why there had been no compulsory national service for these groups was "mainly because of a lack of facilities." Thus, he went on, it is "possible" that such national service may be instituted.[75]

While on paper such a program may make sense, in practice tremendous problems arise. First, how would the government reconcile compulsory military service for selected groups of blacks with the absence of full citizenship for these same

72. E.g., H.H. Schwarz (PFP, Yoeville) in *Assembly Debates*, 17 April 1978, cols. 4821–22.

73. Van der Horst, *Theron Commissions Report*, p. 10 (chapter 2, recommendation 7). This recommendation was debated in *Assembly Debates*, 21 April 1977, col. 5769.

74. *The Star* (Daily Edition), 13 September 1978.

75. *Rand Daily Mail*, 18 August 1977; *South Africa Digest*, 26 August 1977, p. 9.

groups? Citizenship and political rights have been inextricably linked with military service in the history of many Western democracies. In other words, it is hard to have one without the other. Yet, to be sure, the Republic of South Africa is not a Western democracy, though it intermittently makes a pretense to be one. The South African government seems to have, in effect, accepted this principle of linkage as it applies to white immigrants.[76] But it has been, of course, reluctant to give more than cursory consideration to full citizenship rights to Coloured South Africans.

Coloured spokesmen enjoying varying degrees of acceptance by their people have addressed this issue. For some time Coloured politicians have coupled military service and full citizenship. Insofar as they disagree it is largely over the matter of sequence. Does one achieve citizenship best by denying service first until full rights are accorded, or should one serve first and use such a demonstration of loyalty as a political lever to win full political rights? The more common view, expressed by David Curry, then deputy leader of the Labour Party in the Coloured Representative Council (CRC), holds that "I cannot offer White South Africa my loyalty unless I am granted full citizenship."[77] The Labour Party's leader, Sonny Leon, tried the second approach. He called upon the government to reexamine its attitude toward the Coloured people now that Coloureds "have again shown themselves willing to fight for their country."[78] He demanded for each person his or her "rightful inheritance as a citizen of South Africa" and an end to all the "vicious laws" which deny black people "very meaningful participation in the process of government in their own country."

76. See the Defence Act of 1978 (no. 49) in accord with the South African Citizenship Amendment Act (no. 53 of 1978). For brief explanations see South African Institute of Race Relations, *Survey, 1978*, pp. 60–62. In 1979 these provisions led 1,919 foreign citizens to register for military service; see *Assembly Debates*, 27 February 1980, Q col. 205. See also the critique of government policy along these lines by H. H. Schwarz in *Assembly Debates*, 17 April 1978, col. 4822.

77. *The Star* (Weekly Air Edition), 27 July 1974, p. 6. For a Nationalist response to this view see P. J. Badenhorst (NP, Oudsthoorn) in *Assembly Debates*, 9 September 1974, col. 2532.

78. *Cape Times*, 5 December 1975.

Leon, who had been a sergeant major in World War II, warned that "I will never tell my people to fight for the perpetuation of baasskap."[79] To expect Coloured soldiers to risk their lives for their country while still being treated as second-class citizens would be "unfair." The party's current national chairman, Rev. Allan Hendrickse, also followed suit: "If the country was run on an acceptable system then we would have a moral and patriotic duty to defend its borders."[80]

But as the Labour Party, among the parties in the CRC, took a line of "rights first, then service," other members of the CRC were more patient. In 1976 that body resolved to call upon government to amend the Defence Act so that all citizens could be subjected to compulsory military training. It also indicated a preference for training all race groups together. But clearly it was attaching some sort of mystical quality to the act of defending one's country — as if this would open all the doors that had for so long been closed. J. A. Rabie, an independent member (he since has joined the Labour Party), argued that through military training young men learned to show "true patriotism" for their country. The Freedom Party also supported the motion. Labour spokesmen opposed the motion, emphasizing that full citizenship for all South Africans had to precede the proposed extension of compulsory military training.[81]

Later, in 1978, government organized a public relations visit to the Namibian operational area for thirteen prominent Coloureds. On their return many mouthed the government line that more Coloureds should get involved in defense of the republic, but some contended that "to get this they [government] must give our people full citizenship."[82] Some of these men had been heavily criticized by other Coloured leaders for participating in this tour and thereby appearing to endorse the government's policies on behalf of the Coloured community.

It is fair to say that most prominent Coloured politicians

79. *Cape Times,* 17 January 1976.
80. *Rand Daily Mail,* 26 May 1978.
81. *Cape Times,* 1 October 1976. See also the views of poet and academic Adam Small in *The Star* (Weekly Air Edition), 1 July 1978, p. 2.
82. Quoting G. G. Cornelissen, a businessman; *Daily News,* (Durban), 5 September 1978.

operating openly in South Africa agree that most Coloureds would be prepared to participate in defending South Africa provided their political and economic disabilities were eliminated and provided they were given full equality within the Defence Force. The Labour Party has continued to badger the government for complete political rights. "We have no intention of defending the policies of the National Party," said its deputy leader, Norman Middleton, "and that is what we would be doing if we supported a call for Coloureds to volunteer for two years' service with the SADF." Only when Coloureds are recognized as full citizens, in every way equal to whites politically and economically, would his party encourage young Coloureds to fight.[83]

This position fails to address the equally vexing issue of whether the extension of rights to Coloureds ought to be divorced from the issue of rights for all blacks. Among Coloureds who participated in the CRC (disbanded in 1980) and in other white-instigated bodies, the Labour Party seems to be most outspoken. Yet much of the urban Coloured community is even less inclined to cooperate with the authorities and with the SADF than the Labour Party. Elections for the CRC were boycotted and had low turnouts. The CRC was widely regarded as an apartheid organization. Edelstein's 1973 study indicated that only 52 percent of his respondents supported the CRC.[84]

It is difficult to read the pulse of South Africa's Coloureds. Government claims that most Coloureds favor extended, indeed even compulsory, military service for their young men. According to Hennie Smit, former Minister of Coloured Relations, some 88 percent of Coloureds favor a compulsory military scheme for Coloureds. He was referring to surveys conducted by the Human Sciences Research Council (HSRC) in the Eersterust region near Pretoria and in the Cape Penin-

83. *Rand Daily Mail,* 26 April 1979.
84. In addition, only 32 percent of the Coloureds surveyed supported the Labour Party. 37 percent supported no party at all; Edelstein, *What Do the Coloureds Think?*, pp. 58, 60, 73, and 74.

sula.[85] The HSRC, a government body, felt they could not make the findings available to this researcher since the work was done on contract. Without knowing more about the surveys themselves it is hard to respond to their conclusions. It would appear that they present a far too sanguine account of support for SADF use of Coloureds. Edelstein found that only 54 percent of his panel would "support" the regime in the event of external aggression.[86]

It should be pointed out that opinion among Coloureds is divided according to age, income, place of residence (i.e., rural or urban), religion, and language. To be sure, motives for enlistment largely depend on an individual's economic condition. At present one could maintain that the issue of Coloured service in the SADF does not stand as a terribly contentious issue in the community. It certainly would if military service were to be made compulsory or if a paramilitary cadet program were to be introduced into Coloured secondary schools. But even so it is possible to discern divisions among Coloured people. Those more likely to approve of either voluntary or compulsory Coloured participation in defense are probably older and more rural, with less formal education and either of very low or relatively high income. Although the average Coloured person takes pride in the past military record of his people and holds in respect veterans of past wars, most urban Coloureds (some 74 percent of all Coloureds, according to the 1970 census, and likely approaching 80 percent today) are neutral or opposed to Coloureds defending the present regime.

The rural population, although buffeted by an incongruous mixture of political stimuli, is better disposed toward the Cape Corps. On the whole rural Coloureds tend to be unilingual, to be more influenced by the Afrikaans (and hence pro-government) media and by the Dutch Reformed Church. Rural and

85. *Assembly Debates*, 26 May 1978, col. 7999; letter from the HSRC, Pretoria, to the author, 3 April 1980.
86. Fully 43 percent were willing to state openly that they would remain neutral; Edelstein, *What Do the Coloureds Think?*, pp. 60 and 74.

small-town Cape, too, is where a majority of the SACC comes from, and the corpsmen's own views are relayed home on a regular basis. Aware of this diversity of opinion, one can only imagine the extent to which the introduction of compulsion into the debate on military participation would split the community on what would have to be a most emotional issue.

Among whites there are many who favor both a greater use of black, particularly Coloured, soldiers and the corollary tender of full citizenship, usually in that sequence. Government's reluctance to accept what to them is compelling logic is roundly criticized. Editorializing on the death in action of a Cape Corpsman, the *Cape Times* opined:

> The death of the Cape Corps soldier demonstrates the risks borne by the thousands of youngsters who guard the borders, and should spur those at home into finding convincing solutions to political problems — bearing in mind, also, that if a person is expected to die for his country, he should first be able to live to the full in that country.[87]

The New Republic Party's defense spokesman, W. Vause Raw, and his Progressive Federal Party counterpart, Harry Schwarz, rule out compulsory military service until full citizenship is accorded blacks: "Recognize them as full citizens, with all the rights, privileges and responsibilities of Whites. Then and only then can we ask them to accept compulsory responsibility for defending South Africa."[88]

In addition to the issue of full citizenship other practical problems crop up in making military service for Coloureds compulsory. First, so far all Coloureds in the SADF have been volunteers. Except in the beginning, when recruiting problems nettled, there has been little difficulty filling intake quotas. This was partially a function of the relatively small size of the SACC. Finding a few hundred or even a few thousand out of an economically insecure population group currently numbering around 2.8 million presents few burdens. But it is a far leap from an "elite" and highly selective (including self-se-

87. *Cape Times,* 18 October 1978. See also the speech by the mayor of Cape Town, *Cape Times,* 11 June 1974.
88. Schwartz quoted in *Rand Daily Mail,* 26 May 1978.

lected) unit to a compulsory and more inclusive military body drawn from a population group with considerably lower educational and training standards than either the dominant white community or the Coloureds already in the SACC. In short the absorbtive capacity of the SADF would be tested. To be sure, the SADF would not be expected to ingest all eligible Coloureds at once. The pattern of service first on a voluntary basis, then by ballot or lottery, and finally universal and compulsory was followed as white military obligations were expanded. It is likely that the same gradations would be repeated for Coloureds and Indians, too. Yet there is a qualitative vault from one model (small scale and voluntary) to another (compulsory registration with a lottery or ballot) that the SADF would find burdensome.

Second, voluntary service so far has implied some degree of agreement with or acquiescence to the political and economic status quo, or at least a more evolutionary approach to changing it. Those inclined to oppose the system are, through self-selection and through some degree of conscious governmental policy, excluded. "Radicals need not apply" implicitly appears on all the literature and advertisements. Should the element of voluntarism be abandoned, a new type of recruit, ideologically and temperamentally unconvinced, would fill the ranks. A more vigorous indoctrination program would have to be instituted. Given the widespread disenchantment, indeed enmity, among blacks, it would likely be of limited effectiveness, or else it would have to be extremely heavy-handed.

A third consideration ought to be the Rhodesian experience. When compulsory service was introduced for Africans, large numbers of those called up did not appear; many openly refused to serve; others defected after being attested, and discipline problems were legion. Coercion and intimidation were necessary to fill the intakes. Coloured and Asian inductees were also dissatisfied, and resistance to service was widespread.[89] So embarrassing was the response that the Rhodesian

89. Anti-Apartheid Movement, *Fire Force Exposed: The Rhodesian Security Forces and Their Role in Defending White Supremacy* (London: Anti-Apartheid Movement, 1979), pp. 7–12.

military command imposed a total news blackout on information about the first black intake in January 1979, and journalists were ordered not to go near the training barracks.[90]

Further, some account ought to be taken of the disastrous experience that government had with the Training Centres for Coloured Cadets. This scheme, although not a military enterprise per se, was sometimes confused for one. An act was passed in 1967 and came into force in 1968 requiring all Coloured youths who turned eighteen years of age in 1968 to register within three months and those between the ages of eighteen and twenty-four to register annually at any police station.[91] Cadets were chosen from among the registrants on the basis of their skills, educational background, and aptitude. Presumably those least qualified for the job market or those with the fewest immediate employment opportunities were to be chosen. A training center was established at Fauré, near Eersterivier, ostensibly to provide cadets with marketable skills. The three months training stint was to aim at imparting proper discipline by drilling and physical exercise, sport activities, and work performance and instruction. The program did not work well at all. There was widespread confusion among Coloured youth that they would be undergoing training of a military nature.[92] During the first year some 80,000 of an expected 100,000 eligibles registered. But the next year the act was largely ignored. Of an expected 15,000 registrants per year, only 3,800 in 1969, 5,800 in 1970, 4,873 in 1971, and 4,255 in 1972 troubled to register.[93] Only 38.6 percent of eligible young Coloured men actually registered while the act was in force.[94] The government threatened to conduct raids to enforce compliance. In total around 1,000 cadets per year for the first few years and later around 650 per year (once the training was extended from three to four months in 1972)

90. *Guardian* (London), 10 January 1979.
91. Training Centres for Coloured Cadets Act, no. 46 of 1967. This act was repealed in 1981; see *Assembly Debates,* 18 and 25 September 1981, cols. 4276–84 and 4863–72.
92. *Cape Times,* 29 March 1968.
93. *Cape Times,* 9 August 1972.
94. *Assembly Debates,* 18 September 1981, col. 4277.

completed the courses. It has also been disclosed that 391 cadets absconded from 1969 to 1973, and 337 of these were prosecuted, and from 1977 until April 1979 a further 532 cadets absconded, leading to 132 being sentenced to imprisonment.[95]

Complaints were legion of poor quality training; of the recruitment of youths who presumably should have been exempted, for example, those already employed, students, and those undergoing training and apprenticeship elsewhere; of overbearing administration of the program; of the camp being run on the lines of a prison or an army camp; and of psychological intimidation linked to fears of unfavorable references, corporal punishment, and the stigma attached to boys who have been to the training center in the eyes of employers and the general public. Throughout its existence camp principals were military men, including Col. M. J. B. Bredenkamp, who had earlier (1963 to 1968) been the first commanding officer of the Coloured Corps. In sum, rather than being regarded as an institution providing young men with a first step onto the employment ladder, the Training Centre was commonly regarded as a sort of reform school dealing with ne'er-do-wells and troublemakers. A certificate from Fauré formalized that stigma. In 1979 the Training Centre was closed, controversial testimony to the government's heavy-handed approach to dealing with Coloured youth.

The training scheme for Coloured youths might be seen in one respect as a "dry run" for compulsory military service for Coloureds. In some ways it was a means of regimenting Coloureds, using the training center to condition a section of the Coloured community to accept government policy. If that was a primary aim of the scheme, or even an ancillary one, it failed miserably.

There are lessons to be learned from this experience. For example, the confusions and inefficiencies of registration should give government pause before introducing another scheme that requires young, male Coloureds to cooperate with the authorities. At a minimum, noncompliance reached 60

95. *Cape Times,* 11 August 1973; *Cape Herald,* 26 January 1980.

percent and other administrative and training complications led to altogether disappointing experiences with the scheme.

Despite genuine embarrassments and difficulties, government contends that the Training Centre was successful. So do several conservative Coloured politicians. In the eight years from 1969 to 1976, 7,592 cadets had been trained there.[96] On the strength of the "large number of people who had been trained in the short while the centre had been in existence" and the number of letters of thanks received from parents, employers, and cadets government concluded that the Training Centre had answered its purpose. A 1972 research project confirmed its view, indicating that 72 percent of former cadets had "successfully adjusted themselves" in the employment market.[97] One suspects that the Department of Defence would look at this experience more critically before plunging into any form of compulsory registration and service.

Perhaps a more acceptable, to all quarters, antecedent to Coloured compulsory military service might be the institution of a paramilitary cadet program (unlike the Cadet Training Centre) in the Coloured secondary schools. There has been considerable discussion of this alternative, along the lines in force for white students. The idea was embodied in the Theron Commission's recommendation number 7. It was also prompted by government itself. The 1979 white paper on defense notes that expansion of the cadet system to "other ethnic groups" is under consideration.[98] The 1977 white paper more positively indicated that cadet training at Coloured and Indian schools was being investigated and that government hoped to introduce this "shortly."[99]

Yet barriers do not fall easily. There is opposition in the

96. *Cape Times*, 2 May 1974. Only 5,718 completed the course; South African Institute of Race Relations, *Survey of Race Relations in South Africa, 1975* (Johannesburg: South African Institute of Race Relations, 1976), p. 112; and letter from South African Institute of Race Relations, 6 February 1980.

97. *Cape Times*, 2 May 1974.

98. Republic of South Africa, Department of Defence, *White Paper on Defence and Armaments Supply, 1979* (Simonstown: S.A. Navy Printing Unit, 1979), p. 21.

99. Republic of South Africa, Department of Defence, *White Paper on Defence, 1977* (Simonstown: S.A. Navy, 1977), p. 24.

Coloured community. Nonetheless, in February 1978 P. W. Botha announced that legislation was being drafted to extend the school cadet system to Coloureds and Indians.[100]

The first public rejection of the idea came from the Cape Teachers Professional Association (CTPA), whose congress in 1978 opposed the introduction of the program by 492 to 1.[101] Not until such time as full citizenship is granted to all races would the CTPA agree to support it. It is a plot, said one official, to divide blacks just as they were moving to greater unity. Panicky whites, he argued, are looking about for allies. "Even if we foolishly accepted the cadet scheme our children would reject it."[102] The Minister of Coloured Relations regretted this decision but tried to minimize its effect by claiming that the CTPA represents only a small percentage of Coloured teachers.[103]

Coloured politicians in the CRC were rather divided on the cadet program. When P. W. Botha first disclosed his intentions the Labour Party called upon the CRC to review its earlier decision to support the idea. That earlier support had been for a voluntary cadet system only. Others within the Labour Party suggested that they still liked the idea, provided it was applied exactly the same as in white schools and provided parents and teachers organizations approved. But at heart many CRC representatives thought that educational priorities should lie elsewhere.[104] Finally, in late 1979, the Labour Party's annual conference resolved that black school committees, teachers, parents, and pupils should reject any form of high school cadet activity. This resolution, unanimously supported, led to a confrontation with the prime minister. The party national chairman eventually recommended a strategy of noncooperation with government.[105]

100. *The Star* (Daily Edition), 13 September 1978, and *Rand Daily Mail,* 1 February 1978.
101. South African Institute of Race Relations, *Survey, 1978,* p. 56.
102. Quoting Willie Soal, a school principal, ibid.
103. *Assembly Debates,* 26 May 1978, col. 7999.
104. *Sunday Times* (Johannesburg), 19 February 1978; South African Institute of Race Relations, *Survey, 1978,* p. 56.
105. *Cape Times,* 29 December 1979, p. 1; *Eastern Province Herald,* 29 December 1979.

There are other reasons the Coloured community is not being cooperative. Many Coloureds justifiably feel that limited educational funds might better be spent on teachers' salaries and on more schools and facilities. Teachers are the ones who must administer and implement the cadet system, and this would necessitate a considerable reeducation program for them. Although Coloured teachers are rightly reluctant to be drawn in to support the government and to carry out a policy they do not agree with, they could be vulnerable to pressure. The teachers are paid directly by the South African government, not by the provincial authorities, as are white teachers. Heretofore, one of the chief recruiting agents for the SACC has been the Coloured school system.[106] It is likely that the authorities may introduce a cadet program first in rural, more maleable and less politicized areas, then gradually extend outward from there. Certainly a cadet system would be a first logical step preceding compulsory military training. Yet even with their desire to inflate the black role in South Africa's defenses, it would seem that there is still considerable scope for expansion of Coloured participation on a voluntary basis — individually, by enlistment in the SACCSB and by joining cadet units on a voluntary basis, and, more widely, in group terms by each Coloured secondary school deciding if it wants to establish a cadet corps of its own. Given P. W. Botha's penchant for the piecemeal, incremental involvement of blacks, this would appear to be an expected process.

Roles and Ranks

The transition from "traditional" to standard military duties and assignments for black members of the SADF came gradually and, presumably, after care was taken to clear the ground for change in the white electorate. In the beginning a public image was fostered of the Coloured Corps as a noncombat unit of skilled artisans, supplying specialist support services (as cooks, drivers, and so forth) to white fighting formations. Yet

106. See *Cape Times*, 23 August 1977.

SACC members were trained to handle "single-shot small arms for self-defence and the protection of Government property."[107] Later, on being challenged in Parliament, the minister almost apologetically replied: "Members of the Coloured Corps are only trained in the handling of the .303 inch rifle for self-defence and the guarding of Government property which may be entrusted to them. During recruit training 140 rounds per man are fired and thereafter 70 rounds per trained man per year. Members are not trained as instructors on the weapon."[108] In other words the SACC men were trained on the weapon, but not well enough to be a threat.

This was true only until the first intake of the SACCSB in 1973, in which modern Coloured servicemen trained for combat — in counterinsurgency operations and in the use of automatic weapons.[109] It is strange that in March 1975 the minister should announce that Coloured men were going to be trained as full-fledged fighting infantry men. "As soon as suitable terrain is obtained," the white paper stated, "the training of Coloured members of the SADF as infantrymen will begin."[110] The future tense is used. Even before these sorts of announcements appeared the public was being slowly brought to accept armed Coloured soldiers. In July 1973 a photo appeared in the *Cape Times* of a SACC trainee bayonetting a dummy. Only minor public criticism followed. Increasingly in the press it was repeated that the SACC was composed of "fighting soldiers" and that the corpsmen wanted to be regarded as such.[111]

Likewise, specialist training involving combat and authority roles also began more seriously in the later 1970s. When South Africa's parachute battalions were reorganized into an operational parachute brigade, the new brigade included Cape Corpsmen. In addition Coloured Permanent Force members

107. J.J. Fouché in *Assembly Debates*, 19 February 1963, cols. 1576–77.

108. *Assembly Debates*, 30 April 1965, col. 5096.

109. *Rand Daily Mail*, 6 December 1974; and *Cape Times*, 5 December 1974.

110. The 1975 Defence Department white paper, quoted in *Cape Times*, 28 March 1975.

111. *Cape Times*, 20, 26, and 27 July 1973. For example, Howard Salkow and Henry Jooste, "The Coloured Soldier (3): Motivated, Dedicated, Tough," *Paratus* 27 (November 1976): 28–29.

since 1974 have been transferred from the SACCSB to the
Military Police Corps to become full MPs.[112]

The stepwise employment of Cape Corpsmen in Namibia
also characterizes the empirical style of SADF headquarters.
This use began with Coloureds in "traditional" roles — as cooks
in the late 1960s and early 1970s. They went as individuals,
"diluted," attached to white formations. In 1973 a detachment
of twenty drivers, national servicemen of the SACCSB commanded by a Permanent Force corporal from the SACC, was
sent to the "border." Platoons of drivers and some cooks and
supply personnel were sent again in 1974 and 1975.[113] Coloured soldiers, the first to see active service since World War II
as a combat unit and the first to serve as a full-fledged fighting
unit since World War I, were sent "up north" in September
1976.[114] Their two-and-a-half-month tour of border duty was
reportedly well received, and they were given a warm welcome, parading through Cape Town on their return.[115] Again
in 1977 and every year since at least one contingent of
SACCSB men has been sent for a three month stint of operational duty, and many of the men have returned to the operational area for more than one tour. Combat casualties and
deaths have been sustained, usually caused by landmines. The
fact is that SACC personnel have been inched into combat
roles, which have been presumably efficiently and willingly
performed. The government is keen to get effective political
mileage out of these troops. The press is filled with planted
stories. Selected newsmen are taken to combat areas and encouraged to editorialize about their experiences. Coloured
politicians and community figures are given the red carpet
treatment in Namibia, too, and are told to spread the message
at arranged press conferences and among their "constituents."

112. *Cape Times,* 19 and 21 April 1978; *Paratus* 29 (December 1978): 11; and
Rand Daily Mail, 18 April 1978. *Paratus,* Supplement (July 1978), p. iv.
113. *Cape Times,* 31 October and 2 November 1973, 18 June and 25 September 1974, and 5 December 1975.
114. *The Star* (Daily Edition), 2 November 1976; *Argus,* 18 November 1976,
p. 23; and *The Star* (Weekly Air Edition), 20 November 1976, p. 1.
115. *Cape Times,* 18, 26, 30 November 1976; and *Paratus,* 28 (January
1977): 14–15.

But providing Coloured soldiers with full-scale military training and easing them into combat roles, still on a small scale (a couple of hundred at a time), is not the entire story. Unless Coloured forces are to be regarded as little more than obedient Tommies, efforts would have to be made to tap the leadership and supervisory potential of this population group as well. Attempts have been made to develop this potential parallel to the expansion of combat assignments. In the first intake of the SACC were individuals earmarked for instructors' training. In July 1964 the first batch of twenty-nine qualified as regimental instructors, and in November they were promoted to noncommissioned officers' rank.[116] Since then a steady trickle of instructors has been produced, which has included instructors for the navy, in continually upgraded and more technical subjects. Today virtually all the instructors at Eersterivier and Fauré are Coloured.

When the SACC was first initiated in the postwar era the highest rank to which a Coloured corpsman could aspire was warrant officer class 1. Two Coloured company sergeant-majors attained this rank in June 1970, both having been with the SACC since August 1963.[117]

In May 1973 the Minister of Defence disclosed for the first time the government's intention to allow Coloured corpsmen to become commissioned officers.[118] He admitted that theretofore the main task of the SACC had been to provide men for "service" roles in white units. Henceforth advancement in the force, he contended, would be based entirely on merit. In this important speech he also revealed that it was his thinking that eventually the SACCSB would be run entirely by Coloured officers, that government intended that SACCSB trainees who had completed their stint would be organized into Citizen Force units of the corps, and that there would be no objection in principle to the employment of Coloured persons in any of the three arms of the SADF. Perhaps one could not go so far as to argue that P. W. Botha was "scrapping job reservation in his

116. *Cape Times,* 17 November 1964; *Argus,* 18 July 1964.
117. *Cape Times,* 8 June 1970.
118. *Cape Times,* 12 May 1973.

department," but these pronouncements did represent significant policy changes, ones with potentially far-reaching social and military ramifications.[119]

In short order, eleven officer candidates were selected and training began. The candidates ranged in age from nineteen to fifty years, with a rank spread from trainee and private to sergeant major (first class). Only one was a national serviceman; the rest were regular soldiers of the Permanent Force. The eleven were selected out of a panel of thirty-nine who appeared before the selection board. The first orientation phase of their training lasted six months and took place at Eersterivier under instructors from the Military Academy at Saldanha Bay, where white officers are trained.[120] This was followed by specialist training for nine months at places like the Army Services School in Pretoria. All in all, it was eighteen and one half months until seven emerged with commissions.[121] From there these men went on to largely administrative assignments.

Three years later five of these seven gained promotion from lieutenant to captain.[122] Afterwards, one was appointed adjutant of the SACC, and he was later replaced by another Coloured officer from this first cohort. Another was posted to the Castle in Cape Town, the regional military headquarters, and in the process commanded white soldiers. In another year and a half four of the five became the first Coloured officers to achieve "field" or senior rank as majors. The youngest, aged twenty-nine, went on to be named the chief administrative officer of the SACC, and the others served as an infantry company commander, a logistics company commander, and the command information officer.[123]

In 1978 two Coloured Citizen Force officers were commis-

119. *Cape Times*, 15 May 1973.
120. *The Star* (Weekly Air Edition), 20 October 1973, p. 7; *Cape Times*, 17 and 30 October 1973.
121. *Cape Times*, 15 and 16 May 1975; South African Defence Force, *Presentation of Acts of Commission to the First Corps Officers in the SADF* (Simonstown: South Africa Navy Printing Press, 1975).
122. *Paratus* 29, (May 1978): pp. 4–5.
123. *Cape Times*, 8 November 1979, p. 11; *Paratus*, Supplement (January 1980), pp. v and i; *Paratus*, 31 (March 1980): 38–39.

sioned. These were the first black officers outside the Permanent Force. Both are members of a maintenance unit commanded by a white, in which almost all the one hundred and fifty members are former SACC trainees. It was also announced that year that Coloureds and Indians would be permitted to receive training as naval officers at the Gordon's Bay Naval College.[124]

Despite such highly publicized examples there has been a dearth of qualified officer candidates. Vacancies among candidate applicants have been reported.[125] A gap in the training chain has resulted. Considering that the first class of officer candidates was taken in in 1973, by early 1978, after five full years, only the five captains and a batch of new candidates were in place. By 1979 a few more lieutenants were commissioned. Altogether, as of February 1980 there were only seventeen Coloured officers in a PF army contingent of eight hundred, hardly a burgeoning program. If one adds to that figure the three thousand or so voluntary servicemen at the SACC, of whom seventeen have been trained and commissioned (out of a class of forty-nine) as candidate officers, the figures are not at all impressive.[126] The advantage in pay and eventual rank accruing to university graduates notwithstanding, few apply for officer training. No matter how committed the SADF upper hierarchy and the Minister of Defence seem to be to equalizing opportunities for Coloureds in the SADF and to making the SADF a meritocracy for this group, the appeal of the service, as a career, is limited. Because of a more favorable set of economic alternatives for the type of men who would qualify for officer level work, really qualified applicants are in short supply.

Part of the problem was brought to light in the controversy over the authority attached to the officers' commissions and the extent to which men of color could command white soldiers and, presumably, white citizens in emergencies. As part

124. *Cape Times*, 7 October 1978; South African Institute of Race Relations, *Survey, 1978*, p. 155.

125. *Cape Times*, 13 March 1977.

126. Nöthling, *Blacks in the South Africa Defence Force*, p. 3; *Paratus*, 32 (March 1981): 62; and *South Africa Digest*, 24 April 1981, p. 13.

of the decision to establish the SACC government initially undertook to amend the 1957 Defence Act to preclude white soldiers from being subordinate to black soldiers. This involved amending the Military Discipline Code to redefine the term "superior officer." The revised version contained a proviso that "no person subject to this Code who is not a white person . . . shall be deemed to be the superior officer of a white person subject to this code: Provided further that a white person subject to this Code who, irrespective of his rank, is appointed in authority over any person subject to this Code who is not a white person as so defined, shall be deemed to be the superior officer of such last-mentioned person."[127]

Thus, when it was announced that Coloured officers were about to be commissioned the issues of command and race were reopened. P. W. Botha told the House of Assembly at that time that white ranks in the army had been instructed to salute Coloured officers.[128] Nonetheless, the Military Discipline Code remained, and a good deal of the personal interaction between Coloured NCOs and white NCOs demanded an element of pragmatism. "It is all a question of rank," one Coloured NCO said. "My rank is respected and I respect another man's rank . . . . We know the thing [the Military Discipline Code] exists, but it is politely ignored. One of the reasons for the success of this unit is that we have learned to work together in spite of this."[129]

As long as the code remained officially on the books the possibility for awkwardness and incident existed, and the reality of racist subordination rankled. As if to convince doubtful whites in the SADF, Brig. W. J. Fouché wrote an article for the official armed forces magazine in which he maintained that there is nothing "servile or humiliating" about one soldier saluting another who happens to belong to another race.[130] It is the madness of South Africa itself that such an article would

127. Quoted in Barakat Ahmad, "South Africa's Military Establishment," in United Nations, Department of Political and Security Council Affairs, Unit on Apartheid, *Notes and Documents,* no. 25 (December 1972): 9.

128. *Cape Times,* 30 October 1974.

129. *Argus,* 3 April 1972.

130. *Cape Times,* 20 and 21 January 1975.

need to be written, but in reality Coloured commissioned officers were to emerge within five months, and possible aggravations had to be forestalled. By arguing that it was not the individual who was being saluted, nor the uniform, but the "sovereign authority of the Republic of South Africa, namely the State President," Brig. Fouché sought to depersonalize the act of saluting. In his view a salute is merely an expression of esteem for the state president's sovereign authority "and also, in this verligte century, an expression of consideration and goodwill." In this context the old version of the Military Discipline Code simply had to go. In April 1975 the Minister of Defence introduced an amendment to redefine the term "superior officer" in terms of Schedule 1 of the Defence Act. Both Houses of Parliament unanimously approved the change.[131] Black army commissions and ranks were given equal legal status with those of whites.

The government fastened on this symbolic change to broadcast its enlightenment to the outside world. Minister of Information C.P. "Connie" Mulder boasted (in those days he was inclined to boasting), and it was reproduced in the weekly propaganda organ *South Africa Digest,* that "Coloured officers had been appointed in the Army, the Police, and the Prisons' Department, to whom White rank and file were fully subordinate." Cas de Villiers, one of Mulder's mouthpieces as director of the Foreign Affairs Association, who also was implicated in the information scandal of 1978–79, echoed this line.[132] The argument is that this constitutes one of the key changes reflecting a favorable climate for peaceful change in South Africa and evidencing that South Africa is capable of reforming herself without pressures from abroad. Even if these are profound changes, which they are not, it is hard to imagine them occurring without some sort of external pressure that necessitated expanding and modernizing the Defence Force.

131. *South Africa Digest,* 25 April 1975, pp. 3–4; and South African Institute of Race Relations, *Survey, 1975,* p. 197. *Assembly Debates,* 15 April 1975, cols. 4100–4101.
132. *South Africa Digest,* 26 August 1977, p. 2; and 16 September 1977, p. 31.

And when thirteen ranking Coloured civilians were trooped to the operational area to see firsthand the SACC's involvement in the fighting, one spokesman was quoted as saying: "I even saw a white soldier saluting a Coloured officer. The officers eat together and share all the same facilities. At the Ruacana base there's a Coloured officer who is second in Command."[133] This came as a surprise to him. In any other modern army in which rank alone mattered it would not be worthy of comment. But in South Africa it merited quotation. Even this compliant spokesman could not help drawing this conclusion, one which the *Cape Times* also drew editorially: "If it can happen there [at the front] I don't see why it shouldn't happen here in South Africa."[134] The transference of behavior patterns developed for better race relations and more efficiency among men at war would seem, so the reasoning runs, to demonstrate that the essential changes are possible and, indeed, necessary in the civilian context. It would be difficult to convince either South Africa's whites of the wisdom of that line or a social scientist of its empirical accuracy.

Salary Scales and Race Differentials

While the SADF may, at the top, be verbally committed to ending the most overt forms of racial discrimination in the organization (although the basic ones, segregated formations and an all-white command structure at the top, still apply), inequalities and inequities are still part and parcel of the system. To some the difficulty the SACC had at first in attracting sufficient volunteers resulted from low salary scales. The Minister of Defence is frequently questioned in Parliament about salary scales in the SADF and is asked to furnish information comparing white and black salaries and benefits. By 1981, however, Permanent Force members of the SACC and the S.A. Indian Corps had achieved salary levels equal to those of white personnel in all but a few ranks. For example, a Coloured private began at R1,830 rising to R4,950. A white private re-

133. *Daily News*, 5 September 1978.
134. Ibid., and *Cape Times*, 5 September 1978.

ceived R1,998 to R5,670. At lance corporal and corporal ranks similar discrepancies prevailed. But at the level of sergeant and above, including commissioned officers, the salaries were equal. Discrepancies did prevail only at the rank of second lieutenant and candidate officer.[135] Prior to this, Coloured and Indian Permanent Force members were paid at the rate of around 80 percent of the salaries of white personnel of the same rank. A minimum salary scale for the SACC was R1,170 per year, reaching a maximum of R2,700. By comparison, white minimums of the SADF were R1,440, rising to R3,600.[136] As for members of Citizen Force and Commando units, daily pay for whites and Coloureds compares as follows: private, R8.04 to R6.85; lance corporal, R8.63 to R7.45; corporal, R11.59 to R10.41; and for all ranks above (except second lieutenant and candidate officer) the daily rates are the same.[137]

Fringe benefits were unequal, consciously pegged to a ratio established by Parliament. Before the passage of the Military Pensions Act of 1976 (no. 84), which dealt with improving pensions of the veterans of previous wars, a new dispensation for SADF members injured on military duty, and provisions for dependents of those killed, the applicable ratio stood at 4:2:1 between whites, Coloureds and Indians, and black Africans. This act narrowed the ratio to approximately 6:4:3.[138]

Various members of Parliament have complained about the discrepancies.[139] All Coloured spokesmen operating openly in South Africa, pro-government and government critic alike, have pleaded for not only better pay but equal pay for the SACC. "South Africa cannot afford half-price soldiers," declared Sonny Leon.[140] It should be borne in mind, however,

135. *Assembly Debates*, 25 August 1981, Q cols. 145–153.

136. *Assembly Debates*, 4 May 1977, Q cols. 1015–20.

137. *Assembly Debates*, 25 August 1981, Q col. 151.

138. South African Institute of Race Relations, *Survey of Race Relations in South Africa, 1976* (Johannesburg: South African Institute of Race Relations, 1977), pp. 37–38.

139. Notably L. G. Murray (UP, Green Point); J. W. E. Wiley (South African Party [SAP], Simonstown); W. Vause Raw (NRP, Durban Point); and H. H. Schwarz (PFP, Yoeville).

140. *Cape Times*, 17 January 1976 (Leon, leader of the Labour Party, and Nic Kearns, national president of the Coloured Ex-Servicemen's Legion); *Cape*

that although Coloured and African salaries do not compare
favorably to one another or to the white salary structure in the
SADF, the Coloured recruit is inclined to look at them in terms
largely of how they compare with the other alternatives he may
have or hope to have in the general economy. If the job market
is depressed, or if SADF pay looks relatively high, then its
relationship to white salaries is largely discounted. So far it
would appear that salaries and benefits are not a significant
disincentive to joining at the lower levels.

The embattled Minister of Defence at first sought protection
from criticism in the line that the duties and responsibilities of
the SACC are not comparable to those of white members of the
SADF, since Coloureds are employed in a limited number of
musterings and serve in noncombatant capacities. In addition,
SACC men do not exercise command or authority over white
SADF men. In conclusion, lower salaries and benefits are
justified. But even admitting the efficacy of this argument, its
serviceability collapsed along with its premises once the SACC
took on combat assignments and once officers were commissioned.

Thereafter the minister presumably did work to bring
benefits and salaries more in line among the races. With effect
from 1 April 1978 special camp allowances (in lieu of danger
pay) were equalized for all race groups in the operational
areas.[141] All allowances under SADF jurisdiction alone are the
same for all races serving in the operational area. P. W. Botha
has pleaded for patience: "The gap is being narrowed." Parity
will be brought about "when circumstances permit in accord-
ance with the Government's declared policy." But this rather
vague declaration does not indicate the nub of the issue, which
is that the SADF is not an entity unto itself. Salary scales are
adjusted by the Public Service Commission and are not subject
to SADF administrative action. That body thinks more broadly
(which amounts to more narrowly) than the SADF, and when
calls are made to equalize salaries and benefits the commission

Times, 10 August 1971 (Tom Schwartz, pro-government member of CRC);
Rand Daily Mail, 26 April 1979 (Jac Rabie, CRC).
    141. *Assembly Debates,* 7 April 1978, Q col. 573.

continually resists because such changes would imply that salary inequities in other parts of the public service also ought to be revised. Racial parity is not a position they are keen on adopting, arguments to the contrary notwithstanding. Changes, as well, demand parliamentary action. Since there are plenty of white politicians receptive to the commission's view, it has been able to hold the line.

As was mentioned, racist attitudes are an everyday part of the regime and of the military as well. Official efforts to underplay them, indeed even to suppress and transcend them, cannot at this stage eliminate racism altogether or hope to shield black soldiers from its ubiquity. A minor example of how racism seeps into what, on the surface, are innocent circumstances is the following. In this "verligte century," to borrow Brigadier Fouché's term, a questionnaire was sent to thousands of Citizen Force soldiers asking to what population group they belonged. The examples provided were "South African or Cape Coloured." Coloured soldiers were thereby officially informed that they were not South Africans. The commandant responsible tried to slough off blame to a "temporary secretary who typed the questions," but at least he expressed his personal exception to the question. Another officer responded: "This unthinking action breaks down race relations carefully built up over the years." The Defence Force officially apologized.[142] But these sorts of slights are daily occurrences. Racism both within and outside of the regime in South Africa are endemic and virtually impossible to root out in a piecemeal assault on deeply ingrained attitudes and beliefs.

Conclusion

Overall it is not easy to make a judgment on the SACC. Militarily, it appears to be rather effective as a unit. The SACC has scored well in performance tests. Time spent in the operational area has led officials to praise the SACC. Their general morale has improved. From superficial observation and from accounts in the press, some of which are planted by SADF

142. *Argus*, 12 February 1979; and *Daily News*, 13 February 1979.

public relations officers and some others of which are written by defense or military correspondents fearful of losing access to headquarters should critical reports appear, it would appear that morale is high, at least as high as morale in white units. The corps seems to be developing a set of traditions in which their officers and men and the outside community take pride. In sum the Cape Corps would seem to be, for the SADF, a successful experiment.

In many regards things done with, to, and by the SACC are examined carefully at SADF headquarters to determine their applicability to other black formations and groups. The SACC is regarded as an organizational guinea pig, a van in the matter of Defence Force race relations. What has been produced is thought to be a saleable commodity—to that part of white South Africa somewhat skittish about arming and training blacks for combat; somewhat less to the Coloured community itself, intensely sensitive to racist governmental policies and determined not to be "used" again by the white society; even less to the rest of the black community, watching to see how Coloureds fare as a result of their identification with the defense of the regime; and to the outside world, particularly that conservative and liberal segment of it that wants South Africa to demonstrate some flexibility and adaptability and that would like nothing better than to see the South African defense efforts multiracialized so that their own cooperation and collusion with white South Africa can be rationalized, to themselves and to their critics. In these respects a great deal depends on how successful is the SACC and how generalizable are conclusions based upon this particular experiment.

9

The 21 Battalion and Other
Black African Formations:
A Foreign Legion?

BY THE TIME the chief of the army, Lt. Gen. Magnus Malan, granted permission to establish the S.A. Army Bantu Training Centre in November 1973, the SADF had acquired some limited experience with black fighting men. The SACC had been in existence for almost ten years and its SSB for nearly a year. Blacks had served in large numbers in the S.A. Police and had been involved in military duty both in Rhodesia and on patrol on South Africa's borders, and the SADF had employed on an individual basis indigenous blacks in Namibia.[1] In addition, most white opposition to the military use of blacks had been silenced or won over to this more flexible approach. It was no longer an issue of whether to use blacks but of how many, in what roles, and in what organizational format. For the Republic of South Africa, land of the "white man's war" and last bastion of "white Christian nationalism," the time had arrived to defend the regime by any and all means. Caliban must be issued an automatic weapon.

1. *Sunday Times* (Johannesburg), 16 June 1974; *Rand Daily Mail* (Johannesburg), 2 August 1974.

Structure

On 21 January 1974 the Army Bantu Training Centre was officially established under the leadership of Maj. M.W. Pretorius. He, along with nine Permanent Force members, prepared for his new assignment at the Prison Services Bantu Training College at Baviaansport, north of Pretoria. Three months later the first sixteen black recruits reported for basic training.

Establishment of the unit had been a bit unexpected. Only in 1970 the Minister of Defence had stated that black Africans would be employed by his department only as common laborers. In 1968 some 9,088 black civilians were employed in his department, mainly as laborers, cooks, "head boys," and "boss boys."[2] The idea of a black African South African military unit would seem to be inconsistent with the stated government policy of eventual "independence" for each black nation or ethnic group. "If the Bantu wants to build up a defence force," Mr. Botha had asserted, "he should do it in his own eventually independent homeland."[3] Initially, however, the new unit did not appear to veer radically from the preexisting arrangements, except, that is, for the inconsistency with the homelands scheme. The first recruits reportedly came over from the Bantu Labour Service, and the first advertisements in black newspapers touted the unit as a special guard formation, designed to train men for armed duty at military installations.[4] Ancillary skills as drivers, clerks, storemen, and dog handlers would be transmitted as well as first aid and hygiene instruction. In August 1974 another thirty-eight men joined the unit, and at that time it was decided that the first intake of sixteen should be trained as regimental instructors.[5]

The public image of the new unit was fuzzy. In December 1974 Maj. Gen. J.R. Dutton, then acting chief of the army,

2. Republic of South Africa, *House of Assembly Debates* (Hansard), 22 March 1968, cols. 2657–58.

3. Ibid., 31 August 1970, col. 2941.

4. *The Star* (Johannesburg, Weekly Air Edition), 15 June 1974, pp. 1, 11; *Sunday Express* (Johannesburg), 16 June 1974.

5. *South Africa Digest*, 20 December 1974, pp. 12–13; and *Rand Daily Mail*, 5 December 1974.

announced that the army would recruit African soldiers who
would, he said, be allowed to carry arms and who would enjoy
the same pay and conditions of service as white soldiers. Of
course, this would all take place "within the framework of Government policy," and no integrated units were contemplated.
There would be no fear, as well, of black Africans with rank
(the highest theoretically possible then was sergeant major)
giving orders to whites of lower rank. Maj. Gen. Dutton saw
this new unit taking a form similar to that of the SACC, yet he
went on to talk of training which, with the exception of the
security guards, covered the same "traditional," menial assignments.[6]

In 1975 the Minister of Defence continued to refer to
"Bantu" being used for "guard duties and other auxiliary duties," hardly the character of the SACC at this time.[7] What he
identified as the "recent casual utilization of Bantu," he went
on, "will take shape more clearly within the support service
corps" which he promised to establish. Meanwhile, he announced as cabinet-approved policy that "Bantu sections"
were to be added "to certain commandos . . . with the help of
those commandos." But announcement is not fulfillment, and
this policy has proven difficult to implement. It was an awkward time, when black African recruits were neither fish nor
fowl—neither laborer nor soldier. One thing was certain at
that time. Black Africans were not to function in a fully operational combat formation—the old vestiges of "tradition" hung
heavy as the minister, the SADF, and the politicians grappled
with the unit's configuration. At that time the numbers were so
small as to permit a shift if necessary from the guard duty or
auxiliary support service model to something more active.

Three important changes were made in about 1975. First,
African blacks were for the first time permitted to join the
Permanent Force. Before then these men were grouped into a
special S.A. Support Services Corps outside the Permanent
Force structure. Second, on 1 December the S.A. Army Bantu

6. *The Star* (Weekly Air Edition), 14 December 1974; *Rand Daily Mail,* 10
December 1974; *New York Times,* 10 December 1974.
7. *Assembly Debates,* 22 April 1975, cols. 4583–84.

Training Centre was moved to Lenz, its current base, and was deemed then to be self-sufficient. Lenz had been a World War II military base that had been allowed to deteriorate. At times it supplied emergency housing for Indians (it is across the railway tracks from Lenasia, an Indian township) before it was reactivated as a training center for black soldiers. Third, the unit's name was changed to 21 Battalion, since it had been established on the twenty-first anniversary of the Infantry Corps.

The 21 Battalion continued in an anomalous position. To begin with the battalion is still a "training school" for the S.A. Support Services Corps (SASSC). All black Africans in the SADF were first brought into the SASSC. The 21 Battalion is not an operational battalion per se, like most other infantry battalions in the Defence Force, even though an operational company was formed in 1977. This step was taken at some temporary sacrifice to the unit, since it drained the battalion of most of its instructors. Overall, the 21 Battalion is organized for training, and, by and large, for training in non-combatant services. Even into 1977 the press releases and propaganda tended to stress that black soldiers at Lenz were not being trained for combat duty.[8]

Until 1978 the 21 Battalion existed on an ad hoc basis. In that year the chief of the army convened a board of officers to plan for the unit's future. It decided to build the 21 Battalion into a full-fledged training school for black African soldiers from diverse ethnic groups.

The board also agreed to set up a number of regional units beginning in January 1979, perhaps at first of company size although capable of growth.[9] Since each would be identified with a regional command, each would probably take on a particular ethnic composition. At present there are a battalion of around three hundred Zulu (called the 121 Battalion, affiliated with the Natal Command, and based at Jozini), com-

8. E.g., *South Africa Digest,* 18 February 1977, p. 24. In contrast, the same report was accompanied by photos, all posed, illustrating men in combat scenes.

9. From interview, Lenz, 25 July 1979; and the statement by the Deputy Minister of Defence in *Assembly Debates,* 2 March 1979, cols. 1748–49.

panies of Swazi (the 111 Battalion, attached to the Northern
Transvaal Command, and based at Amsterdam), and units of
Venda (the 112 Battalion at Madimbo) and Shangaan (the 113
Battalion at Impala, near Phalaborwa in the eastern Transvaal). The Zulu battalion began training in April 1979, and it
already has been on operational duty patrolling the northern
Natal border.[10] Expectations are that these regional units will
be used in Namibia, too. There are immediate plans to form
similar units in the Cape and the Free State.

   It is envisioned that in around eight years there will be about
eighteen similar black battalions. Each is to be an operational
unit, decentralized and attached to a regional command —
Northern Transvaal, Eastern Province, Free State, Natal, and
so forth. At first it was thought that each black African recruit
would be trained originally at Lenz and then, on completing
his year's training, would be assigned to a regional unit or to
Lenz as an instructor (after further specialized training). The
Lenz men would retain their Permanent Force status. Lenz
would become, then, an elite enterprise among black formations. The regional units, however, have now started to do their
own training and are now Auxiliary Service formations. In the
cryptic words of the Deputy Minister of Defence: "We are
recruiting on another basis."[11] Regional unit members are recruited locally, and lower qualifications seem to apply than for
21 Battalion members. This would appear to be the new mechanism for the expanded use of black Africans in the SADF.

   It is difficult, without being privy to classified data, to discern
the social backgrounds of 21 Battalion recruits. Conflicting
reports make it necessary to be wary of "authoritative" data. In
contrast to the SACC information, where all accounts agree
that recruits tend to come largely from rural areas beyond the
Western Cape, there is little agreement regarding the backgrounds of 21 Battalion members. A top ranking personnel
officer indicated that around 70 percent of the members are

10. *Sunday Express*, 2 March 1980. Notice of the formation of these units was
not published until late May 1980. See *South Africa Digest*, 30 May 1980, pp. 1,
3, 22–23; and "Impis March Again," *South Africa Digest*, 4 July 1980, pp. 14–
15.
   11. *Assembly Debates*, 2 March 1979, col. 1749.

from rural districts, with no clear-cut pattern of ethnic composition.[12] Commandant Swanepoel, in contrast, claims that most of the battalion was recruited from urban areas, particularly from boom towns of the northern Orange Free State such as Welkom and Kronstadt. He noted that the largest single ethnic group was South Sotho. Many of these men have not, in Swanepoel's words, been "detribalized." Being from the Free State South Sotho are most likely to speak Afrikaans as their first European language, and since this is the functional command language of the unit, as it is in the army, they are more likely to fit into the system. Zulu is also widely spoken in the 21 Battalion. Others have said that urban men, even men from Rand townships, are numerous in the battalion. Still others have denied this.

The SADF has a series of two-week courses on various African languages, but presumably this has made little impact on white personnel. Commandant Swanepoel admitted that of the seventy-seven white men in the battalion in mid-1979 not one could speak a black language. Yet whites assigned to black African units do attend an orientation course, taught at one time by the Ethnology Unit attached to the Witwatersrand Command. Instructors are often graduates in anthropology and African languages.[13] It would appear that the current thinking at the 21 Battalion is that the cultural gap between white and black is so great that integration within units ought to be avoided. Instead, it seeks to evade what it sees as potentially explosive mixing and to encourage ethnic differences. The ultimate strategy of the SADF is not clear. At present all blacks at Lenz are trained together. And there is no formal separation of black soldiers into tribal or ethnic groups. In the longer run, however, a great deal depends on the resolution of the homelands citizenship issue and the growth and success of regional-cum-ethnic companies and battalions.

Thus the ultimate organizational dilemma is obvious. If the homelands scheme envisages all South African blacks eventu-

12. Interview, Pretoria, 16 July 1979.
13. SADF continues to advertize for ethnologists "to help maintain good relations between various ethnic groups employed in the services"; *Argus* (Cape Town), 30 January 1979.

ally achieving citizenship in an ethnic homeland, even those black Africans resident in white group areas, what becomes of black Africans in the SADF? Presumably they too will all become citizens of other countries. Technically black Africans will lose all their rights attending South African citizenship and will become "foreigners," many in the land of their birth. Will the 21 Battalion and other black African units then become "foreign legions"? Logically, that is the dilemma, and politicians and SADF personnel officers are aware of the delicate issue. Chief Gatsha Buthelezi of KwaZulu complained sarcastically: "They expect us to be 'patriotic' foreigners. We are called upon to offer our lives in defence of the borders of a country in which we will now be foreigners. . . . I have never seen such insensitivity in my whole life."[14] Chief Buthelezi has refused both SADF invitations to visit the 121 Battalion base and an offer of an honorary colonelship in the 121 Battalion. Certainly those blacks serving in the 21 Battalion consider themselves to be South African citizens and expect to continue as citizens into the future. Otherwise the recruitment problems would be enormous. When asked if he was willing to defend South Africa, one civilian resident of Soweto wryly dodged the question — "I'm a Bantu homeland citizen, so I'd be indulging myself in foreign politics — South Africa's."[15] Officially, when a homeland becomes "independent" each "citizen" of the new state is supposed to be released by the 21 Battalion (or presumably the new regional units) and then reemployed by that homeland's new army. He even may have already been involved before independence in preparation of the homeland's guard. Yet the 21 Battalion still has Tswana members, and probably some Xhosa and Venda are in its ranks. It has been rumored that some two-thirds of the Venda members of the SADF declined to transfer to the Venda National Army upon that homeland's "independence." There are also Venda in the 112 Battalion. Until such time as comprehensive strategic planning between SADF and various homeland national guards and armies is evolved, is it likely that black African personnel

14. As quoted in *Washington Post*, 10 April 1979.
15. As quoted in *The Star* (Weekly Air Edition), 13 March 1976, p. 5.

will be moved easily from formation to formation or army to army without some considerable dissatisfaction and dislocation?

Finally, there arises the issue of what becomes of black Africans who leave the SADF for civilian life. Although some Coloured veterans have moved into commandos (sometimes existing heretofore all-white commandos and sometimes newly organized, racially separate Coloured commandos), few commandos have welcomed black African soldiers.[16] Periodically the press publishes (and presumably the SADF releases) statements by commando officers of support for government policy of allowing Africans to join commandos.[17] But many commandos have not been cooperative. General Malan, early in 1978, appealed to all-white commando units to accept Africans in their ranks. But when asked what roles Africans would play in the all-white units, whether any had already joined, and whether all facilities would be integrated, General Malan, through his press liaison officer in Pretoria, declined to answer these questions.[18] A policy spelled out by the Minister of Defence more than two and a half years earlier had apparently achieved little worth crowing about.

Government policy has been particularly ambiguous on the roles to be performed by black Africans in commandos. Certainly they are not to be treated the same as white members. For example, the minister has emphatically pointed out that the SADF "cannot distribute arms on a very large scale to blacks without the necessary control measures. I do not want to be misunderstood on this point. The distribution must be under the strictest regulations prescribed by the head of the Army."[19] Despite being pushed by various members of Parliament on the commando issue, the prime minister has not been able to open up the commando option widely enough to satisfy government preferences.

16. See the minister's instructions in *Assembly Debates,* 22 April 1977, col. 5904.

17. See, e.g., *Rand Daily Mail,* 23 January 1978, p. 1.

18. *Rand Daily Mail,* 25 January 1978. The statement a few days earlier by General Malan and press comment on it, all favorable, appear in *South Africa Digest,* 27 January 1978, pp. 7, 26–28.

19. *Assembly Debates,* 22 April 1977, col. 5904.

Rank and Status

White Permanent Force recruits must have a Standard 8 education (Junior Certificate, "0" Levels). For Africans, expected qualifications have gone as low as Standard 5 or 6 if the selection board thinks, on testing the applicant, that he has promise.

Lenz is expected to train up to the rank of sergeant major. The first batch of corporals were promoted in 1977 (after serving two years in the unit) and the first twenty-one sergeants two years later, early in 1979.[20] Significantly, the two highest ranking black Africans in the SADF are outside the ordinary line of command. Both were lateral entry appointments, a public relations officer (captain) for the South West Africa Command and the first black chaplain (colonel) in the SADF. Plans are being studied to train and promote Africans into regular commissioned ranks, but so far the highest line rank is a staff sergeant, promoted in January 1981.[21]

The facility at Lenz is not equipped to train in all specialities. Many have to be sent elsewhere for instruction to become chefs, MPs, storemen, and others. They complete their qualifying courses at several centers, including Lenz, doing the same courses that white NCOs pass for promotion. Some continue on with courses to qualify as staff sergeants. According to Defence Force press releases, "nothing will stand in their way of promotion to any suitable rank for which they qualify."[22] Most of their assignments will be in administration and maintenance, although platoon leaders have done courses to train as section leaders, drivers and maintenance men, medics, radio operators, and advanced instructors.

By and large the Defence Force hierarchy conceives of African units being relatively self-contained. It is not easy for the men of the 21 Battalion to be transferred individually to other units, although it has happened. If special assignment to white units is necessary, headquarters prefer that blocks of Africans (platoons or companies) be posted to the white units. "The

20 "Medals for 100 of our Black Defenders," *Hit* (March–April 1979), pp. 14–17; and *Paratus,* Supplement (April 1979), p. vii.

21. *South Africa Digest,* 3 November 1978, p. 7; and 1 December 1978, p. 12; and *Paratus* 32 (February 1981): 44.

22. Ibid.; and *Sunday Times,* 26 September 1976.

principle of integration has been accepted," Commandant Swanepoel admits, "but the implementation of it is difficult." The commandant is inclined to see a marked difference between the Coloured and the African experiences in the SADF. He emphasizes cultural problems of adjustment, doubts about black African preparation and aptitude, the need to go slower with Africans, and the need to be more sensitive to African as well as white racial sensitivities. In short, the commandant openly admits that he possesses some stereotypical images of African blacks. Permanent Force people, he optimistically maintains, are not likely to be insensitive. Although he may be aware of his own prejudices, he would not regard these as insensitivities. But national servicemen and white civilians are less aware. "You cannot isolate this unit from society." To illustrate this point the commandant recounted an incident early in 1979 when the battalion sent its band (a rock group) to the military tattoo in Durban. The band was put up in an international class hotel that is permitted to entertain black guests. But an encounter in the bar in which white customers told the men that "Kaffirs aren't allowed in here!" hurt his men. On their return, the commandant had to apologize to his men, trying to explain the difficulty to them (maybe they should be explaining it to him). He then chewed out the organizer of the tattoo, stating that unless he personally guaranteed that this would not happen again the 21 Battalion would not send its band again.[23] For blacks in South Africa these are everyday occurrences.

Recruitment and Force Levels

There is no aggressive or comprehensive recruiting campaign for the 21 Battalion, at least not in terms of trying to sell young Africans on the idea of the military as a career. Although the SACC canvasses Coloured secondary schools, no such comparable policy exists for the 21 Battalion. Recruiting officers would probably encounter sullen hostility if they were to approach black African high school students. "We don't bang the

23. Interview, Lenz, 25 July 1979.

big drum," one officer quaintly phrased it.[24] Much of the recruitment is being done by word of mouth, by newspaper advertisements and announcements on SABC's Radio Bantu, and especially by personal contact of members with friends and relatives. There are SADF recruiting offices in the centers of the six largest South African cities. The SADF occasionally sets up information booths at fairs and shows. Literature is distributed, and members of various units are on hand to discuss with the public and particularly with likely applicants their service prospects.[25] Recruits sometimes walk into the training center for an interview. The reason a more vigorous recruiting program has not been undertaken is because, the personnel staff claims, it has not been necessary. In one respect they are right. Something like three times more candidates apply than can be enlisted. The current waiting list reportedly contains six hundred names.[26]

Other reasons for the low key recruitment posture reflect an awareness of impending political problems. In this regard the existence of a waiting list contributes an element of false security. Although the recruiting literature clearly states that applicants must be in possession of a Standard 8 certificate, many applicants are below this level, and some even go as low as Standard 5. Moreover, during the first ten-week orientation period of each intake there seems to be a high dropout rate, indicating either flaws in the selection and orientation process or a low overall level of aptitude for military service. A more vigorous recruitment campaign and a more rigorous selection process to choose just the right candidates might be, in the long run, more cost effective. There has been some recent evidence that recruitment of black Africans has not been going as well as we have been led to believe.

24. Interview, Pretoria, 16 July 1979.
25. E.g., *Paratus,* Supplement (May 1978), p. iii; and *21 Bataljon* (Pretoria: Hoof van Staf Personeel, S.A. Weermag, n.d.), distributed in English and Afrikaans at the Pretoria Show, late August and early September 1978.
26. Interview, Lenz, 25 July 1979. Yet there is also conflicting evidence that blacks picked up for infringements of the law are sometimes given the choice between "volunteering" and jail; *Observer* (London), 6 July 1980, p. 10. It is difficult to confirm such rumors.

The festering hostility among young blacks toward virtually all manifestations of white authority has been building and taking more overt forms in the decade of the seventies. Expressions of black consciousness and black power, although inhibited by the absence through banning of public, legitimate institutional channels, have been no less evident and bitter of late than during the mid-seventies, leading up to and immediately following the township protests and violence collectively known as the Soweto rioting of 1976. Disenchantment with the system, criticism of the police and the armed forces, abandonment of hope for nonviolent reform, and demands for radical revolution are more openly expressed by a greater and wider variety of black spokespersons than ever before. To the strident appeals of exiled revolutionary groups such as the ANC, the Pan-Africanist Congress (PAC), and the various black consciousness organizations inside and outside of the country can be added the voices of regular and ad hoc labor groups, church leaders, spontaneous organizations and committees of students, parents, teachers, neighbors, and so forth. Association and identification with the government and its administrative agencies is anathema. Except for among those virtually handpicked black echoes of governmental policy, black African public rejection of black military and police service approaches unanimity. Explicit repudiation of military enlistment need not be verbalized. The message is clear from the tone, content, and thrust of the overall black African societal stance against the regime. As these views are spread beyond the urban areas and townships, as they penetrate the less politically involved rural peoples, and as the regime's need for larger intakes of black African recruits grows, waiting lists will evaporate. Low profile and word-of-mouth recruitment will probably not suffice, even given the economic pressures on the people. As was stated earlier, an open labor market does not exist for blacks. The authorities have devised ways of coercing—by law and selective law enforcement, by economic manipulation, by outright physical pressure—and thereby expanding the manpower pool. But they do so at the risk of bringing into the SADF individuals whose skills are incomplete and, more importantly, those whose loyalty is suspect, elements which, in short, are more trouble for the SADF than the authorities would think they are worth. The politicization of black South Africa adds, from the regime's perspective, an ominous dimension to black recruitment, a policy that it has contended has been an unmixed success.

When in 1976 Harry Schwarz of the PRP called for a campaign to recruit 10,000 blacks into the army on a full-time professional basis,[27] his views were rejected by government out of hand. It is an annual ritual during debate on the Defence Vote for Schwarz to develop this argument, and usually W. Vause Raw of the UP and later the New Republic Party (NRP) to repeat the theme. Just as reliably the Nationalists accuse Schwarz of wanting "to swamp" the Defence Force by having it be composed of "a speckled white elite officers' corp and the rest consisting almost entirely of non-whites."[28] The "big solution" was not necessary or wise. The Defence Minister, as late as 1977, maintained that Africans, Indians, and Coloured would *not* be given a bigger role in the defense of South Africa. He did not intend to create larger units manned by "people of colour."[29]

What exactly are the facts of the use of black Africans in the SADF? Certainly, as Defence Minister P. W. Botha (now the prime minister) was fundamentally correct in his statements. Compared to the Portuguese or the Rhodesians in their use of blacks (as a proportion of total security forces) the SADF has indeed been wary of "swamping." Although precise figures that are comparable over time are difficult if not impossible for an outsider to come by, it has been clear that the force levels of black African units are low. Intakes have been small; for example, 82 recruits were taken out of 217 applicants in January 1977. The January 1981 and 1982 intakes expanded to 518 and 672 men "after the pre-selection phase," which involved interviewing over 816 and 918 applicants, respectively.[30] The size of the 21 Battalion, then, has remained quite small and has

27. *Assembly Debates*, 6 May 1976, col. 6177.
28. E.g., ibid., 21 April 1977, col. 5803.
29. Ibid., 22 April 1977, col. 5871; and *Rand Daily Mail*, 23 April 1977.
30. Interview, Lenz, 25 July 1979; and *Assembly Debates*, 5 May 1980, Q col. 701; and 4 March 1982, Q cols. 257–58.

grown gradually, from 35 in 1975 to an "enrollment" of 350 at Lenz in June 1978 to published estimates of between 400 and 515 in 1979.[31] The January 1980 number of black African Permanent Force members in the army is around 490, representing less than 2 percent of the total Permanent Force complement. Yet each intake is larger than its predecessors, and it looks increasingly like larger numbers are being retained in the service. Therefore, one might expect force levels to be approaching 1700 with the 1982 intake, especially if one includes regional black formations.

P. W. Botha's statement that blacks would not be given a larger role in the SADF was rather the exception. Far more frequent have been announcements to the opposite effect. A panel appointed by Botha when he became prime minister to examine defense needs has urged a gradual expansion in the recruitment of blacks, as has a joint conference of SADF officers and the National Development and Management Foundation.[32] The pattern for the future appears set.

Training Program

After the preselection phase of recruitment the intake is put through a ten-week orientation program that consists of basic military training (basic drill, military discipline, and simple commands), one week of public health and personal hygiene, another week dealing with personal finances, a week of psychological testing, two weeks of instruction in Afrikaans ("just simple commands"), and an exposure to "information and political education."[33] This is followed by a mutual culling out. Those who do not like the discipline or hard work can drop out. Those who are "too aggressive" or who have had a record

31. *Assembly Debates*, 29 April 1975, Q cols. 852– 54; *Post* (Johannesburg), 18 June 1978, p. C4; *Washington Post*, 10 April 1979; and *New York Times*, 16 September 1979, pp. 1, 16 (elsewhere in this article a figure of 1,000 blacks in the SADF is mentioned).

32. *New York Times*, 16 September 1979, pp. 1, 16; *The Star* (Weekly Air Edition), 8 February 1978, p. 2.

33. Interview, Lenz, 25 July 1979. Brig. J. F. J. van Rensberg of the general staff had earlier noted that "no effort [is] made to politically indoctrinate blacks and coloureds during training"; *Rand Daily Mail*, 26 May 1978.

of absenteeism or drinking too much or who are resistant to the military life are dropped. At this point only around half the intake is left. At this stage as well there is a "security clearance" on each man selected, and discussion begins with the recruit and with his instructors as to placement and specialty training options.

Once these issues are resolved remaining recruits begin the Basic Training, phase two of their program. For white national servicemen this lasts twelve weeks. For Africans it is a seventeen-week haul. These seventeen weeks, plus the ten weeks of orientation, twenty-seven weeks in all, compare to twelve weeks for white entrants. Only when one arrives at the training of corporals for promotion to sergeant is African and white training the same. There are some black African instructors at the Basic Training level. The higher up in the ranks instruction is conducted, the more whites dominate. During Basic Training the 21 Battalion units are not trained in the skills of conventional warfare — rather the emphasis is on counterinsurgency fighting (COIN). Afterward the men undergo another battery of psychological and intelligence tests and then are moved along into phase three, specialization courses, which include training as personnel clerks, ordinance clerks and storemen, tradesmen, vehicle mechanics, chefs, drivers, and similar noncombatant roles.

At this level there are few black African instructors, and the normal promotion courses beyond the first qualification courses have no black African instructors. Black African platoon and section leaders are also scarce. This is, to some extent, an artificial shortage. When the 21 Battalion was ordered in 1977 to prepare a company for service in Namibia, there was disarray.[34] All the qualified black instructors were pulled out of the training wing and given operational responsibility. The result was that training was set back months. Nowadays it is easier to do this, for there are increasing numbers of black

34. This is not arrived at from reading an "official" account of the preparations; i.e., "This is How 21 (Black) Battalion Prepared for Border Duty," *Paratus* 29 (April 1978): 4–7; but rather emerges from conversations with various SADF officers.

platoon leaders, corporals, and sergeants. In addition, the 21 Battalion has assisted in the training at Lenz of the 1 Transkei Battalion, the first forty-eight members of the 1 Ovambo Battalion from Namibia, and the first one hundred members of the 121 Battalion.[35]

Combat Duties

In mid-1977 the 21 Battalion began preparing a company for operational duty, and in late March 1978 it went off to the Eastern Caprivi Strip for three months of what was officially called "advanced training." The company, consisting of around one hundred forty men, was organized into three platoons and two project patrols. The patrols were expected to liaise with the local populace, serving an intelligence function by gaining the people's confidence and thereby exploiting their racial commonality.[36] In 1979 a second operational company of the 21 Battalion served in the border area. The battalion's commanding officer requested, so he said, that instead of an operational company the battalion should send a psychological operations (psyop) unit to Namibia for several months early in the year. Having made effective contact with the indigenous inhabitants, these same men could return to Namibia later in the year, just before the then-planned UN-supervised election. In that way the 21 Battalion could best "influence" voting. The commandant claims that this request was denied by SADF headquarters.

The 21 Battalion has evolved from an auxiliary support unit producing instructors with administrative and artisan skills to a formation with a triple purpose — primarily training but also operational combat, with an emphasis on COIN and riot control, and maintenance. The propaganda utility of the 21 Battalion has begun to be realized, and in some respects so has its practical utility.

35. A. Leon, "1 Transkei Battalion and 21 Battalion: Object Lesson in Togetherness at Lenz," *Paratus* 27 (March 1976): 19–21; and *The Star* (Weekly Air Edition), 7 February 1976, p. 14.

36. *Daily Dispatch* (East London), 24 November 1978; and "Force News," *The Citizen* (Johannesburg), 10 July 1978, pp. i and ii.

Pay, Benefits, and Conditions of Service

"Black Permanent Force members of 21 Battalion enjoy the same career benefits as their White colleagues." So says a 1977 piece of SADF puffery.[37] In a Johannesburg *Post* account of the 21 Battalion it is stated that "officers of the Defence Force have agreed that in the army there are no race bars. All racial groups . . . are treated alike. They use the same barracks, eat the same food and go through the same conditions of service."[38] The distinguished journalist, Colin Legum, has also been impressed by what he has heard (but not seen). "The army . . . has become the outstanding institutional model for the kind of multiracial society South Africa could one day become . . . . From the moment a civilian enters the army he leaves behind the racially segregated life he knows at home. Messes are indeed shared by whites and blacks, according to their ranks. They eat, drink and fight together."[39] These are unambiguous assertions, but what of reality?

Regarding pay scales in force at the time these statements were printed, base compensation for black Africans in 1977 averaged between 54 and 63 percent of white salaries at comparable ranks as shown in table 11.[40]

In July 1976 Permanent Force salaries were supplemented with a pensionable allowance for whites (10 percent), for Coloureds and Indians (15 percent), and for black Africans (20

TABLE 11.
"Bantu" and White Base Salaries for the Lower Ranks, 1977

	White	"Bantu"
Corporal	R2700 – 4740	R1530 – 3000
Lance corporal	1950 – 4200	1080 – 2580
Private	1440 – 3660	780 – 2100

SOURCE: Republic of South Africa, *House of Assembly Debates* (Hansard), 4 May 1977, Q col. 1015 – 20.

37. *South Africa Digest,* 18 February 1977, p. 24.

38. *Post,* 18 June 1978, p. C4.

39. *The Observer,* 26 April 1981.

40. Crocker puts differentials at 70 percent (personal communication, November 1980, p. 37).

TABLE 12.
Black and White Base Salaries for the Lower Ranks, 1981

	White	"Black"
Corporal	R4230 – 7290	R2718 – 5430
Lance corporal	3105 – 6480	1998 – 4710
Private	1998 – 5670	1326 – 4230

SOURCE: Republic of South Africa, *House of Assembly Debates* (Hansard), 25 August 1981, Q cols. 145 – 53.

percent). Although these may have improved the remuneration picture slightly, they hardly represent parity.

Comparable salary rates in 1981 were reported by the Minister of Defence and are shown in table 12. Similar differentials prevail up the ranks.[41] The same magnitude of discrepancy was applied to special camp allowances paid daily in the "operational area" (table 13). The special camp allowance was equalized by the Minister of Defence effective 1 April 1978.[42] The same applies to other allowances, including danger pay, for all members of the SADF in the operational area. Yet the minister announced at that time that "other emoluments payable to non-whites are not yet equal to those of whites but the gap is being narrowed as and when circumstances permit."[43]

Military pay rates are regulated by the Public Service Commission and are not subject to unilateral SADF administrative action. Those allowances and perquisites under *direct* SADF control reportedly have been equalized. Pay changes also necessitate legislative approval, and government is continually being pressed by the PFP and the NRP, as it was by their predecessor parties and factions, to accept the principle of "equal pay for equal work" within the Defence Force, or at least to take steps to close the salary gap.[44] When queried in 1979 to estimate the cost of introducing equal pay for all races in the SADF in the first year, the Deputy Minister of Defence cited a

41. *Assembly Debates*, 25 August 1981, Q cols. 145– 53.
42. *The Citizen*, 8 April 1978.
43. *Assembly Debates*, 7 April 1978, Q col. 573.
44. E.g., Schwarz in ibid., 2 March 1979, col. 1705; 1 May 1980, col. 5292; and Raw, 17 April 1978, col. 4833; and also *Rand Daily Mail*, 28 September 1976.

TABLE 13.
Special Camp Allowances in the "Operational Area,"
Before 1 April 1981

	Married		Single	
	Rations Supplied	Rations not Supplied	Rations Supplied	Rations not Supplied
White	R4.50	5.50	3.50	4.50
Black	R3.50	3.50	2.50	2.50

SOURCE: Republic of South Africa, *House of Assembly Debates* (Hansard), 2 May 1977, Q cols. 992–93.

figure of R7.5 million, and in 1981 that figure was set at R8.23 million.[45] Given the windfall revenues from inflated gold prices, this action would hardly extend governmental finances. Yet for political reasons government resists implementing a policy it seems to have accepted in principle, "on certain conditions, of course."

Even in the matter of pensions no equality prevails. Maximum monthly war veterans' pensions as of 1 April 1978 were: for whites, R101.50; for Coloureds and Asians, R66.70; and for Africans, R31.80. Because of a rigorous application of means tests seeking to cull out "undeserving" applicants and those able to maintain themselves, and so forth, far fewer blacks qualified for and received veterans' pensions than did whites. The issue has been taken up by the South African Legion, the senior exservicemen's organization in the country, and by other groups.[46] Across the board pensions and benefits had conformed to an overall ratio of 4:2:1 (white, Coloured and Indian, and black African). Efforts have been made since 1976 to bring proportions more in line, but by no means have they approached parity, nor is government committed to it.

According to a classified study prepared by the SADF and

45. *Assembly Debates*, 14 May 1979, Q col. 412; and 11 February 1981, Q col. 102.

46. South African Institute of Race Relations, *Survey of Race Relations in South Africa, 1978* (Johannesburg: South African Institute of Race Relations, 1979), pp. 484–85; *Survey of Race Relations in South Africa, 1976* (Johannesburg: South African Institute of Race Relations, 1977), p. 392; *The Star* (Weekly Air Edition), 3 February 1979, p. 14.

approved by General Malan and the Minister of Defence, all
legal vestiges of segregation based on sex and race were to be
eliminated in the SADF with effect from 1 April 1978.[47] Just
how difficult it has been to carry through this sweeping decree
is apparent. The sorts of things that can easily be changed —
for example, common uniforms and symbols of rank and serial
numbers without suffixes denoting the race of the member —
were instituted promptly. Ostensibly recruitment and promotion standards are supposed to be identical, but this has proven
to be difficult. It would appear that recruitment standards for
black Africans have been lower than those for whites, but those
for promotion have been higher. In addition a common seniority list for officers is supposed to enable any officer from any
formation in the Permanent Force to be eligible for any position for which his rank qualifies him. Structurally, as well as in
terms of policy, this has been meaningless, for the structural
basis of segregation, the separation of formations and units,
still holds fast.

It would appear that efforts have been made by SADF to
integrate and equalize service conditions in the operational
area, though less so on posts and in camps in the Republic. The
basic forms of segregation — the existence of separate units
and formations and the continuation of auxiliary service designations for larger numbers of black troops, all compounded by
the reality of rank patterns — mean that at the highest levels,
where, presumably, it should be easier to equalize conditions,
the most progress has been made. At lower ranks, where the
greatest cultural differentiation exists and where the least desire to break down segregation prevails among white soldiers,
the problem is most intractable. A small-scale experiment to
integrate Defence Force members on post failed totally and
nearly led to violent opposition by white national servicemen.

Most recreational facilities in the Defence Force have been
integrated since 1976. However, some individual facilities,
such as swimming pools, are still racially restricted. At Lenz,

47. The legal authority on which General Malan's decree is based can be
found in "R. 341," in Republic of South Africa, *Government Gazette*, no. 5888,
24 February 1978, p. 29.

for example, the pool had originally been solely for white use. Blacks wanted to use it more, and it was decided to build a second smaller pool for white battalion members rather than integrate the larger, older pool.

Officially, the men mess together in the garrison as in the field. They stand in the same lines, and they may sit together if they wish. In barracks they are free to use the same toilet facilities, and there are supposedly integrated dormitory areas. But as in all fundamentally segregated societies a high measure of self-segregation occurs, out of "choice," but a choice bounded by the insecurities of the environment and an unwillingness to precipitate tension or displeasure. Whites assigned to the 21 Battalion invariably are there as instructors or in some specialist or command capacity. It is unlikely that they would be quartered with men of lower rank. So only at instructor level is mixing likely.

With regard to family housing, regulations prescribe a standard square footage based on rank. Thus housing standards are supposed to be identical. The same applies to NCO housing. But houses are still grouped by race, thereby conforming to the same "group areas" model that is in force in the civilian world. Schooling for children of Defence Force personnel is racially segregated. In short, despite an increase in interracial contact over past patterns, and despite the undeniable fact that there is less racism in the SADF than in most other South African institutions, particularly other state institutions, opportunities for socializing between races, and for social relations as equals among friends and colleagues, remain near impossible.

The 21 Battalion as a Public Relations Exercise

Government and the SADF have expended great energy trying to sell black South Africans on the Defence Force and on the necessity to adhere to the established order, subject to marginal reforms, as preferable to a revolutionary order fraught with instability, insecurity, and, for whites, of course, the loss of control. One of the prize exhibits in this sales campaign is the black African soldier. In the exaggerated words of Commandant Swanepoel, "the main field application of black soldiers is in influencing the local populations."[48] The influence is in terms of intimidation, perhaps. But as likely, he means that the rock band, for example, because of its visibility, becomes as politically vital as an operational company. Parades, award and promotion ceremonies, parents days, off-base fairs and festivals become convenient excuses for showing off black units. Visits to Lenz from black African officials, sporting personalities, the media, and others assume all the vitality of field maneuvers as visitors are shepherded, with genuine pride, to see some "square bashing," the band "in rehearsal," a luncheon with the boys (after drinks in an "integrated" bar), and a "fireworks display." Opportunities are made to chat with battalion members and their officers, and in general this form of "show-and-tell" is open and serious business.

When the 21 Battalion trains in the field, local chiefs and *indunas* tour the camp, pose for the photos, and make appropriate statements for the press. They are told by the SADF that soldiers are there to protect the local population and that "progress" can take place only in an "atmosphere of peace."[49] Then they are sent back home to sing the virtues of the SADF, its African troops, and the need to cooperate with the authorities. Meanwhile the SADF public relations arm busies itself broadcasting the happenings and endorsements to those who may not share the experience first or second hand. If the effects can be magnified by the press and by media coverage or, at least, by reportage in the SADF and governmental publications, so much the better.[50] The secret psychological action plan of SADF has had, as a prime target, the improved recruitment of African units. To achieve this goal press visits, newspaper coverage, and glossy publications were to be encouraged to glam-

48. Interview, Lenz, 25 July 1979, p. 3.

49. *Paratus* 29 (April 1978): 5.

50. See, e.g., "Broadcasters Told About the Real Threats," *Paratus* 29 (November 1978): 7; the entire issue of *Informa* (Pretoria) 26 (March 1979), a publication of the Information Service; "Blacks Join Border Battle," *South Africa Digest,* 19 May 1978, pp. 16–18; "Medals for 100 of our Black Defenders," pp. 14–17; and dozens of newspaper features, many sounding like they were printed, unedited, from SADF press releases.

orize life for black African servicemen.[51] Prominent black visitors are also taken to white Defence Force units to be suitably impressed. The visitors are used by the SADF as their names and the prestige of their offices become associated with the regime. *Paratus,* the official SADF monthly, also has established a regular column called "The Black Man's View," which is a combination of quotations from black collaborative politicians and citizens and the toadying drivel of a columnist. It almost never contains items of a substantive interest. In addition, public relations officers with professional experience outside the SADF are attached to each regional command. But the basic question is — how successful have they been?

The fact is that virtually everywhere, except in official government publications and in others backed by government front organizations, black Africans have rejected the regime, the Defence Force, and black collaboration with them. Considering the criminal sanctions attending those counseling against military training (though the principal intended targets are clergy and liberals who advise whites eligible for national service against compliance), African opposition to SADF service is widespread and vocal.

Those blacks most inclined to support the regime, or those at least in favor of cooperating with the SADF against "Marxism and communism" if not in defense of apartheid, are often officials in "acceptable" organizations. This invariably means those councils and bodies created by the state to facilitate the governance of black peoples. For example, the chief minister of Lebowa, Dr. C.N. Phathudi, has said that his people are genuinely grateful to the SADF for their sacrifices in defending all the people of South Africa. "I'm only sorry," he went on, that "our people of Lebowa cannot participate fully in the defence of South Africa. We have a country worth defending and worth dying for. What we have is rich and worth possessing forever."[52] Prof. Hudson Ntsanwisi, chief minister of Gazankulu, concurs: "As far as the Black South African soldiers are concerned, it was quite clear to me that if the South African

51. *Rand Daily Mail,* 24 March 1980, p. 2.
52. *The Star* (Weekly Air Edition), 30 November 1974, p. 4.

Black man is given a chance, he will be only too ready and willing to take his rightful place in the defence of the country."[53] A parade of African community councillors, tribal council members, representatives of regional authorities, and employees of diverse governmental departments are trotted across the pages of *Paratus,* the *South Africa Digest,* and the various organs of the press to echo similar views. But their willingness to collaborate can easily be explained and need not trouble us here.

More impressive are those black public figures who, despite their vulnerability to regime pressures, continue to call into question the government's motives and methods. Many must speak in circuitous and aesopian terms. Chief Gatsha Buthelezi, has, for example, told the prime minister that blacks could not at this stage be expected to assist in the military defense of South Africa, as this would amount to defending apartheid. Much earlier he had said that his people did not create terrorism and were not moved to resist it.[54] Indeed, Chief Buthelezi's Inkatha Yenkululeko Yesizwe, the Zulu cultural and political movement, has consistently discouraged recruitment into the SADF. They have refused to allow Defence Force members to visit schools in KwaZulu for recruitment purposes, and they refuse to cooperate with the SADF either by visiting the fighting zones or by attending the Durban military tattoo.

An alliance of generally moderate black political parties (chiefly the Coloured Labour Party and Buthelezi's Inkatha) declared in July 1978: "While blacks do not enjoy citizenship nor share political power, it [the alliance] will not urge the black community to participate in the military defence of the apartheid regime."[55] These are testy statements given South Africa's repressive legal fabric, specifically the laws making it a crime to discourage participation in the SADF, and the arsenal of informal sanctions the regime can bring to bear on known critics.

53. *Informa* 26 (March 1979): 2.
54. *Nation* (Johannesburg) 3 (January 1979), a publication of Inkatha; *The Star* (Weekly Air Edition), 18 May 1974, p. 14; and 16 May 1981, p. 3.
55. Quoted in *Washington Post,* 10 April 1979.

Steve Biko was even more outspoken, and, of course, he paid for it dearly. When discussing black policemen he did not mince words:

> There is no such thing as a Black policeman. Any Black man who props the system up actively has lost the right to being considered part of the Black world: he has sold his soul for thirty pieces of silver and finds that he is in fact not acceptable to the White society he sought to join. These are colourless White lackeys who live in a marginal world of unhappiness. They are extensions of the enemy into our ranks.[56]

Presumably, the same sentiments would apply to blacks in the SADF. Biko's views have wide appeal in the black community, especially among younger people, many of whom see black enlistment as betrayal.

The entire philosophy of black consciousness, very much alive today, condemns any collaboration with the apartheid state. One cannot "operate within the system," its adherents argue, and still claim to be a black person. Terms like "running dogs of the system," "sellouts," and "political turncoats" are prominent. Since Steve Biko's murder and since the banning of the South African Students Organization (SASO), the Black People's Convention, and other black consciousness organizations, it has not been easy to give organizational expression to this philosophy in South Africa. The Azanian People's Organization (AZAPO) is the current institutional manifestation of black consciousness in the republic. AZAPO rejects all links with government, including negotiations. While black consciousness envisages a future nonracist society, strategy and tactics of black liberation necessitate the exclusion of whites, even sympathetic whites, from the process. The group most violently opposed to black collaboration with the regime and any of its coercive forces is the African National Congress. A target in its recent stepped-up sabotage campaign was the SADF recruiting office in central Durban.[57] Police stations and

56. From Frank Talk (Stephen Biko), "I Write What I Like: Fear—An Important Determinant in South African Politics," in Millard Arnold, ed., *Steve Biko: Black Consciousness in South Africa* (New York: Random House, 1978), p. 276.

57. *The Guardian* (London), 28 May 1981.

a military base have also been attacked with some success. The popularity of the ANC among the young people is extensive and undeniable.

If one reads between the lines of official releases even laudatory press agentry can reveal much:

> In camp at Lenz they need no pass to go out in the evening. To most their uniform is a matter of pride. They do not feel they are restricted in any way. To nearly all of them, their lives have assumed a greater purpose and an importance since coming to Lenz.[58]

The important qualifier here is "in camp at Lenz." Small praise it is for a system to brag that its soldiers do not need a pass while in camp when the unstated reality is that they do need a pass outside of camp. Even if these sentiments are true in camp, they do not apply when black soldiers are in the larger community. During the 1976 Soweto uprising families of members of the 21 Battalion were moved out of Soweto and into the camp for their own protection — protection from their own people. Blacks drawn into the repressive apparatus of the state, their personal property, and the official state plant — schools, beer halls, offices — became prime targets for the protestors.

In a *New York Times* account of the 21 Battalion a black sergeant, one would assume a loyal and obedient member of the SADF, was described taking off his uniform before setting off for his home on leave. "My friends don't like it," he is reported to have said. "They ask, 'How can you join the army as long as the black man is oppressed in this country; how can you go and fight for the white man when it is the white man who is pushing us down?'"[59] Although this sergeant found hostility a problem, he managed to justify to himself his role in the SADF, citing pay and benefits and arguing that now, after fighting, "we have a right to claim our share in [this country], along side the white man."[60]

In informal and in some formal surveys conducted by the South African press opposition is equally evident. *The World,*

58. "Medals for 100 of our Black Defenders," p. 17.
59. *New York Times*, 16 September 1979, pp. 1, 16.
60. Similar kinds of hostility are reported in *Washington Post*, 10 April 1979.

the Soweto black daily banned in 1977, asked its readers: "Would you fight for South Africa if we are invaded from Angola?"[61] Despite the loaded "we," and disregarding the unrepresentativeness of a postal response, some 244 letters were received, and 203 said they were opposed to fighting in defense of South Africa. The most common reasons expressed were that it would be a "white man's war" and that most blacks had little to defend. Even so, some who opposed fighting said they would change their minds if government abolished the pass laws and took steps to improve their lot economically. Some men harked back to World War II and mentioned the bonuses given white veterans and the "worthless medals" and paltry rewards offered blacks on mustering out. Few young blacks show any enthusiasm for joining the SADF, and most display bitterness. "They must treat us like brothers so that we must feel we have something to fight for."[62] The government can expect little popular acceptance among blacks for the SADF or for black participation in the SADF unless and until major improvements in civilian race relations and economic conditions for blacks are instituted. The problem for white South Africa is not a problem of propaganda and salesmanship. The 21 Battalion and the SADF may be efficient, even feared and grudgingly respected organizations, but the commodity being marketed is not these units. Rather it is South Africa itself. The public image of the SADF cannot help but be tainted by the regime structure that embraces it and which it defends. Until white South Africans and their leaders appreciate that, their efforts to involve blacks in defense of the system are bound to be frustrated. The essence of black association with the SADF, defense of the status quo, is not lost on black South Africans.

61. As reported in *The Star* (Weekly Air Edition), 13 March 1976, pp. 5, 10.
62. From a hurried street survey by *The Star* (Daily Edition), 19 September 1978. The results are the same as earlier surveys.

10

The Homeland Armies

It is not easy to discern exactly what the SADF or the South African government expects to achieve with respect to the creation of and interaction with defense forces of the so-called "independent homelands." Although policy statements seem to indicate that the homeland armies are to be considered as part of the South African defensive armory in case of external attack, there are plenty of inconsistencies and contradictions in this sort of thinking. And like so much of the strategic dimension of South African life, these questions are blanketed by a general and understandable secretiveness on the part of government and the SADF. Statements for public consumption may be smoke screens rather than indicators of policy. So much depends on the actual evolution and resolution of the grand Verwoerdian scheme of separate development. Whether it is to be pursued to its logical conclusion in all putative homelands, whether its implementation will be frozen in time, or whether it will be forced to be abandoned, undone, or revised because it has been shown to lack viability are still debatable issues. Defense of the homelands, in other words, is contingent on the pursuit of the homelands policy—very much the official policy of the state, yet still questioned in its basic presuppositions, even in some precincts of the National Party itself.

After examining the South African government's policy and strategy, and the criticisms leveled against them from parliament and from homeland leaders, the establishment of the homeland armies (Transkei, Bophuthatswana, Venda, and Ciskei) will be described. The timing and sequence of their establishment; the training, force levels and organization of the armies; and their relations with the SADF will be explored. Particular attention will be devoted to the severance of diplomatic and military links between South Africa and the Transkei in 1978, for this event highlights many of the important possible areas of dispute between a homeland and Pretoria, especially as this and similar confrontations affect the strategic contingencies in the region.

Political issues cannot be ignored — questions of structure, territoriality and extraterritoriality, governmental stability in the homelands and the need for domestic coercion, and the possibilities of military coups. If homelands are ostensibly "independent" and "sovereign," how far can their policies diverge from those of Pretoria before Pretoria becomes fearful of hostility toward South Africa being reflected in the homelands' foreign policies. And should these regimes be unable to maintain order in their territories, will Pretoria resist the temptation to intervene lest the unrest in the homeland spill into South Africa itself? Questions of the overall regional defense strategy of Pretoria, its perceived need for buffer territories, the impact of concepts of regional "constellations" of states, and the prospects of something like a "Brezhnev doctrine" for southern Africa contribute to an importance far beyond the surface impression of another few hundred largely ceremonial black soldiers in fragmented and weak countries.

Government Policy and Its Critics

Superficially, the government's overall policy is direct, clear, and naive. In its view it is the logical development of the home-

lands policy that each homeland will "follow the road of independence to its end" and as a necessary concommitant thereof
"will develop a military unit in one form or another." In other
words, "a homeland will be able to develop a military unit to the
extent determined by its needs."[1] If one accepts the basic prem-
ise that these homelands are to become sovereign and fully
independent states, then it would have to follow that their
governments are free to pursue a defense policy in their own
interests as they perceive them.

The homeland armies, in turn, are to be regarded as an
integral part of a larger regional defense scheme, the exact
content of which has never been made public. Repeatedly, government spokesmen have made reference to such a conception. The Minister of Bantu Administration, M. C. Botha, first
spoke of some future multinational defense structure in 1973.
Examining "our Bantu nations in 25 years' time," he indicated
that a number of them would become "totally independent."
Admitting the prospect that some might pursue foreign policies contrary to that of South Africa, he continued:

> It can be that there will be military planning in terms of which the
> Bantu nations, with the help of the Republic of South Africa, will
> maintain local military units. These units will not only be used
> for the defence of the countries to which they belong but they
> could be involved in a wider South African defence plan against
> aggression from outside.[2]

Although his remarks were couched in the subjunctive, they
failed to mask a basic contradiction. If governments pursue
foreign policies contrary to South African interests, could they
not also develop opposing defense policies?

What M. C. Botha referred to as "a wider South African
defence plan" P. W. Botha, then Minister of Defence, called the
"military milieu of the Republic of South Africa and not outside the military milieu of the Republic of South Africa."[3]

1. H. J. Coetsee (who later became Deputy Minister of Defence; NP,
Bloemfontein West) in Republic of South Africa, *House of Assembly Debates*
(Hansard), 17 April 1975, col. 4362.

2. Quoted in *The Star* (Johannesburg, Weekly Air Edition), 11 August
1973, p. 15.

3. *Assembly Debates*, 22 April 1975, col. 4584.

Homelands established "in their full character" (meaning, presumably, independent), nonetheless, will still occupy a position within the "military milieu" of the Republic itself, not the region of southern Africa. Just how an independent state is to be made to have its defense policy conform to that of the Pretoria government is not specified, but politically and economically it is not out of the question. These sorts of issues were raised again when the government of the Transkei severed diplomatic relations with South Africa in 1978 — at the time a theatrical but practically inconsequential act which had little effect on interaction between the two governments and peoples. In the late 1970s Pretoria subtly altered the wording of its defense plan from that of a South African perspective to one of the wider region. It was announced in 1978, for example, that it was government policy to regard the armies of the independent homelands as part of the southern African defense system to fight against the "onslaught of marxism and communist imperialism," often obliquely referred to as "the forces of chaos" and "terrorism."[4] With the government's reintroduction of the idea of a regional "constellation" of states, the SADF again is called upon to fashion and promote a scheme for a joint defense of the region.[5]

Never, however, has the exact constellation or configuration of such a defense plan been published. When pressed by opposition M.P.s, government responses have been vague. W. V. Raw, then of the United Party, welcomed the announcement of the formation of a Transkeian battalion since the Transkei was, at that time, still a part of South Africa. But he warned that government policy was leading to the separation of the Transkei into a foreign state and therefore of the Transkeian battalion into a "foreign force" within what had been South African territory. What military agreements, he asked, has

4. *Citizen* (Johannesburg), 8 September 1978; South African Institute of Race Relations, *Survey of Race Relations in South Africa, 1978* (Johannesburg: South African Institute of Race Relations, 1979), p. 56. A clear statement of this position is made by the Minister of Defence in *Assembly Debates*, 31 January 1978, cols. 103–5.

5. See the speech by Lt. Gen. C. Viljoen, chief of the army, reported in *Uniform*, no. 54 (November 1979): 51.

government made with the Transkei government? In effect the thrust of his speech was an attack on the homelands policy itself, a rejection of the idea of eventual independence for the homelands, and a call for continued association, perhaps in the form of a confederation.[6] *The Star* had taken up this issue earlier when it commented on the recruitment of blacks into the SADF. *The Star* applauded that step and noted that such unenfranchised soldiers would, inter alia, form the nuclei of eventually independent homelands armies and would presumably be allies of "white" South Africa. Such a policy of separate nationhoods will have to lay "more stress on the element of confederation that will mate us and less on the element of group separateness that divides us."[7]

Raw urged the drafting of a "NATO-type treaty," but one with a difference he himself did not seem fully to appreciate. Rather than being a multilateral security agreement, his proposed arrangement called for "the right of access" of South Africa to Transkeian territory, the acceptance by the Transkei of "specific responsibilities," and above all the existence of a force "unified under one command of the South African Defence Force." The Transkei constituted "an essential link in the defence and security of South Africa." Thus any Transkeian defense force must be "integrated into the total strategy of South Africa's defence."

Government's reply was characteristically vague. H.J. Coetsee minimized the threat to South Africa from the Transkei by emphasizing the ceremonial nature of the battalion. Yet he admitted that the unit might not eventually be under the military command of South Africa, as if this were necessary to point out with regard to an ostensibly independent state. His chief rejection of Raw's proposal was because Raw's views reflected the overall philosophy of the United Party, which, Coetsee maintained, was that the black people can best be controlled by integrating them with the whites. This refusal to

6. *Assembly Debates,* 17 April 1975, col. 4361. Note the use by Lt. Gen. R.H.D. Rodgers, chief of the air force, of the terms "constellation or federation of states in southern Africa"; *Citizen,* 2 July 1979, p. 10.

7. *The Star* (Weekly Air Edition), 29 June 1974, p. 11.

recognize nationalities, he insisted, was "typically liberalistic" and akin to imperialistic thinking.[8]

As for the organizational character of any forthcoming arrangements, the Minister of Defence merely parried Raw's suggestions by indicating that no agreements had until then been concluded with the Transkei government regarding defense. Since the Transkei had not as yet achieved independence that was, he noted, premature. But he assured the members that any such agreement would be debated in parliament should it be agreed upon between prime ministers.[9] He did indicate that consultations had already taken place between the chief minister of the Transkei, the chief of the SADF, and the chief of the army. However, these talks, the House was told, dealt mostly with the establishment of a Transkeian military unit.[10] Leave matters of this sort in the hands of the SADF, he pleaded, for it is experienced and it knows best how to liaise and cooperate "without causing friction and tension." In other words, P. W. Botha evidenced the basic perspective that he has displayed throughout his tenure as Minister of Defence — one of utmost confidence and trust in the SADF and in its upper echelon leadership, even with sensitive political and diplomatic negotiations.

High level Defence Force personnel seem to display a slightly different emphasis. Although they clearly support the creation of homeland forces if, indeed, the homelands policy is to be pursued, they do not appear to be pleased with the current conceptualization of homelands in all its particulars. Most especially they seem dissatisfied with the fragmented territorial state of the homelands, and they also are uneasy about the inevitable contradiction between homeland independence, loss of South African citizenship for all blacks, and the 21 Battalion status. As early as 1974 Brig. C. L. Viljoen, Director of Operations for the army, suggested that the consolidation of

8. *Assembly Debates*, 17 April 1975, cols. 4362 – 64. The Minister of Defence also made references to the ceremonial and "military engineering operations" contributing to "development," for which such units would be trained; ibid., 22 April 1975, col. 4584.

9. Ibid., 21 April 1975, col. 4495.

10. Ibid., 22 April 1975, col. 4584.

the homelands would be beneficial from a defensive stand-point. The existing fragmentation was militarily unaccepta-ble.[11] With less subtlety and restraint, G. de Jong (NRP, Pieter-maritzburg South) said that the government's plan for creating a constellation of independent homelands was condemned as a "nightmare" for South Africa's military commanders. "Surely even a moron can see that this map is the most illogical and stupid plan ever devised by man."[12]

Yet within the constraints of a policy it does not necessarily relish the SADF has done its best to help establish homeland guards-cum-armies and to devise mutually acceptable continu-ing training schemes after independence, support and supply services, and contingency plans for cooperation between the diverse formations. The presence of high level commanders seconded to homeland armies from the SADF certainly expe-dites matters. But these arrangements can not go on in-definitely. Legal sovereignty does, indeed, pose future prob-lems. The dilemma regarding citizenship and the 21 Battalion and regional black units has been dealt with in the preceding chapter.

Certainly the South African government has had little difficulty finding homelands' spokesmen willing to support the Pretoria line. Leaders of homelands moving toward indepen-dence in turn have asked the South African government to assist in, indeed, to assume full responsibility for creating homeland military formations and priming them for indepen-dence. Chief Kaiser Matanzima of the Transkei in 1974, Chief Lucas Mangope of Bophuthatswana in 1976, and Chief Minis-ter Patrick Mphephu of Venda in 1978 have requested SADF assistance. They each have chimed loudly that the defense of their people and of the people of South Africa are interdepen-dent and that they would be willing to collaborate with South Africa to defeat terrorists. Chief Matanzima's expression is representative: "The interests and general welfare of the Transkei are so interwoven with those of the Republic (of

11. *Rand Daily Mail* (Johannesburg), 3 August 1974; or *X-Ray*, 5 (December 1974): 4.

12. *The Star* (Weekly Air Edition), 8 April 1978, p. 1; and *Assembly Debates*, 5 April 1978, col. 3955. See also *Financial Mail* 71 (19 January 1979): 142–43.

South Africa) that an attack on one may be regarded as aggression against the other."[13] After earlier misgivings in the 1970s[14] Chief Mangope fell into line. Other homeland leaders with some exceptions (notably Chief Gatsha Buthelezi) have uttered similar views on the necessity to "stand together," although one cannot be sure that in more private negotiations in preparation for devolution they might not have taken a firmer stance to improve their bargaining position with Pretoria.

The Formation of Homeland Armies

It is necessary at this stage to describe the process by which homeland armies were initiated and brought to readiness for independence. Our principal concern here is to concentrate on relations between the South African government and the homeland governments and between the SADF and the homeland armed forces. It is not our task to present a complete picture of each homeland army but rather to describe how they interact with the SADF itself.

The first homeland army to be established was that of the Transkei.[15] As a result, many of the practices worked out experimentally in the formation and training of the Transkeian Defence Force have been repeated in the establishment of the Bophuthatswana and Venda forces. Early in 1974 Minister of Defence Botha informed parliament that Defence Force experts had been in consultation with homeland leaders. "We have been approached by some of the homeland leaders and governments," he phrased it, "who said they would like to have a greater part in the combatting of terrorism and in the promotion of security in their part of the country."[16] Further hints

13. *South Africa Digest,* 16 January 1976, p. 12.

14. E.g., *Rand Daily Mail,* 16 December 1974.

15. Information on the Transkei Defence Force was gleaned from P. Coetzee, "Transkei Army Takes Shape," *Paratus* 26 (July 1975): 2–3; "Transkei Army Volunteers Get Cracking," *Paratus* 26 (September 1975): 8–9; A. Leon, "1 Transkei Battalion and 21 Battalion: Object Lesson in Togetherness at Lenz," *Paratus* 27 (March 1976): 19–21; "Transkeian Defence Force," *Paratus* 27 (October 1976): 6–9; and other items from *Paratus, South Africa Digest,* and various South African newspapers.

16. *The Star* (Weekly Air Edition), 16 February 1974, p. 9.

were given throughout the year, and finally in April 1975 it was announced that the government would help establish and build up a Transkeian army and would supply the weapons and equipment.[17] In fact, it might appear that agreement had been reached almost a year earlier. At that time, it was later disclosed, Chief Minister Matanzima wrote a letter of thanks to the government of South Africa.[18]

After these April announcements events moved rapidly. A South African military selection team visited Umtata to assess candidates for training as potential officers. Work was begun on a 141 hectare military-administrative complex and base camp twelve kilometers west of Umtata. By July 1975 the first seventy Transkeian recruits had been chosen. They soon were attested to the SADF, and in August they began their training at Eersterivier along with the SACC. The SADF officially ended the recruitment of Xhosas into its own 21 Battalion. Much of this early organizational work was guided by Brig. Phil Pretorius, formerly the officer commanding the Northern Transvaal Command. He had been named military advisor to the Transkei early in 1975.

Recruits were subjected to a two-week orientation program, concentrating on personal hygiene, neatness, and discipline, and a four-month basic training program. Sixty-eight of the first batch of seventy passed out in January 1976.[19] Shortly thereafter the Transkei Battalion moved to Lenz for advanced training. That base had recently been taken over by the black 21 Battalion. At the same time the first Transkei Battalion was joined by the second intake, this time of eighty-six men. The target date for the end of this training activity was 26 October 1976, projected Independence Day for the Transkei.

Organizationally the Transkei Battalion was to be divided into two parts — a ceremonial company, including a band, similar to South African State President's Guard, and a rifle com-

17. *Rand Daily Mail*, 11 and 12 April 1975.

18. Part of the letter dated 10 April 1974 to the commissioner general is printed in *Assembly Debates*, 22 April 1975, col. 4584. It is possible that the date announced to the House as "10.4.74" is a misprint. Certainly 1975 is more likely.

19. *South Africa Digest*, 16 January 1976, p. 12.

pany, consisting at first of an infantry platoon and of a
mounted infantry platoon. Later a headquarters company was
added for administration of the battalion.

Shortly after the temporary move to Lenz a group of twenty
men designated for the mounted unit left to take up training at
the SADF Equestrian Centre at Potchefstroom. The first
officer candidates were selected for a course, and it was
planned that they would be commissioned at independence. A
third intake of ninety-eight recruits began training in May.

In the approach to independence, relations with South Africa went well—at least on the surface. The SADF was deeply
involved in the establishment of the Transkei Defence Force
(TDF). Brig. Phil Pretorius as military advisor, Cmdt. "Sakkie"
Pretorius as base commander, and Maj. L. Elwyn Jordaan as
commanding officer of the battalion, along with some twenty-
six other white officers and NCOs on loan from the SADF,
provided the organizational and tutorial skills for the Transkei
Battalion. Construction of the new showpiece military headquarters and base for the battalion progressed well, and the
headquarters were ready for occupation in May 1976. In September the Battalion was officially transferred to the Transkei
government by P. W. Botha. Tons of equipment and supplies
came from the SADF.

On the political front Chief Minister Matanzima was at work.
On 17 September 1976 a nonaggression agreement between
Transkei and South Africa was entered into by which each
party undertook "never, for any reason whatsoever, [to] resort
to the use of armed force against the territorial sovereignty
and political independence of the other." Neither were to permit its territory to be used for military, subversive, or other
hostile actions against the other.[20] Later the chief declared that
a defense bill was being drafted, which included provision for a
Permanent Force and a Citizen Force, the chief provisions
reflecting the SADF model. Later, national service was established, and a school cadet system was announced.

By Independence Day the hard work and sense of purpose

20. This agreement is set out in Republic of South Africa *Government Gazette*
136, no. 5320, 22 October 1976, p. 26.

had produced results. The new base was ready and the Transkeian Battalion prepared to mark the occasion. The battalion consisted of 254 members, plus the thirty South African Permanent Force officers, WOs, and NCOs seconded to the Transkeian Department of Defence. Of the 254 men (who at independence transferred their attestation from the SADF to the TDF) seventy-one were NCOs, and there were seven candidate officers commissioned at independence, including the prime minister's son. A mounted platoon of forty-five provided the hoped-for military dash. All in all it was an impressive result for about eighteen months of joint work and fourteen months of training.

Between independence and the unilateral severance of diplomatic relations with South Africa in April 1978 the intimacy between SADF and TDF continued. Brig. Pretorius added on the responsibility of Secretary for Defence for the Transkeian government. In May 1977 Chief Matanzima announced the introduction of a six-month voluntary national service scheme aimed at building up a reserve force, and at the end of July the first volunteers began basic training.[21] After training they were given the option of joining the Permanent Force. The chief spoke of a five-year development plan for the army. In January 1978 Brig. Pretorius was promoted by the SADF to major general and was reassigned to be director general on the staff of Chief of Staff Operations. Therefore, he stepped down from the TDF and was succeeded by Brig. Y. de Bruyn.[22] Visits for officer candidates, exchanges, joint military planning, and training and assistance continued at all levels.[23]

The string of events in April and May 1978 seemed to occur unexpectedly. The issue at hand was a land dispute between the two governments. In March the Alteration of Provincial Boundaries Act was passed by the South African Parliament. This provided for the transfer of East Griqualand from the Cape Province to Natal. Chief Matanzima had earlier made

21. South African Institute of Race Relations, *Survey of Race Relations in South Africa, 1977* (Johannesburg: South African Institute of Race Relations, 1978), p. 339.

22. *Paratus* 29 (February 1978): 6–7.

23. E.g., *Paratus*, Supplement (January 1978), p. iii.

claims to East Griqualand and had submitted written represen-
tations to substantiate his claims to the area. East Griqualand is
important to the Transkei because it separates the Umzimkulu
enclave from the rest of the Transkei. The South African government dismissed these claims out of hand. Put out by Prime
Minister Vorster's unwillingness to bend, on 10 April Chief
Matanzima announced in the Transkei National Assembly that
he was breaking off diplomatic relations with South Africa.
Other motives may also have been on his mind, including the
realization that international recognition for the Transkei
would not likely occur until the Transkei could distance itself
politically from Pretoria. Such a grand gesture, it may have
been hoped, might highlight its "independence." Vorster, on
his part, refused to yield.[24] Since the decision to break relations
was Matanzima's, Vorster said that Matanzima had to take the
initiative to reopen relations.

Despite the severance of diplomatic links and the withdrawal
of diplomatic representatives between the two countries, commercial and other relations continued unaffected. In fact, even
diplomatic relations of a sort were reestablished (although not
officially so) when an agreement between the two foreign ministers led to the appointment of a South African official with
the necessary staff to look after South African citizens in the
Transkei. The Transkei government reciprocated, and personnel of both countries were to enjoy immunity.[25]

But in the defense field cooperative relations seemed to be
particularly strained. In response to the diplomatic break the
SADF was instructed by its government to cancel a course that
had been arranged for Transkeian soldiers at the South African School of Infantry at Oudtshoorn. Chief Matanzima read
this as a "slap in the face of the Transkei Government" and, in
turn, responded by unilaterally suspending the nonaggression
pact between the two countries.[26] Although the Transkei had

24. *Assembly Debates*, 11 April 1978, cols. 4389–401.
25. Ibid., 3 May 1978, Q cols. 728–29.
26. The pact itself makes no provision for suspension or termination, although the one with Bophuthatswana does; *The Star* (Weekly Air Edition), 13
May 1978, p. 2; *Eastern Province Herald* (Port Elizabeth), 11 May 1978; South
African Institute of Race Relations, *Survey, 1978*, p. 284.

absolutely no way of enforcing its wishes, it was announced that henceforth all South African military aircraft and naval vessels would no longer be accorded overflight and passage rights in Transkeian airspace and territorial waters. Just a few years after Chief Matanzima had pledged his commitment to a side-by-side defense of South Africa—that Xhosa warriors would fight for South Africa to "the last drop of blood"—the mercurial leader was calling for Transkeians to defend their land against South Africa.[27] Other assertive gestures relating to terminating several non-defense agreements reached between the two governments prior to independence and pressures on some South African officials seconded to the Transkei civil service punctuated the prime minister's fit of pique.

Officially, South Africa's involvement in the training of the TDF terminated on 12 May 1978, as a result of the severance of diplomatic relations and the suspension of the nonaggression pact on 10 May. A Transkeian with experience in the SAP took over command of the TDF. In 1979 South Africa's Deputy Minister of Defence reaffirmed that no future involvement with the training was envisaged.[28] Yet one gets the impression that SADF-TDF contacts and cooperation continued at less visible and publicized levels. One or two Transkeian platoons graduate in each class of the Police Training School at Hammanskraal. When asked what links still existed, one top SADF officer coyly responded, "Do you want the official or the unofficial answer?" He would not elaborate.

Meanwhile the TDF sought to expand its contacts. In September 1978 it was rumored that Rhodesia was training a select group of TDF military personnel, and relations with "a country in the Middle East" were mentioned.[29] At the official opening of the Citizen Force the Transkeian Minister of Defence

27. Patrick Laurence, *The Transkei: South Africa's Politics of Partition* (Johannesburg: Ravan Press, 1976), p. 131.

28. *Assembly Debates,* 16 February 1979, Q col. 75; and *Rand Daily Mail,* 17 February and 24 February 1979. See also the statement by Minister of Defence in *Assembly Debates,* 17 April 1978, col. 4939.

29. *The Star* (Daily Edition), 22 September 1978; *Citizen,* 25 August 1978; *Sunday Express* (Johannesburg), 17 September 1978; *Daily News,* 22 September 1978.

called on Sweden, Holland, Denmark, Egypt, and Nigeria to help Transkei protect itself against South Africa.[30] Humphrey Berkeley, a former Labour M.P. in Britain and former diplomatic advisor to the Transkeian prime minister, claimed that Nigeria had offered to establish "a military presence" in Transkei and to supply the territory with substantial financial aid. The Nigerians had apparently offered to train informally Transkeian Police and Defence Forces. The plan fell through because the Nigerian diplomat sent to Umtata to clinch the deal was left unceremoniously unattended while Chief Matanzima was in South Africa negotiating secretly with South Africa.[31] A month later, in April, South Africa paid the Transkei R118 million. Throughout 1979 there were continued references to Transkeian soldiers training "abroad," but such a vague term could mean in South Africa itself, too.[32] Finally, in early 1980 Transkei decided to reestablish diplomatic links because of South Africa's ostensible "determination to negotiate on the land issue." It was also announced that the nonaggression pact would be restored.[33]

In short, despite the vulnerability of the Transkei and the fact that that country is purely a creation of South Africa's apartheid policies, intimate defense relations between the two governments did not progress without some irritation. In such a strained setting, the extensive contact necessary for strategic and military planning as envisaged by those who devised the homelands scheme becomes more challenging. If the South African defense picture is to involve all homeland forces, the possibilities for independent postures are expanded ever so slightly, perhaps enough to call into question the continued pursuance of devolution for all homelands.

After the departure of the seconded South African army

30. *Rand Daily Mail,* 31 October 1978.

31. Humphrey Berkeley, "The Mission that Failed," *The Spectator* 243 (4 August 1979): pp. 12 – 14. *Rand Daily Mail,* 3 August 1979; *Sunday Express,* 12 August 1979.

32. *Eastern Province Herald,* 12 July 1979, p. 2. See also "Christmas and New Year Message 1979 by Hon. Minister of Defence: Chief G. M. M. Matanzima to Officers and Senior NCOs of the TDF," personal photocopy, p. 2.

33. Statement by Prime Minister Chief George Matanzima; see *Rand Daily Mail,* 8 February 1980.

personnel, discipline and efficiency in the TDF suffered.[34] Equipment was destroyed and allowed to deteriorate, soldiers terrorized the citizenry, drunkenness was rife, and TDF reliability was doubtful. In May 1981 Kaiser Matanzima recruited Lt. Col. Ron Reid-Daly, formerly commander of the Rhodesian Selous Scouts, to reconstruct the TDF. Reid-Daly brought with him thirty-five former Rhodesian colleagues. Although the Rhodesian soldiers are resented by many in Umtata, the Matanzimas support them wholeheartedly. The highest ranking Transkeian is the son of the Paramount Chief of the Thembus, and the next ranking local is the son of Prime Minister George Matanzima. Today the TDF represents a "souped-up brigade" of Permanent Force members. It consists of an infantry battalion and a Special Forces battalion in training at Port St. Johns. Relations between the TDF and the SADF are much reduced from earlier times and generally downplayed in the press, but help with supplies, logistics, intelligence, and coastal defense are apparent.

The second homeland to field an armed force is Bophuthatswana. In October 1976 it was announced that Chief Minister Lucas Mangope had asked South Africa to train Tswanas for military service. Some nine months before scheduled independence on 6 December 1977, the SADF began training a National Guard for Bophuthatswana.[35] It was hoped that a guard of some 221 men would be ready for independence. The first intake completed basic training in three months by early June 1977.[36] Although this intake was smaller than had been hoped for, the second and subsequent intakes were more

34. Information about the contemporary TDF was gathered in several interviews in Umtata, 10–12 June 1982; and from Louis Du Buisson, "Where the Selous Scouts Call the Tune," *Frontline* 2 (November/December 1981): 6–8; *Sunday Times,* 31 May 1981; *Sunday Tribune,* 1 November 1981; *Daily Dispatch* (East London), 14 May 1982; and Barry Streek and Richard Wicksteed, *Render Unto Kaiser: A Transkei Dossier* (Johannesburg: Ravan Press, 1981), esp. pp. 91–95.

35. *South Africa Digest,* 8 October 1976, p. 3; *Paratus* 28 (February 1977): 15.

36. Recruiting literature, e.g., *Balebeledi Ba Setshaba Ba Bophuthatswana: National Guard* (Pretoria: Military Printing Unit, 1977), sets out bare details on qualifications for selection, training program, benefits, and career opportunities.

satisfactory. At a base near Mafeking the SADF began a training program similar to that for SADF recruits. The first NCOs were appointed on completing the course, and eight officer candidates were chosen and sent for further instruction.[37] They were commissioned shortly before independence. Presently, all section leaders and platoon and company commanders are reportedly Tswanas, and the highest ranking Tswana is a major.

Around 90 percent of the basic level management posts are held by Tswanas, while at the middle level the figure is 60 percent. Only 15 percent of the top level posts are manned by Tswanas, most of whom started their careers in 1977. Although South African citizens may join the Bophuthatswana Defence Force (BDF) on special contract, preference is shown to Tswanas when vacancies arise or new posts are created. But key post personnel are recruited or seconded from the SADF. Brig. F. E. C. van den Bergh, the officer commanding the North Western Command of the SADF, was named the military advisor to Chief Minister Mangope, and Lt. Col. J. van Niekerk was the first officer commanding the National Guard. Some thirty South African commissioned officers and NCOs supervised instruction. Many SADF personnel have been retained in their advisory and command capacities after "independence." The extent of "interreliance" is still quite high.[38] Indeed, the BDF is effectively a unit of the SADF's North Western Command. The Bophuthatswana Minister of Defence is now Brig. H. F. P. (Hennie) Riekert, a former brigadier with the SADF, and the commanding officer is Brig. H. S. (Jack) Turner, also of the SADF.

Currently the BDF is comprised of three units: an infantry battalion, 50 percent of whose troops are trained for operational duty in a counterinsurgency capacity; a maintenance

37. "Bophuthatswana's National Guard," *Paratus* 28 (June 1977): 18; *The Star*, 27 August 1979.

38. "Proud Tswanas Queue to Join Their Army," *Paratus* 32 (November 1981): 18–19. See also "Racial Goodwill Strengthens the SADF," *Paratus* 29 (November 1978): 6; and Republic of Bophuthatswana, Department of the Presidency, *Proclamation*, no. 22, 28 November 1978, typescript in personal possession.

unit for support and logistics; and a military school where personnel are trained for special tasks and for promotion. But for highly specialized assignments and advanced courses BDF members are sent to South Africa. Presently applications are running at satisfactory levels, and for the July 1981 intake of 350, over two thousand applications were reportedly received. The January 1982 intake was postponed, ostensibly because there were not enough qualified instructors. At that time around sixty instructors were prepared. BDF members join on a contractual and probationary basis. During or after the first six months, which includes fourteen weeks of training, either the BDF or the individual recruit may request his termination. Otherwise the member signs on permanently. If the member later decides to terminate his contract, he must purchase his discharge.[39]

Although Chief Mangope once expressed doubts about defending South Africa before the rights of the black man were assured,[40] he has now thrown himself into a collaborative South African – Tswana effort at building up a defense and police establishment. A nonaggression pact between the two governments was also gazetted.[41]

In October 1978 the chief minister of Venda, Patrick Mphephu, announced that a Venda National Army was being trained in South Africa, and that it would serve to combat terrorism in the homeland after it became independent in September 1979.[42] The Venda National Force combines the functions of army, police, traffic police, and prison services. It is based in Sibasa, the capital of Venda.[43] On independence, the force was commanded by a former South African security po-

39. *Rand Daily Mail*, 30 August 1979; and "Proud Tswanas Queue to Join," pp. 18–19.

40. Quoted in Jeffrey Butler, Robert I. Rotberg, and John Adams, *The Black Homelands of South Africa: The Political and Economic Development of Bophuthatswana and KwaZulu* (Berkeley: University of California Press, 1977), p. 76.

41. Republic of South Africa, *Government Gazette* 150, no. 5823, 6 December 1977, pp. 34–35.

42. *The Star* (Weekly Air Edition), 7 October 1978, p. 8.

43. *Guardian* (London), 6 August 1979, p. 5; *Sunday Times* (Johannesburg), 9 September 1979; *Post* (Johannesburg), 5 February 1980. For a sarcastic comment see Revelation Ntoula's editorial in *Voice*, no. 12 (19 February 1980), a South African Council of Churches publication.

liceman, Lt. Col. T.R. Mulaudzi. In mid-1980 it numbered
around 450. When asked on South African television if Venda
could handle any threat to subvert the existing order in Venda,
Mulaudzi replied that, if necessary, Venda would summon
help from its "good friends" in South Africa. To formalize this
attitude Venda has also signed a pact of nonaggression with
South Africa.[44]

Political Issues and Strategic Speculation

In reality, some difficult questions confront the SADF, the
South African government, and the homelands as they deal
with the issues of homelands defense. Especially if the exfolia-
tion of homeland territories from the South African state
should continue, massive border problems could arise — unless, that is, the SADF treats these territories strictly as parts of
the South African defense system, sovereignty and mutual
consultation notwithstanding. The South Africans began their
plans for devolution in Namibia by setting up homeland governments and corresponding police and defense units. The
defense formations, nevertheless, were always integrated into
SADF command and operational structures. Eventually, the
inevitability of some form of "independence" for South West
Africa as a single Namibian state became clear, and the homeland or tribal armies were deemphasized. Reorganized and
increasingly grouped together, they became the embryo of a
structurally fragmented Namibian Army. The place of SWAPO
forces in such a formation remains to be seen, although after
the Zimbabwean settlement and the integration of the fighting
units of the Patriotic Front into the regular army there it must
surely be discussed. No such alternative is available within the
Republic of South Africa itself short of scrapping the entire
superstructure of ethnic homelands as a device for controlling
growing numbers of urban blacks in an industrial South Africa.
   But in addition to the total structural question, more narrow, political issues abound. One is the inherent instability of
the homelands governments and states themselves. Territorially noncontiguous, devoid of natural resources, unable, even

44. Signed on 13 August 1979.

in the best of times, to satisfy minimum economic needs of their inhabitants, let alone of all their citizens (in fact, they were designed by Pretoria to do just the opposite—to harbor an inexpensive working force for the Republic during times of economic weakness and to house its families during times of economic boom), the homelands are testimonies to the instability and exploitative character of the system. Their governments are entirely dependent on the goodwill, generosity, and coercive support of the South African regime. If Pretoria's years are numbered, the homeland governments can count their futures for less. Certainly without the Republic's blessing and support they would collapse from within.

The government in Venda illustrates the unpopular character of the homeland order. Chief Mphephu's government is a minority regime with little popular support. In the July 1978 general election Chief Mphephu's ruling Venda National Party was decisively defeated by the opposition Venda Independence Party. The opposition won thirty-one of the forty-two elected seats. Yet the government held power by calling upon chiefs and headmen (twenty-seven are nominated) and the fifteen additional members designated by regional councils to support it and by invoking the emergency powers ceded by South Africa. Thus Mphephu was able to detain eleven successful opposition candidates and almost fifty of their supporters.[45] In such a situation the Venda National Force becomes little more than a surrogate occupying force indirectly acting on behalf of the Republic of South Africa and its client regime.

Similarly questionable practices and heavy-handed dealings with opposition have marked political life in the Transkei, especially before independence as the Matanzima government sought to entrench itself in power over the protests of opposition politicians. The very first Transkeian election in 1963 brought Paramount Chief Matanzima's Transkei National In-

45. South African Institute of Race Relations, *Survey, 1978*, pp. 297 – 98; *Post*, 26 March 1980, p. 3, in which Venda's Minister of Justice claims that Proclamation R276, a law providing for detention for ninety days without trial, will never be repealed.

dependence Party (TNIP) to office with a very small majority. Their support was mainly among the chiefs, with few elected members behind them. Over the next decade there was a prolonged swing to the TNIP, with opposition M.P.s defecting to the government side. Preventive detention was used to intimidate the opposition before the general election in September 1976, with the result that the opposition came away with only four of the seventy-five elected seats and three of the seventy-five nominated chiefs' seats. The notorious Transkei Emergency Proclamation R400 of 1960, an omnibus act that had been ruthlessly used to suppress opposition, has now been replaced by the Transkei Public Security Act. This continues to mask extensive popular dissatisfaction with the Transkeian government.

More patently than those of most less-developed countries, the homeland armies are designed for internal security and for the maintenance in power of less than popular governments. Such forces pose little obstacle to external invasion, be it from South Africa or from a guerrilla liberation movement. Vulnerable governments with miniscule defense forces are thin reeds on which to build a reliable barricade against popular discontent. The prospects of military involvement in domestic politics is constant. In May 1981 top officers of the TDF (all Transkeians) were detained by the Transkeian Police; these included the TDF chief of staff. The TDF was reported to have been having disciplinary problems, but these high-level arrests would imply deeper, political problems, since some of those detained stand charged with allegedly having contacts with the African National Congress. Lt. Col. Ronald Reid-Daly, former leader of Rhodesia's efficient Selous Scouts, was named at that time to assume acting command of the TDF.[46] He now bears the rank of major general. To be sure, the SADF is not so naive as to fail to appreciate the prospects for military coups in these territories. There must be contingency "arrangements," the details of which have not been made public, that would enable SADF participation in homeland defense and in sup-

46. *Cape Times*, 30 May 1981; *The Sun* (Baltimore), 6 October 1981.

port of governments in jeopardy. Legal niceties need not complicate the matter.

But even assuming the homeland governments could become stable, there is no further guarantee that they will continue to be "reliable" allies of the Republic. Indeed, about the only way they could hope to become "stable" or popular is by opposing South Africa's policies, especially policies that affect homeland citizens "abroad," that is, in the Republic, or by attacking the territorial arrangements successfully. The fact is that most opposition parties within the homelands have opposed the homelands policy itself and the granting of independence to territorially truncated and segmented "nation states." Even some of the governing parties have expressed these views. In short, the very identity of the new governments with South Africa (a function itself of the "transition to independence" and the transfer of "legitimacy") is a formula for popular complaint and suspicion.

Homeland "independence" may justifiably be suspect and limited. Nevertheless, these states are professedly legally sovereign, or so Pretoria would want us to believe. They are technically free to pursue policies at variance with those of South Africa. The Transkeian severance of diplomatic relations with Pretoria is a case in point. Surely there are grounds to question the authenticity of that action. South African budgetary subventions continued. The seconding of South African administrative personnel was not affected. Business went on as usual. But the unchallenged assumption that these states will remain reliable "allies" of South Africa must be queried.[47]

These new governments, no matter how much they may be creatures of South Africa's domestic colonial policy, no matter how economically conservative and politically repressive they may be at home, still are peopled by politicians who live in at least two worlds, who have to sail a rough sea between the Scylla of the white Republic's government and the Charybdis of their own black citizenry. Indeed, the inhabitants of the homelands and the statutory homeland "citizens" residing in South Africa divide that constituency still further. These gov-

47. See, e.g., *The Star* (Weekly Air Edition), 29 June 1974, p. 11.

ernments must, for their own political tenure, learn to play off and balance diverse constituencies. Although it appears today that they are snugly ensconced in the South African camp, which they are, it is still possible to imagine that the rise of new interests or the power shifts among existing groups and interests may set them adrift, at least enough to encourage South Africa to write them out of long-range defensive contingency plans or to precipitate South African military reoccupation, if necessary.

Furthermore, the homeland armies hardly pose threats to any but unarmed critics of the homeland governments. The fact is that the homeland armies were not designed to defend the country against incursions from outside. A few hundred troops can hardly strike fear into the hearts of well-armed and trained freedom fighters. All parties appreciate this. The homeland armies were not fashioned for military purposes. The Venda National Force best exemplifies this since it is an all-purpose, paramilitary formation. Homeland armies were created to supply the trappings and regalia of independent statehood. Their purpose is ceremonial—to take the salute and be reviewed at the transfer of sovereignty, to welcome visiting dignitaries, to guard the state house and public buildings. As such they may look good in photographs, and they may represent the embodiment and confirmation of independence for outside observers and for external propaganda. Both Pretoria and the homeland governments are pleased by this vital function. When homeland forces do become operational, they are more like police mobile units, anti-riot forces, or crowd control instruments. Perhaps as they are enlarged they may yet become armies for military or defensive purposes. But thus far such a role is unrealistic.

In another sense the homeland armies serve a political purpose. For as long as SADF personnel or outsiders such as Reid-Daly continue to exercise command in homeland forces, such forces serve as an additional weapon in the hands of a shaky government. For years after independence, for example, the Malawian government of H. Kamuzu Banda retained the services of British army personnel at high levels. To be sure, rationalizations of their professional qualifications and efficiency were advanced. But President Banda was not un-mindful of the danger of military coups. He must have rea-soned that by having foreigners in command positions, with loyalties first to their own career services abroad, which in turn supported the established government in Malawi, the chances of a Malawian military coup were reduced measurably.

In addition, if a homeland government should become criti-cal of South Africa or should pose a threat (by its very instabil-ity) to South African order, the homeland forces commanded by SADF men may stand as a fifth column within the homeland government itself. The replacement of SADF personnel would take time and might give the Pretoria government either time to react or at least some warning of impending difficulties.

Finally, as one surveys a map of South Africa it becomes apparent that the homelands occupy strategic territory on or near the borders of the Republic.[48] They form a semicircle around the industrial and mining heartland of South Africa, from the coastal parcels of Ciskei and Transkei (bordering on Lesotho) on the Indian Ocean and the dispersed KwaZulu in Natal (bordering on Swaziland and Mozambique) to the Trans-vaal homelands of Kangwane (also bordering on Swaziland and Mozambique), Gazankulu, Venda, Lebowa, South Nde-bele, and Bophuthatswana (bordering on Botswana) in the northwest. Moreover, these territories are often peopled by ethnic groups that also live in neighboring states. Such a situa-tion is, of course, a two-edged sword, as the history of the Soviet Union in Central Asia indicates, but it does widen for-eign policy and strategic alternatives.

The South African government would like to transform the homelands into an "inner ring of buffer states" to replace what had been a defense in depth supplied by the Zambezi salient, with its ring of buffer states once policed by Portuguese and white Rhodesian security forces. As a first line of defense against guerrilla incursions (a very thin line, I have argued) the bantustan armies do no more than pose token resistance. They serve as a triphammer that sets into motion emergency plans in which the homeland government invites in the SADF. As *Rand*

48. Many of these ideas are drawn from Laurence, *The Transkei*, p. 131.

Daily Mail journalist Patrick Laurence has argued: "The first shot fired by a Black army at African nationalist guerrillas would make survival of its leadership dependent on the survival of the White regime in South Africa."[49] Likely they already are so committed even before the opening volleys. But the dependency relationship is not reduced by having two armies "jointly" at war. Joint maneuvers and SADF military maneuvers within nonindependent homelands are common.

This policy is not altogether clear in all cases. If homelands are to represent a kind of *cordon sanitaire,* why did the South Africans, with the consent of the Venda authorities, excise a narrow strip of territory between Venda and the Limpopo River? By removing Venda from direct contact with the Zimbabwe border, South Africa must be directly and primarily responsible for dealing with the borders of the Republic. Factually, this has always been the case. But this maneuver has not been done with the other homelands on the border. In addition, as tacit recognition of the strategic importance of the small Venda homeland (population, 461,000) the South Africans built and operate a military airfield at Madimbo.[50]

Some version of the Brezhnev doctrine may be contemplated or invoked by the Republic of South Africa toward one or more homelands.[51] The Brezhnev doctrine of limited sovereignty and intervention provided the justification for the Soviet invasion of Czechoslovakia by the Warsaw Pact states in 1968. In that dispute, involving a regional grouping, the Soviet Union asserted that a member of the group should limit its sovereignty rather than endanger the group's class solidarity. The group, acting cooperatively and "by way of self-defense," has the right to use force to assure fraternal socialist unity and to prevent the possible collapse or overthrow of a member state's government. Insofar as there already is serious question about the "sovereignty" of Bantustan governments, it would seem that such a doctrine might more easily be applied toward

49. As quoted in *Eastern Province Herald,* 26 June 1976, p. 3.
50. *Rand Daily Mail,* 30 November 1978; 1 December 1978.
51. Such an idea was broached as early as 1972 by Merle Lipton, "Independent Bantustans?" *International Affairs* 48 (January 1972): 13 – 14.

a homeland government than, for example, in a situation where there is no question of the juridical independence of a state, as with the Warsaw Pact states or in some modernized, hegemonial version of the Monroe Doctrine. Clearly, Pretoria feels that it has the right to intervene preventively, if necessary, in any part of its former territories if its interest should be threatened. What it needs is some sort of treaty arrangement that might legitimize that intervention.[52] The idea of a confederation of southern African states being proposed by the Botha government could expedite such a scheme. Although it may be Pretoria's policy to regard the armies of the "independent" homelands as part of a regional defense system "to fight against marxism,"[53] their anticipated role may be little more than that of the canary in the coal mine — to signal to the South African government that action must be taken to stem the tide of opposition to the governments in the homelands. Under such an arrangement, the SADF might intervene as a preventive measure, all the more easy since so far no homeland has gained any form of international recognition outside of South Africa.

52. See the arguments advanced in G. E. J. Stephan and H. Booysen, "The Angolan Conflict: Its Relevance for South Africa in her Relations with Future Independent Bantustans and the Need for a Monroe Doctrine," *South African Yearbook of International Law, 1975,* vol. 1 (Pretoria: University of South Africa, 1976), pp. 103 – 114.

53. *Citizen,* 8 September 1978.

11

The Use of Indigenous Forces
in Namibia

THE DEFENSE OF the status quo or some fair copy of
it in Namibia has proceeded on two levels, the political and the
military. Militarily, South African policy has reflected a growing awareness of the seriousness of the black nationalist challenge to continued South African occupation, and hence
South Africa has felt the need to expand and upgrade its defensive effort.

At first Pretoria assumed that elements of the police would
be sufficient to contain the unrest. Expansion of police units
and an improvement of their paramilitary and counterinsurgency skills proved inadequate. Creation of indigenous homeland police forces to protect the homeland governments in
South West Africa and the inclusion of black South Africans in
the SAP units likewise failed to stem the nationalist tide.

In March 1974 the SADF was given responsibility for patrolling borders and combating the insurgency. Indigenous Namibians, at first only San trackers and later full tribal battalions of
San, Ovambo, Kavango, Caprivians, and then others, were
enlisted. There was even a highly secret formation of Portuguese speakers (mostly former Frente Nacional de Libertação

de Angola [FNLA] soldiers from Angola's Bakongo region) known as the Buffalo Battalion. This group was active in cross-border operations in Angola.

Eventually efforts were made, beginning in 1977, to create a national South West Africa Territory Force, a national Namibian army consisting of tribal formations and nonethnic battalions. This was followed by compulsory military service for black as well as white Namibians (although some key tribal groups were at first exempted). In the pages that follow an effort is made to discuss these disparate formations and the commandos that have also been established and to explore the popular Namibian responses to these military developments. By way of introduction, we shall first examine the international background of the struggle.

The International Setting

Two factors have given rise to the establishment by the South African government of indigenous black military forces in Namibia and to their structural growth and evolution over the past decade and a half. They are, first, the outbreak and escalation of an open armed struggle for the independence of Namibia. Second is the widening persistence and intensification of international opposition to South Africa's administration of the territory and especially to Pretoria's phased integration of what it calls South West Africa into the economic, political, legal, and social structure of the Republic of South Africa. The South African government has apparently retreated from such an assimilationist path, but indirect control is very much a part of its policy.

This is not the place to trace the emergence of black nationalist movements or the international debate over Namibia in diverse forums—in the International Court of Justice, the United Nations, the Organization of African Unity, or in the various capitals of Africa, Europe, and North America where diplomatic pressures have begun to mount against South Africa's illegal administrative and military presence in Namibia. To give added urgency to this debate and its attendant diplomatic jockeying, the black peoples of Namibia sought to organize themselves in pursuit of their independence from Pretoria. Beginning in 1959 with the establishment of SWANU (South West African National Union) and followed a year later by the more important organization, SWAPO (South West African People's Organization), the political campaign began in earnest. SWAPO launched its armed struggle in 1966, and this was supplemented in the early 1970s by strikes and protest demonstrations organized by the legal but continually harrassed internal wing of SWAPO. The struggle was revitalized and expanded when the Portuguese government fell in 1974. A government friendly to SWAPO was established in Luanda, Angola two years later.

Meanwhile, Pretoria was not without options. Its two-pronged policy consisted of first, coercion — the stifling of internal dissent by repressive legislation and enforcement and a military buildup coupled with preemptive and reactive cross-border strikes into Angola and Zambia in opposition to the SWAPO guerrillas. The other option involved political and diplomatic maneuver. In Namibia Pretoria sought to arrive at an internal constitutional arrangement both acceptable to black traditional and middle-class leaders who still remained subservient to Pretoria and at the same time still salable to some portions of the outside world. Internationally, this policy involved attempts to deflect, delay, and blunt foreign and especially Western initiatives in favor of a "peaceful" transition to majority rule in Namibia or worse, in South Africa's eyes, revolution under SWAPO's aegis.

When it became apparent to Pretoria that some version of independence would have to be conferred upon Namibia, the South African government searched about for a neocolonial solution, one that would leave any government in Windhoek manipulable from Pretoria. The result was a decision to structure independence along ethnic lines. A 1974 plan sought the division of Namibia into ten "tribal homelands." An effort was made to identify compliant black nominees who would agree to the acceptability of Pretoria's scheme. Still, this design failed to gain approval at the Turnhalle Conference, opened in September 1975, even though the plan represented the logical extension of Pretoria's earlier homelands formula for South

West Africa embodied in the Odendaal Report of 1964. A constitutional committee consisting of four delegates from each of the eleven major population groups sought to draft a constitutional instrument. After much debate it was decided to accept the idea of a unitary state. All delegations eventually endorsed the territorial integrity of the country, and they targeted a date for independence, 31 December 1978. This arrangement broke down for several reasons. First, it was not possible to arrive at an acceptable transitional or interim government. Second, the white politicians held out for the continuation of some form of ethnic organization of local government, national representation, and governmental powers. Several black delegations considered this a veiled reinstitution of the old homelands policy. Third, SWAPO would have nothing to do with these negotiations or their product, and SWAPO spoke for the largest single group of black Namibians. No arrangement without SWAPO endorsement could work. Fourth, popular black opposition to the proposed scheme was apparent, even to politicians in Pretoria. Fifth, the Western governments and the United Nations backed SWAPO in its rejection of the Turnhalle formula.

At this point the United Nations and the five members of the Western Contact Group began negotiating in earnest with Pretoria. Again, despite adept maneuvering, little transpired that all sides — including SWAPO — could agree to. What Pretoria sought was to assess the extent to which it would have to concede genuine power to maleable black leaders in order to relieve the pressures for revolutionary change, as embodied in the SWAPO challenge. They proposed a blatantly conservative strategy, little different from Ian Smith's similar ploy in Zimbabwe. The fighting and the South African military buildup continued throughout these negotiations.

Creation of Tribal Formations

Initially, the form that the first use of black armed men took was strictly pragmatic, yet it fell quite logically within the ambit of the overall governmental plans for political devolution. The first introduction of Namibian black men into the SADF in

Namibia took the form of the recruitment of San (white South Africans call these people Bushmen) as specialized trackers. Such individuals were attached, as in a dilution policy, to individual white units. There is no designated homeland for the San, although there is a Bushman Reserve to which the San steadfastly refuse to move. Yet the San were used in a way as an ethnic group force, not unlike those that followed.

A part of the policy to divide and dominate had been to follow the installation of homeland governments possessing some modicum of internal self-government with the creation of homeland police forces and then homeland-based defense forces. The former were officially under the direct control of the homeland authorities, although these institutions have virtually no independence or latitude to make policy contrary to the dictates of the commissioner-general. The homeland-based defense forces are still units within the SADF command structure, not at all taking directives from homeland governments. Nonetheless, these homeland formations were created and trained by the SADF ostensibly at the request of homeland leaders, themselves put in place by the South African authorities in South West Africa.

Despite the fact that SWAPO began its armed insurgency in 1966, it was not until the mid-1970s that South Africa began to employ black troops in Namibia. Armed black policemen had appeared in South West Africa in the late 1960s. But fighting units composed of indigenous blacks were not organized until 1974. The police used on the borders were members of SAP, although later homeland policemen, directly under the command of the homeland authorities, made their appearance. Some, particularly of the Ovambo police force, received training at the police college at Hammanskraal in South Africa along with black SAP members. During the late 1960s the military insurgency in Namibia itself had been almost entirely put down. By and large, police action was sufficient to contain the threat. The struggle heated up into the 1970s.

In March 1974 the South African Army took over patrol of the borders from the police, although both the SAP and tribal authority police continued to maintain a role on the borders. In both Ovambo and Kavango tribal police assumed responsi-

SOLDIERS WITHOUT POLITICS

bility for control of border crossing points in collaboration with
local headmen. The improved COIN capacity of the SAP and
their more modern automatic weaponry added to their effectiveness. But by far the most important development in the use
of blacks in defense roles was the creation of the homeland
armies.

The first indigenous Namibians were officially brought into
the SADF in 1974. A camp for sixteen San volunteers plus one
white officer and six national servicemen was established in
September in the Caprivi. This was a pragmatic step with few
long-range principles at stake. Trackers were required, and the
San possessed these skills in abundance. They were almost
immediately assigned to border patrols manned essentially by
SADF personnel, even though the San had been, originally,
members of the auxiliary service rather than of the regular
SADF.

Later, San were trained in combat skills and were deployed
as units, performing other services in additon to tracking as
signalmen, medical orderlies, drivers, and infantrymen. Another unit was formed in 1976 of San refugees from Angola.
Several hundred San serve today in the S.W.A. armed forces.
The 201 Battalion operates out of Fortified Base Omega in the
Caprivi. Small units are flown to the fighting zones in Ovamboland for six-week tours. There is also a "proper" homeland battalion, the 203, for Bushmanland.

San also help instruct white soldiers in survival techniques in
the bush and in tracking. San families reside at Omega, which
contains modern facilities, including a school, a hospital,
shops, and a clothing factory. Total base population consists of
around 3800 people, about 850 San troops, 2700 dependents,
and 250 whites. As of 1981 there were two San corporals, and
the other officers, instructors, and leaders were white. It is
claimed that care is taken not to westernize the San soldiers to
such an extent that their superior sensitivities to the natural
signals of the bush are dulled. In fact, San soldiers are encouraged to return to the bush from time to time to hone their
tracking skills.[1]

1. *New York Times*, 6 October 1977, p. 35; and 24 February 1981; *South Africa
Digest*, 28 April 1978, pp. 16– 17; *Sunday Tribune* (Durban), 19 October 1981; and
Sunday Express (Johannesburg), 30 May 1982, p. 6.

As can be seen from the following tables the San population is quite small, and very few reside in their "homeland," which is really an artificial space between the Okavango and Herero areas. It is designed to contain a traditionally nomadic people. Little progress has been made in establishing such a "homeland." In that respect, the San Battalion (then known as the 31 Battalion) was just an appendage of the SADF, performing specialized functions, and was not really associated with the defense of a particular tribal territory or "homeland." Yet most of the other black peoples of Namibia, unlike those in South Africa itself, tend to reside in their officially designated "homelands."

In 1975 it was estimated that the population of Namibia consisted of the groups listed in table 14. The official breakdown of the "native" groups, as of mid-1974, is shown in table 15. Thus a program to create homeland armies seemed at first, to the SADF and to the political planners in Pretoria, to provide a convenient organizational weapon to maintain order in the territory and to expedite the move to a divided and thereby controllable South West Africa. It took little effort to get individual local headmen and tribal appointees and even elected officials and legislative bodies, in some cases, to request the South African government to help in setting up and training such forces. These black politicians were consciously defending themselves from the revolutionary forces at the same time as their collaboration made them a larger target.

TABLE 14.
Population of Namibia, By Race, 1975

Whites	100,000
"Coloured" groups	
Coloured	33,000
Rehobeth Basters	19,000
Namas	38,000
"Native" groups	687,000
TOTAL	877,000

SOURCE: South African Institute of Race Relations, *Survey of Race Relations in South Africa, 1976* (Johannesburg: South African Institute of Race Relations, 1977), p. 460.

TABLE 15.
Ethnic Groups Among Black Africans of Namibia,
Mid-1974

	Population	Estimated % of Population Domiciled in Its Own Homeland
Ovambos	396,000	97
Kaokovelders	7,000	92
Kavangos	56,000	98
East Caprivians	29,000	98
Damaras	75,000	34
Hereros	56,000	56
Tswanas	5,000	91
Bushmen [San]	26,000	4
Others	15,000	0
TOTAL	665,000	

SOURCE: South African Institute of Race Relations, *Survey of Race Relations in South Africa, 1976* (Johannesburg: South African Institute of Race Relations, 1977), pp. 460–61.

If one thinks of the San trackers as a specialist unit, the first tribal army to be established in a formal sense was in Ovamboland. In June 1974 the commissioner-general of South West Africa announced that it had been decided that about ten specially selected Ovambo men would go to Pretoria to take a SADF instructor's course.[2] Then, under the control of the SADF, they would return to Ovamboland to begin training others for a homeland force. Allegedly, this request for training came from the Ovambo Legislative Council, a partly elected, partly nominated body. After initial training in the homeland, troops of the First Ovambo Battalion (in early 1977 it was designated the 35 Battalion until a S.W.A. army was created in 1979, when it was renumbered the 101) were sent at the beginning of 1976 to Lenz. Others in the unit, it had been confirmed, had been fighting alongside the SADF units on the Angolan border and, indeed, had probably participated in the South African invasion of Angola earlier, in 1975 and 1976.[3]

2. *Rand Daily Mail* (Johannesburg), 27 June 1974.
3. See the statements by the Minister of Defence, in which the extent of black participation in the operational area had miraculously jumped from one

The Minister of Defence had disclosed that black soldiers fighting in the operational area were "members of the border area authorities," a probable reference to the Ovambo tribal government. Press speculation as early as October 1975 referred to "English speaking Africans" in the South African column striking northward through Angola and to the likelihood that they were Ovambos.

Ovamboland was the first area to be placed under martial law during the war. Emergency regulations enabled the police and later the SADF to exercise drastic powers to search and arrest without warrant, to detain without charge or trial, to deny access to legal advice, to break up meetings, and to enforce controls on the movement of persons. Even more violent extramural activities by police and the SADF went on outside the "protection" of the law. In general, civilians are required to cooperate with the security forces in their search for "terrorist infiltrators." Failure to report to the police persons suspected of being in Ovamboland unlawfully constitutes a criminal offense. In addition, other regulations provide for forced removal of populations, the creation of "prohibited areas," or "no-man's lands," and "free-fire zones," curfews, and other draconian measures applied first to Ovamboland and shortly thereafter extended to Kavangoland and Caprivi.[4] So it was only to be expected that the Ovambo "homeland" should get first test of a tribal army.

Kavango, to the east of Ovambo, has generally been a more peaceful sector of the operational area, especially early in the war. There, at a meeting of the Legislative Council in April 1975, South Africa's Minister of Defence announced that Kavango was to have its own armed force.[5] The Kavango Battalion (the 34 Battalion) was officially established in November 1975 when eighty-two recruits began training under SADF

hundred ninety to four hundred to five hundred during the precisely same period; Republic of South Africa, *House of Assembly Debates* (Hansard), 26 January 1976, col. 56; 6 May 1976, col. 6209; and 7 May 1976, col. 6284. See also *Cape Times* (Cape Town), 31 January 1976.

4. "All Options and None: The Constitutional Talks in Namibia," *Fact Paper on Southern Africa*, no. 3 (August 1976), p. 12. Published by the International Defence and Aid Fund.

5. *Rand Daily Mail*, 19 April 1975.

instructors.[6] Later the 34 Battalion was designated the 202 Battalion of the S.W.A. Territory Force. By February 1976 it had completed basic training and had moved on to weapons instruction at a base outside of Rundu, on the Angolan border. In both the Ovambo and Kavango battalions instruction is in Afrikaans. Members wear SADF standard uniforms and function entirely under SADF, *not* tribal homeland direction. Nonetheless, during the two-year training course, which includes combat assignments in the operational area, the men serve as members of auxiliary service battalions and are given the option of joining the Permanent Force or of returning to civilian life after this course of training.[7] The official reason for the men being in the auxiliary service is to avoid upsetting local salary scales. This eventually led, however, to a legal adjustment in the Defence Amendment Act of 1979 (clause 4) in order to make these battalions subject to the Military Discipline Code.[8]

Both battalions are organized along infantry lines, spending most of their time on foot. There are, however, special mounted units within the battalions. Weaponry consists of standard infantry issue, including automatic and semiautomatic small arms backed by mortar and rocket fire.[9] Both battalions tend to be deployed in sections, together with white troops in addition to their own white officers and NCOs. They patrol and fight alongside whites and also act as interpreters for white leaders. They are quartered in base camps (of company size) that include white troops. Sleeping quarters are not integrated, but in the operational area the mess and toilet facilities are formally integrated. In practice, however, informal segregation exists.

When they are deployed in combat roles they may be as-

6. *Focus on Political Repression in Southern Africa*, no. 3 (March 1976), p. 12. Published by the International Defence and Aid Fund.

7. South African Institute of Race Relations, *Survey of Race Relations in South Africa, 1977* (Johannesburg: South African Institute of Race Relations, 1978), pp. 602–3.

8. *Assembly Debates,* 20 March 1979, cols. 2894–95.

9. See, e.g., *Citizen* (Johannesburg), 7 May 1979; and Al J. Venter, "Black Against Black: Along the Angolan Border," *Soldier of Fortune* 4 (February 1979), 32–35.

signed beyond their tribal homelands. Some of their men are sent to Windhoek for language training in Afrikaans, and others are sent for specialist courses as mortarists, drivers, chefs, and so forth and for leadership training at Oudtshoorn in the Cape.[10]

Other platoons of Kavango and Ovambo are billeted with each chief. They act as bodyguards, perform general police duties, attempt to gather intelligence for command and to harass known SWAPO supporters and politicians, and try to generate support for progovernment political activists.[11]

The Kavango and Ovambo battalions have approached full battalion strength—perhaps as many as five to six hundred members. They have been unabashedly tribal formations, encamped within their homelands and generally deployed in their own homelands, although not exclusively.

Two other battalion-strength "ethnic" units bear consideration. The Caprivi (33) Battalion (now the 701 Battalion) trains at a camp in Mpacha, adjacent to a South African Army camp.[12] This battalion was formed in 1977 and attempts to cover a particularly sensitive area of the border. It is organized along much the same lines as the 34 and 35 Battalions, expects recruits to possess the same entry qualifications (e.g., the ability to read and write, a clean police record, a high degree of physical fitness, and the age of at least eighteen years) and is deployed generally as are the 34 and 35 Battalions. The battalion largely speaks Lozi, a language spoken widely in western Zambia. This provides the SADF with a policy dimension in its preemptive strikes into Zambia. Since English is the second language of the Caprivians, the 701 Battalion is the only unilingual, English-speaking unit in the Defence Force.

Even more interesting is the 32 Battalion, known as the Buffalo Battalion, a 1,000-man unit formed as a direct outgrowth of the Angolan civil war and South Africa's military intervention therein. Large numbers of refugees fled the fighting in Angola into Namibia from the south and, from the north, into

10. *Paratus* 30 (January 1979): 10; and *Paratus,* Supplement (May 1979), p. iii.

11. *Focus on Political Repression in Southern Africa,* no. 15 (March 1978), p. 15.

12. *Paratus,* Supplement (May 1978), p. ix.

260   SOLDIERS WITHOUT POLITICS

Zaire. Many were housed and fed by the South African authorities. In 1976 the SADF decided to recruit among these refugees, who were both black, white, and mixed-race Portuguese speakers. Most of its ranks are former members of the FNLA's army. Black members of the Portuguese Army were signed on, too. They are under short-term contracts, normally for one year. If they have had military experience they are paid a bonus on signing of around $600, and at the end of their terms they are given an additional $1,900 bonus. Later a black Angolan who claimed to be a captain in the 32 Battalion reported that he was paid around $1,000 per month and $12,000 at the end of his contract. He placed the battalion's base at Rundu, in Namibia's northeast, but that is the base for the Kavango battalion, not the 32 Battalion's base. Originally there were twenty-one white Europeans in the unit. Around eight were thought to belong in 1981. Similar short-term contracts in other formations are available to South African citizens with military experience. The 32 Battalion was seldom if ever mentioned in the official press releases until public disclosure of its activities in early 1981. In fact, it was generally regarded as "top secret." In January 1981 *The Guardian* of London reported on the "Buffalo Battalion" on the basis of interviews with a British deserter from that battalion.[13] The South Africans denied the story at first, but later, in response to allegations of atrocities committed by the unit, furnished information on the unit.[14]

The 32 Battalion is specifically designed for "cross-border" operations, mostly from its base in Caprivi (Bakari). Sometimes its units attempt to pose as União Nacional para a Independência Total de Angola (UNITA) fighters; in other cases they want local populations to think they are Angolan troops. Its commander had been Andreas Breytenbach, an officer

13. *The Guardian* (London), 29 January 1981 and 2 February 1981. I disclosed the existence of this unit as early as January 1980 during a seminar presentation on "The Societies of Southern Africa in the 19th and 20th Centuries," Institute of Commonwealth Studies, University of London, 17 January 1980.

14. *South Africa Digest,* 6 February 1981, p. 4; *New York Times,* 27 May 1981; and *Africa Research Bulletin* (Political Series) 18 (15 March 1981): 5975A–B; *Sunday Express,* 24 May 1981; and *Sunday Tribune,* 24 May 1981.

who had earlier commanded a battalion of FNLA in northern Angola and Zaire. After the FNLA's defeat Holden Roberto, its leader, asked Breytenbach to stay on. Instead, Breytenbach (the brother of imprisoned poet Breyten Breytenbach) returned to Namibia to organize the 32 Battalion in late 1975. Its present commanding officer is Cmdt. D. Ferreira. Some of its formations are commanded by ex-Portuguese NCOs, some by men who had left the Rhodesian forces after Robert Mugabe's victory in the Zimbabwe elections, and the rest by SADF men. A share of its arms are Soviet-made weapons captured in the field.

Throughout this period the SADF and the tribal authorities hammered away at the popular resistance to the use of black Namibians to defend the system. Efforts, as well, were made to inspire support for those inclined to ask the SADF to help them organize their tribal defenses, as if this support would be evidence of popular acceptance of the collaborative antirevolutionary activity. The Namas, for example, were called to meetings where SADF ranking officers talked to them about "initiating" a military unit for Namas. This was in December 1976. A few months later the formation was on track.[15]

A National Army for Namibia

A time arrived, in late 1976 or early 1977, when a decision had been taken to seek some form of independence for South West Africa, or Namibia, as a single, unitary state. The issue of security forces, and especially of the SADF during the transitional process, has been a difficulty for the parties negotiating the independence process — the South African government, the Turnhalle parties, SWAPO, the United Nations, the front line states, and the five Western Powers. Pretoria has been reluctant to agree to a partial and phased withdrawal of its troops without reservations and loopholes. But fearing that this might prove inevitable, it has taken steps to establish an indigenous defense force for the entire territory — one that is intended to become the nucleus of a future Namibian national army.

15. *Focus on Political Repression in Southern Africa,* no. 8 (January 1977), pp. 14 – 15.

Pretoria reasons that if the SADF selects, trains, and supplies the new force even a formal SADF withdrawal designed to mollify international and local opinion without risking a military collapse would leave Pretoria with considerable influence on defense and security in the territory. Barring a political settlement, this option is still quite remote. According to a spokesman for Defence Headquarters in Windhoek, local Namibians constitute only about a fifth of all soldiers fighting against SWAPO in Namibia. To be sure, the Namibian component of those fighting in the northern areas in "much higher."[16] The task of constructing the new military is still totally under SADF supervision. So far no control or direction has been devolved to indigenous peoples. Maj. Gen. J.J. "Jannie" Geldenhuys was appointed officer commanding South West Africa in early August 1977. His assignment was "to build and develop an independent and complete defence force for South West Africa" involving "all elements of the SWA population."[17] Even as early as late 1976 one begins to hear references to the "ultimate formation of a multiracial S.W.A. army."[18] It is difficult to imagine the Republic relinquishing any military authority to a new regime in that territory in its present or any similar state of instability and flux.

Those inclined to question the Republic's motives were answered by Chief of the Army Lt. Gen. C.L. Viljoen, who postured: "The S.W.A. Army will not be an army of oppression, but an instrument in the hands of a legally chosen government. It is going to be an army from the people for the people — a fair organisation with a national identity."[19] Yet which "national identity" is to prevail? The basic building blocks of this "national" force have been separate ethnic units. To be sure, the future Namibian defense force makes provision for integrated (i.e., multiethnic) formations. But it also is being designed to accommodate ethnically identifiable units. Rather than integration taking place within each formation, the command structure at the top is supposed to be integrated and should

16. *The Guardian,* 17 June 1981.
17. Words of the Minister of Defence P.W. Botha, *Windhoek Advertiser,* 1 August 1977.
18. *The Star* (Weekly Air Edition), 4 December 1976, p. 8.
19. *Paratus* 28 (September 1977): p. 4.

supply national guidance. Battalions such as the Ovambo, Kavango, and Caprivi units would continue to be ethnically based even though recruitment into these units was suspended with effect from 15 February 1978 and though their ethnic designations were officially eliminated in late 1978. It was argued that this was done because these units were up to full strength, and new recruits were not required.[20] Yet their composition remains virtually unchanged, and members and officers regret the name changes. To a base commander of the 35 Battalion, the battalion would and should always be thought of as the "Ovambo battalion." General Geldenhuys, earlier in his tenure as commanding officer, likened the 33, 34 and 35 Battalions to the Scottish and Irish regiments in the British Army — part of the total force, but with ethnic roots, composition, and pride.[21]

In August 1977 a formation was created, known as the 41 Battalion, that sought to accomplish two aims with regard to this ethnic and national question. On the one hand, it became a unit for those ethnic groups not already brought into the defense picture. On the other, it was seen as the organizational embryo for the future S.W.A. or Namibian army. The ethnic principle had been retained and moved southward, effectively extended to include all of Namibia's ethnic groups.

First mention of the 41 Battalion implied that it would be just another ethnic battalion. It was referred to as the "Nama 41 Battalion." The official SADF publication, *Paratus,* noted, "Thus the Namas become yet another SWA group to get their own army."[22] Quickly thereafter, however, it became clear that the 41 Battalion was more than a Nama unit. In fact, the battalion was to be comprised of five different bases spread widely throughout the country. At Narubis in the extreme south several groups train together — Namas, Coloureds, Rehobeth Basters, and Tswanas. Coloureds (as many as two hundred began training in late August 1977) are at an originally "unidentified" base, presumably Drimiopsis, northeast of Windhoek, near Gobabis. Otjisondo, also northeast of Windhoek,

20. *Focus on Political Repression in Southern Africa,* no. 15 (March 1978), p. 15.
21. *The Star* (Weekly Air Edition), 24 September 1977, p. 16.
22. "The Namas Get Their Own Army," *Paratus* 28 (September 1977): 2 – 4.

houses the Herero recruits. Damaras and others train at Ka-manjab in the northwest. Finally a base at Nouaspoort is the center for a company of San and others.

Initially it was announced that each ethnic group would re-cruit one hundred and sixty men and that they would be trained separately, for one year each and then a second year of specialization and advanced training, in some cases in the op-erational areas of Ovambo, Caprivi, and Kavango. The official press releases began to fancy the 41 Battalion as a new army of Namibia.[23] Hitherto, black troops had been trained as auxiliary forces. As negotiations for Namibia's independence and pre-tense relating to the bargaining process became more ad-vanced, the need for a national army became evident. The 41 (now 911) Battalion represented the nucleus of the new forma-tion. The battalion's recruits are reputedly not being trained to bolster tribal governments or tribal agents of the South African government. They can and have been deployed anywhere in Namibia, though most see service in Ovamboland. The na-tional army, it is contended, can live with ethnic and regional components, maintaining their identities yet surrendering all to a centralized command structure at the top—a pattern the National Party government rejected for the white SADF itself back in the 1950s. These units officially became part of the new South West Africa Territory Force (SWATF) in 1979.

An integrated "command structure" had heretofore meant that all formations would be directed from a central headquar-ters and presumably that all formations would be dealt with equitably in terms of assignment and deployment. The top leadership of the South West Africa Territory Force have all been white and all mostly SADF. There were three Coloured and two black lieutenants by 1981. Corporals, lance corporals, and sergeants have also emerged from among the black sol-diers. The highest ranking Namibian black in the SWATF is a captain who entered the service at that rank. He is a public relations officer to the S.W.A. Command.[24]

23. E.g., *Paratus*, Supplement (April 1978), p. iii; and ibid., (July 1978), p. vii.

24. *Paratus*, Supplement (November 1978), p. i; *South Africa Digest*, 17 No-vember 1978, p. 4; and *Paratus* 32 (January 1981): 41.

South West African white males are subject to compulsory national service. Most do their national service training in South Africa, although the hope has been expressed that eventually all white South Westers will do their training in Namibia itself. This is increasingly so since the 1981 compulsory intake. "It has not been decided," General Geldenhuys has said, "whether they will be grouped together [as the other ethnic groups are], or integrated with other population groups."[25] So far the band is officially integrated, and section leader and instructor training has been centralized too. Units are so small that it has not been practical to hold a separate course at each base. A leadership training school has been established at Okahandja, north of Windhoek.[26]

For the sake of consistency and to keep up the image of defense as a multinational enterprise, politicians proposed compulsory military service for all races. The dominant party in the Pretoria-sponsored internal political settlement, the Democratic Turnhalle Alliance (DTA), was asked to introduce such a policy by its white component, the Republican Party. Other parties, although by no means as powerful in the National Assembly, opposed the idea. A Namibia National Front spokesman said that the majority of blacks in Namibia would never become involved in what he called the colonial war between South Africa and SWAPO. The SWAPO Democrats, a group of former SWAPO activists who currently operate openly in Namibia, also found compulsory military service unacceptable. Until Namibia becomes truly independent and democratic, it is neither right nor just to ask black Namibians to defend an oppressive system, they maintained. Naturally, SWAPO itself condemns any use of black fighting men by the SADF or by the "puppet" homeland leaders and their governments.[27]

Despite this opposition the South African president in October 1980 issued a proclamation making national service com-

25. *The Star* (Weekly Air Edition), 24 September 1977, p. 16.

26. William Gutteridge, "South Africa's Defence Posture," *The World Today* 36 (January 1980): 29.

27. *The Guardian,* 15 September 1979, p. 6; and *The Star* (Weekly Air Edition), 23 July 1977, p. 2.

pulsory for all races in Namibia. This move, brought into force in 1981, followed a call by the DTA-dominated National Assembly in Windhoek during its 1980 sitting. All Namibian male citizens between eighteen and twenty-five are now eligible for training in the S.W.A. Territory Force. Of course, conscription will be initiated on a selective basis.[28]

The first intake of January 1981 consisted of around 1,200 men, of whom 20 percent were white. The recruits were trained by instructors from the Second South African Infantry Battalion Group at Walvis Bay and at Rooikop, a base about twenty kilometers from the port. After four months of basic training and six additional months of specialized training, the men returned to their various ethnic units to complete their tour of duty. In this fashion the new model SWATF perpetuates ethnic separatism. As for race, neither integration nor segregation officially exists, but "spontaneous group formation" has led to only one six-man tent (out of two hundred) being racially mixed. Three companies were racially mixed, two consisting of men with Standard 8 qualifications or higher, the third company plus a battery and a squadron group having lesser qualifications.[29]

So far, however, compulsory universal rather than selective military service for all Namibians is beyond the means of the South African authorities. In the first intake young men of draft age from the northern areas (Kaokoland, Ovambo, Kavango, and Caprivi) were not called. This has effectively excluded four ethnic groups and approximately 60 percent of the eligible men.[30] But the danger of civil war, especially of a post-settlement civil war, grows as Ovambo and other groups find themselves less involved in the security forces of the new order. Not only would Pretoria be unprepared to equip and train such large numbers, but this policy would cause a boycott of the program, increase domestic resistence, and precipitate the flight of numbers of young men from these northern areas

28. *The Star* (Weekly Air Edition), 25 October 1980.
29. *The Star* (Weekly Air Edition), 4 April 1981, p. 4; and "Blye Verwagtinge oor SWA se eie NDPs." *Paratus* 32 (May 1981): 34 – 36.
30. *To the Point* (Johannesburg), 5 December 1980.

driven to take up arms actively against the occupying force of South African troops. Some conscientious objection has been reported, and a group of twenty-eight self-confessed SWAPO members claim to have been discriminated against at a junior leadership training school near Okahandja. Some, it is said, have been sent to the operational areas for "reorientation." In a related development, the Lutheran World Federation reported in Geneva that in early 1981 there was a "marked increase" of young refugees to Angola and Botswana.[31] Voluntary intakes had proved to be generally manageable and as efficient as could be expected, given the hostility that Namibians have for the regime. The next step, selective yet compulsory service, raises issues that will test the authority of a government devoid of legitimacy in the eyes of many black and white Namibians.

Commandos and Other Units

Units under the size of battalions and nonregular formations also have been established and grafted onto the Namibian armed forces organization. The commando, so much a part of the myth of the Afrikaner citizen army, has been adapted to black military service in South West Africa.

The first black commando unit in either Namibia or South Africa was formed in late 1976. In November 1976 about fifty Basters began basic training near Rehobeth. Under white commando instructors and controlled by the SADF, this group became the kernal of a Baster commando. Although the initial intake was mostly younger men, it included at least one who had served with the SADF during World War II. By early 1977 this unit was supposed to have reached company strength of around one hundred and twenty.[32]

The following year, in November, the Rietfontein Commando was formed, and its first fifteen members began train-

31. *African Research Bulletin* (Political Series) 18 (15 February 1981): 5944C; *The Star* (Weekly Air Edition), 13 June 1981, p. 2.

32. *Rand Daily Mail,* 26 November 1976; *The Star* (Weekly Air Edition), 4 December 1976, p. 8; and *Focus on Political Repression in Southern Africa,* no. 8 (January 1977), p. 14.

ing in January 1978.[33] At one point it was reputedly the biggest black commando in Namibia, composed mostly of Mbanderu men who are closely associated with the Herero. Many work in the Hereroland administration; others are cattle farmers, and others are laborers. The unit was formed allegedly at the request of inhabitants of the Rietfontein block. More likely the urging of the SADF and of Chief Elifas Tjingaete, a tribal chief and DTA delegate to the National Assembly, were involved in prompting initiatives. Members attend meetings and training sessions at least once a month. All instructors are local white farmers and workers in the Gobabis district. The homeguard kind of formation is seen as vital against sporadic guerrilla activities, especially those aimed at individuals who collaborate with the South African authorities. In June 1979 it was announced by General Geldenhuys that these commando members were used operationally, the first black commandos so deployed in Namibia.[34]

Other black commando units have probably been formed, although the SADF propaganda machine has not produced column inches of coverage about them. When such a propaganda machine is silent in a situation where in the past it has been inclined to draw attention to black formations, such units either do not exist, are not doing well, are not ready yet for a public debut, or are being used for purposes the SADF would rather not mention.

In the far northwest of Namibia, near the Skeleton Coast, lies Kaokoland. There, all tribal headmen were brought together, and South African authorities suggested the idea of constituting an indigenous company.[35] Within weeks one hundred and twenty recruits were found, subjected to a three-week trial workout, and candidates were selected for training. By January 1979 the first group had completed training as infantrymen. Most of this group are Herero and Ovahimba. Although they speak the same indigenous language, Afrikaans is used in instruction. Few of these men can read and write, and

33. *Rand Daily Mail,* 16 July 1979, p. 9.
34. *Rand Daily Mail,* 15 June 1979.
35. *Paratus* 30 (January 1979): 12–13. It is now called the 102 Battalion.

so exclusively oral instruction is conducted, tedious and repetitious as it may be. In that the caliber of Afrikaans language skills is also rudimentary among the indigenous peoples in this region, one can imagine an army regimen rather limited in sophistication and heavy on physical drill.

The fact is, however, that steps are being taken to involve as many different Namibian peoples as possible in what appears to be the defense of the territory and a particular, though still unclear, political order. Moveover, they are being organized ethnically, despite a professed desire to create an all-Namibian national defense force. The overall structure seems to feature organizational confusion comprised of a jumble of units with diverse compositions, command structures, assignments, and importances. This is the pattern within the S.W.A. Territory Force. Over the melange of groups stands the SADF itself, with its own scramble of formations. One can only imagine how this intricacy of disparate units can pose problems for an independent Namibia. Indeed, this may be just why such a structure was chosen. Robert Mugabe's efforts to rein in diverse fighting corps in Zimbabwe may provide some hint of what Namibia might have to face. Encouraging a homeguard mentality, in which each unit identifies with a particular people or territorial entity, may be sensible in motivating people to fight. It is not the best route to forging a larger sense of nation.

Part of this is understandable given cost factors and patterns of black population distribution in Namibia. But if there is, in fact, a desire to create a Namibian nation, and there is no doubt that such a phenomenon exists already in spite of Pretoria's efforts and the efforts of some smaller ethnic groups and some traditional leaders to thwart and crush it, then the defense forces might be one such valuable nation-building instrument at their disposal. On the contrary, the South African authorities have chosen not to employ that instrument to that end, simply because they see the military more as a coercive force designed to perpetuate a divided traditional political elite that has, in the past, owed its tenuous status and what hobbled power it enjoys to the SADF, the tribal police, the SAP, and the overbearing power of the South African state itself, reincarnated as the South West African territorial authorities. They know full well that those authorities could not survive long without South Africa's imposed support. Yet short of appearing as an undiluted occupying power, South Africa continues to experiment with compliant coercive organs, hoping to resist the inevitable — a total retreat from Namibia and the implantation of a nationalistic, independent black government in Windhoek.

Pretoria is playing a subtle and delicate game in Namibia. South Africa does not behave as an outright occupying force. Nor does it blatantly establish "puppet" governments or proxy forces. On the contrary, South Africa realizes that the credibility of its conservative stage management depends entirely on its ability to convince both the outside world and Namibians that Pretoria is not only well-intentioned but determined to fulfill its colonial obligations (they would never call them that). To place compliant politicians into power without appearing to be overly manipulative, at least not any more manipulative than a half dozen other non-Namibian forces, is no easy task. Few Namibians are so naive as to be blinded by the press agentry, and few miss the underlying motives behind incomplete social reforms and niggardly welfare schemes. For South Africa to be credible, its own candidate government must be credible.

The emergency laws relating to compulsory collaboration with the authorities against insurgency are very much at the root of SADF-civilian relations. But in addition much of these relations are patterned after the civil-military programs used by the United States in Viet Nam. The struggle to "win hearts and minds" (known as WHAM) includes a variety of civic action programs — many of which get full publicity treatment.[36] Such publicity is very much targeted at youth — in schools, recreation programs, and youth camps. Individual programs are diverse. But their fundamental purpose is to ingratiate the SADF to the people and thereby parlay this sup-

36. Regarding national servicemen teaching in schools in the operational area, see e.g., "The SADF Cares," *Paratus* 30 (January 1979): 16 – 17; *The Star* (Weekly Air Edition), 25 February 1978, p. 7; and 8 October 1977, p. 9.

port into military and, of course, political advantage. Yet because of this it has not been able to overcome the predatory approach of the SADF, and especially of individual members of the SADF, in dealing with the local people. Misconduct and indiscipline are not uncommon in SADF dealings with the people of Namibia and of Angola.[37] The people, as one old man told a gathering, "suffer much under them." He was openly applauded. Zealous soldiers, in an effort to gather intelligence or to reduce their own risks in the field, are inclined to use force first, then try to persuade. Torture is common. Summary punishment is to be expected. Presumably South African soldiers and officers in combat zones in Namibia are required to sign an undertaking that they will not commit atrocities. The fact that such pledges exist is indirect acknowledgment that there is a problem.[38] The SADF and its personnel seem to subscribe to an American aphorism from Viet Nam which goes: "We must win hearts and minds, but if you grab 'em by the balls the hearts and minds will follow." The lesson of Viet Nam should have told the South Africans that such a crude reliance on force will not work. Although many of the top officers appreciate this matter, it is not easy to assure compliance with all their directives by all of their subordinates.

Despite efforts to disguise their aims, the SADF and its various indigenous agents are an occupying force and are seen as such by the people of Namibia. No manner of WHAM will hide that reality. The Namibians are not asking for or demanding efficient or just government from what they regard as the colonialist regime in their land — they merely want them to get out. The tribal authorities and those black politicians who participated in the Turnhalle exercises have been tainted. South African officials take pains to point out that "the people" themselves have contributed the idea of starting tribal military units. "The people" in this instance must refer to the official tribal

37. See *Assembly Debates*, 24 June 1977, Q col. 1408; *The Star* (Weekly Air Edition), 20 August 1977, p. 3; *LSM News* (Liberation Support Movement, Oakland, Calif.), nos. 11–12 (1976?), p. 26; *Namibia News* 9 (SWAPO, London; September 1976): 3–5; and *The Guardian*, 29 January 1981.

38. *New York Times*, 27 May 1981. See also the study by the S. A. Catholic Bishops Conference, *Sunday Express*, 16 and 31 May 1982, pp. 7 and 13.

leaders and their associates — themselves held in place by the SADF. They need homeland or tribal formations for their own self-protection. To call these individuals spokesmen for their people is, in most instances and among most ethnic groups, a mockery of the concept of representation. SWAPO is not without fault in its intimidation of segments of the people of Namibia. Their own fighters have on occasion been undisciplined, ruthless, and even cruel. But if a clear cut choice could openly be expressed by Namibians today, SWAPO would easily gain more support than any other party or coalition of parties. The SADF and the Pretoria-rooted government in Windhoek would certainly not win a popularity contest, even in light of civic action.

Despite almost continual behind-the-scenes negotiations over the future of Namibia, it appears that South Africa feels that militarily the circumstances in Namibia are still very much within their control. With a statement reminiscent of American bravado in Viet Nam, one SADF strategic planner told me in March 1980 that the SADF would "win" the war in South West Africa within one year. The 1980–81 offensive of stepped-up raids into Angola seems designed to eliminate SWAPO and to deny SWAPO a sanctuary. Thus it would appear that Pretoria thinks it can hold out for a political arrangement more in keeping with its own preferences. Although the situation is not entirely analogous, the overwhelming victory of Robert Mugabe's Zimbabwe African National Union – Patriotic Front in Zimbabwe must give South Africa's leaders pause to realize that parties identified with an internal settlement prompted by minority settler regimes are tarnished goods, unsalable to all but the fearful, the naive, or those with a vested interest in the status quo. In the face of popular opposition, Pretoria may have no other choice than to back its own proxy forces. But this cannot make for a more peaceful transition to black government. It only prolongs the struggle, making it more bloody and making postwar settlement less stable and more bitter.

12

Conclusions:

The SADF and Political Change in South Africa

IN ITS PRESENT mood white South Africa would rather battle to maintain its basic model of racial and economic relations than alter it radically. Settler regimes in southern Africa have followed this unyielding pattern for decades. Ever since the last trek, since there was nowhere else to retreat, Afrikaner leaders have dug in their heels. Colonial settlers, especially when denied a metropolitan escape, have been formidable adversaries resisting claims of indigenous peoples for equality or self-government. Constraints that inhibit a more powerful metropolitan power's employment of force are virtually absent in the case of a settler regime. For settlers, the issue is not whether to fight opponents but how.[1]

Thus, it is hardly surprising to find the government of South

1. See Andrew J. R. Mack, "Why Big Nations Lose Small Wars: The Politics of Asymmetric Conflict," *World Politics* 27 (January 1975): 191, who makes the case that conflicts involving settlers' regimes are fundamentally different from asymmetric conflicts between metropolitan powers and indigenous insurgents. See Kenneth W. Grundy, "Intermediary Power and Global Dependency: The Case of South Africa," *International Studies Quarterly* 20 (December 1976): 553 – 80, on the larger political and economic issues.

Africa and its Defence Force using black soldiers to fight revolutionary opponents. It is, simply put, a pragmatic response to
the changing security needs of the state. Despite all the publicity about the establishment of a "people's army," the bringing
of larger numbers of black recruits into the South African
Defence Force represents for South Africa's leaders a counsel
of last resort. It is neither a reflection of harmonious, liberal,
nonracist attitudes nor a statement of inclusive and widened
patriotism on the part of all population groups.

The use of blacks in military roles in South Africa points to at
least one often ignored yet important facet of the system.
South Africa's ruling elites are capable of change, reform, and
flexibility. Ideology is not the sole determinant of policy. On
the contrary, the attitude here might be described as one of
flexible inflexibility. The goal of the white-dominated capitalist order is unchanged. The means for achieving and maintaining it are subject to varying policy lines and interpretations.
These policies are themselves products of shifting political and
economic configurations. What may appear to be the ultimate
bend in the system today would have been unthinkable fifteen,
ten, or even five years ago, just as what is acceptable to the
regime today is likely to be quite different and inadequate in
the future. The Republic's policies are often reactive responses
to perceived threats from inside the country and from abroad.
Ideological blinders certainly affect its perceptions and interpretations of policy options but they are, in turn, adapted to
empirical conditions.

But these sorts of fluid situations help explain the regime's
movement toward allowing black participation in the security
activities of the state. Perhaps, at this point, it might be helpful
to ascertain the extent of black Defence Force involvement.

An Inventory

Just as white force levels in the SADF are not public information, it is difficult to determine precisely how many black members of the SADF there are. It can be estimated, however, that
as of January 1980 there were approximately 5,250 blacks in

TABLE 16.
Approximate Numbers of Blacks in the SADF, January 1980

	Permanent Force	National Service or Auxiliary Service	Total
SACC: Army	800	1,875	2,675
Navy	800	—	800
Air Force	25	—	25
Indian SSB: Navy	360	—	360
21 Battalion	490	300	790
121 Battalion (Zulu)	—	300	300
Other regional battalions	—	300	300
TOTALS	2,475	2,775	5,250

SOURCE: Author's estimates based on data presented throughout this study.

the SADF. Since January 1980 one might add another 4,000 black men to the SADF. But as of January 1980, some 15 percent of the Army Permanent Force was black African and Coloured, and around a third of the navy's PF were Indian and Coloured. Seen in this context the black contribution to the career Defence Force is significant. By including air force PF members the black proportion fell to 14 percent of the PF. Altogether, however, the PF constitutes only 20 percent of total SADF active duty forces. Major portions (over 80 percent) of active duty forces, especially in the army, are white national servicemen, two-year conscripts. From this perspective the black component of the army appears to be reduced further to around 8 or 9 percent. Around 24 percent of the total active naval forces in early 1980 were black. Further dilution occurs when Citizen Force and Commando units are added. The black component of the total SADF military personnel then appears to approach only 2 percent of the total Permanent and Citizen Forces.[2]

It must be remembered that these figures do not include

2. See the strange 1978 standoff between Harry Schwarz (PRP) and P. W. Botha, Minister of Defence, in Republic of South Africa, *House of Assembly Debates* (Hansard), 17 April 1978, cols. 4872–74 and 4949–50. Official 1982 figure for all blacks in the PF is 8 percent: *Assembly Debates*, 17 February 1982, Q col. 112.

blacks serving technically outside the SADF in the various battalions of the Namibian forces and in the homeland national armies and guards. Indeed, the larger numbers of blacks in the Namibian forces mean that in the operational areas some 35 to 40 percent of the combined SADF and SWATF deployment is black. In this sense, a disproportionate number of blacks are engaged in combat. Because of that, they can be regarded as a form of "cannon fodder," as alleged by the African National Congress.[3]

Moreover, the situation must be considered to be extremely dynamic. Now that a number of units and formations are in place, the regime is prepared, or so it would seem, to move quickly into the expanded recruitment of blacks. This, indeed, is the often stated intention of the authorities. One SADF official called it "a natural process that will take place gradually."[4] As the war in Namibia persists and escalates and as domestic South African unrest grows the government's estimates of its military manpower needs can be expected to increase. Since mobilization of young white males has reached a plateau, the logical source of new recruits is the black community — logical, that is, if we merely look at cold numbers. The National Development and Management Foundation has submitted to the SADF that larger numbers of Coloureds, Indians, and black Africans should be mobilized. Rear Adm. R. A. Edwards, chief of Staff Personnel, agrees but insists that this can only be done gradually, over five years or more. When asked if South Africa had five years, he replied: "Time is running out — time has run out. . . . I don't think we have five years to play with, but I don't think we can do it in fewer than five years."[5]

The dilemma hidden in this logical pessimism is clear — the need for increasing trained manpower weighed against an inability and, for political reasons, an unwillingness to move more rapidly to bring blacks into the service. One further reason the regime cannot move faster is that the SADF has not

3. "Army and Politics," part 3, *Sechaba* (June 1980): 11.

4. Maj. Gen. E. A. C. Pienaar, quoted in *Rand Daily Mail*, 28 January 1979.

5. *The Star* (Johannesburg, Daily Edition), 8 February 1978. See also the remarks of Harry Pitman, leader of the Progressive Party in Natal, in *The Star* (Weekly Air Edition), 30 March 1974, p. 16.

even been able to provide problem-free training for its recent larger intakes of white national servicemen. Since the move to a once-a-year intake and a two-year national service obligation, the SADF has been hard pressed to find enough NCOs, instructors, and facilities to expedite training. Moreover, it is likely that blacks themselves might resist expanded mobilization. To add larger numbers of less digestible black recruits creates problems that would test the limited absorptive capacity of the SADF. In fact, the numbers of blacks as a proportion of the Permanent Force has grown slowly since late 1978 or so. "Total strategy" in this environment must be tempered by obvious short-term and more profound long-term limitations. The racial and ethnic complexion of the existing military establishment — consisting of numerical distributions, treatment of personnel, rank differentials, and terms of service — is fluid, but fluid within channels shaped by ingrained habits of social relations and preferences, both within and outside of the armed forces. Historically, the pattern need not be one of continual growth and openness of the forces. "A "golden age" for blacks in the United States army ended in 1917. For the next thirty years life for blacks in the U.S. military was made less comfortable. The surrounding social conditions inform and shape the entry and quality of life for black men in the armed forces. South Africa's situation could also follow such a pattern of ebb and flow.

The Armed Forces as an Integrative Effort

The defense of the status quo for South Africa is reputed to be a "total," holistic social enterprise. Certainly, it involves all coercive arms of the state — the South African Police, the SADF, and other police and security forces in varying degrees of readiness. It is also to include all elements of the population and the economy. Coordination and planning among coercive institutions of the state are advanced, and the functional overlap among the forces is considerable. Blacks in the SAP are, of course, assigned primarily local tasks. But they are prepared for and have taken part in extended quasi-military functions both inside and outside South Africa. The government's perception of a "total onslaught" against South Africa has prompted a "total strategy" for defending that order. Military planning and preparations have encouraged a more offensive mind-set. Not only reactive operations outside South Africa and Namibia but preemptive and preventive raids are common. "Total strategy" is an aggressive not a passive or responsive strategy. South African forces and South African military aircraft have been deployed in and have penetrated the airspace of at least Angola, Mozambique, Zimbabwe, and Zambia in the past two years, as they have for years. Black members of the SADF are not only being required to defend South Africa — they are also being ordered to participate in the disruption of the affairs of neighboring peoples.

The armed forces in developing countries have been portrayed as social unifiers, as integrating institutions, as agents of social mobility and unity. Assuming the best of intentions on the part of civilian politicians and military authorities, this image is highly misleading. Few countries possess a truly open military service, least of all South Africa. In the South African setting military service is a travesty of reality. The SADF is still a highly racially selective institution. The element of trust in blacks in all assignments and roles is marginal. A few leaders express acceptance of the principle of meritocracy in the armed forces and some even admit that the foundations of racist social structures must be altered. Yet quite clearly there are intrinsic barriers to free mobility within the service.

Rather than breaking down racial barriers the South African government and the SADF are attempting to use racial and ethnic differences to maintain the political and economic regime. These differences are seen as a resource, to be exploited in order to tamp down civil unrest and to control and reverse the military thrusts on the borders. The use of racially segregated formations, in addition to the new regional-cum-ethnic, racially exclusive battalions officered or otherwise directed by white officers, facilitate the ability to divide and rule. Not only organizational distinctions within the SADF but the existence of homeland formations contribute to this structural complexity. If skillfully managed this complexity can be used to thwart the expression of unified antiregime activity. The ideological context, that of separate development, is little more than a domestic colonialism that divides, rules, and exploits more efficiently. Although in the operational areas there is some degree of cooperative racial interaction and integration, in South Africa this is discouraged by the structure and stratification of the SADF. Interracial fraternization is difficult, and interethnic fraternization among blacks has come to be awkward, particularly outside the black 21 Battalion.

Precisely how regional ethnic units are to be deployed is not clear. Presumably they will be assigned in the territories allotted to their own regional commands. If that is the case, then the SADF is not prepared at this point to use the classic technique for pacifying dissident ethnic elements, that is, to use troops of one ethnic group against other peoples. Certainly, the SAP thinks along these lines, as it did in Soweto in 1976. Why should the SADF be any different? Perhaps the local issues have not yet become sufficiently explosive to lead the authorities to adopt this divisive policy. Time will tell.

A traditional South African approach to manipulating majority unrest has been to divide and rule. White SADF officers are "civic soldiers" in the sense that most have thoroughly internalized the norms and behavioral modes of the dominant Afrikaner community. If this is the case, no matter how enlightened they may appear to be in relatively relaxed times, in a future conflict old habits may surface. It is not likely that the more "liberal" among high ranking SADF officers will have an unimpeded opportunity to bring about changes within the military service that will contribute to societal transformations.

The Loyalty of Black Soldiers

"Throughout our history men of all races have been fighting shoulder to shoulder for the preservation of civilization in this country."[6] So reads an article in the official SADF organ. In

6. "This is How 21 (Black) Battalion Prepared for Border Duty," *Paratus* 29 (April 1978): 4.

stirring prose, the hard sell campaign has begun to try to persuade South Africans of all races to cooperate in the defense of the system. It has only partially succeeded.

One thing that has surprised outside observers is the speed and ease with which the white community came to accept the employment of blacks in the SADF, even in fighting assignments. The transformation of white public opinion seems to have all the earmarks of, if not a religious conversion, at least a political one, with much the same conviction and intensity. Why shouldn't it have come about? Provided the instruments of control remain in white hands, a major proviso to be sure, there is every reason to expect that the regime can manage this new policy. In Zimbabwe the incidence of black desertion from the Rhodesian security forces was quite low, considering the military collapse near the end of the Muzorewa-Smith government. Only after compulsory military service for blacks was introduced did problems of discipline widen and deepen. Black Portuguese forces, likewise, held fast until after the military coup in Lisbon. Even then, despite widespread insecurity and discontent, large numbers of black troops did not defect or desert. Exceptions abound, but overall, blacks in these armed forces remained obedient to the regime. Even the most "ideological" of wars have been fought with impressed soldiers.

Yet something crucial is still missing. That is the vital perception of interest on the part of black people that for them the system is worth defending or, stated differently, that they have a deep enough material stake in a contemporary or even a foreseeable white-ruled South Africa to risk their lives and their social standing among peers by opposing fellow blacks committed to smashing the repressive arrangements. Once in the service, however, blacks are inclined to remain reliable, and to some extent they are intimidated into doing so. The factor of inertia may explain this in part. But this inertia may be outweighed, in the South African circumstances, by the fact that blacks can join the South African Army for indefinite terms of service. They have the contractual option of resigning at any time, with just one month's formal notice. Can they pull out if they do not like the drift of a particular war? If so, how would government seek to coerce them into fighting? As in the Zimbabwean example, getting blacks into the armed forces in larger numbers may prove to be the more nettlesome problem. As it presently stands material inducements to enlist appear to be sufficient — at least for the ranks. Black pay levels, although less than white levels, are considerably above what most young blacks could hope to get in the private or the public economy, assuming that they could find work. Conditions of service in the SADF are relatively attractive, as well, and will remain so unless the war becomes more intense. The SADF is still a rather encapsulated institution, shielding its members from the worst excesses of a thoroughly racist society. The skills acquired in the SADF may also enhance one's marketability upon demobilization. But a military organization cannot exist in isolation. Even equal status in the military (which for blacks does not exist) cannot offset the frustrations of an unequal status in society. This is where the SADF is bound to have problems. In the end, even an enlightened military is called upon to interact with the very society it seeks to defend, yet escape.

The black community appreciates this paradox. White South Africa, perhaps because of its own self-delusion, does not see the paradox. Whites, especially rural whites, "understand their blacks." Illustrative of this self-delusion are the remarks of one Nationalist M.P. Speaking of the volunteer white commando member in rural areas, he said:

> He knows the Black population and he has a good relationship with them, a relationship built up during the years of working together, a relationship of co-existence in a spirit of goodwill and happiness. . . . Therefore a spirit of mutual respect and trust is built up which definitely cannot be destroyed overnight with the barrel of a Russian AK – 47 gun.[7]

To be blind to the reality of rural race relations is part of the Afrikaner prejudice that keeps the system going. The very defense mechanisms sharpened by those exploited and racially

7. Dr. W. J. Snyman (NP, Pietersberg) in *Assembly Debates*, 23 April 1979, col. 4742. This statement was later quoted favorably by another Nationalist M.P.

disadvantaged are seen as evidence of "good relationships" that will sustain the system. This self-delusion, however, may just be opinion verbalized on the surface for external consumption. Like the grand South African propaganda offensive, it can be viewed as part blindness, part whistling past the graveyard, part shrewd advertising gimmickry. Yet the lessons of the information scandal and of advertising in general should be appreciated — if one tries to purchase good publicity for a dubious cause one ends up fooling few, misleading oneself, and damaging one's case.

The black population has not been misled into accepting the SADF as an instrument for real societal change. Undoubtedly, over the years there has been a subtle alteration in military purpose and leadership style. Gone is the pure specialist in violence (though that is still the central assignment of the SADF). Instead, there are also quartered in the SADF persons of a wide variety of social skills (educators, agriculturalists, health workers, and so forth) and, at the top levels, of a managerial ability to orchestrate these diverse skills. Yet the SADF's civic action programs affect few black lives positively and deceive fewer black people. Winning hearts and minds is fine when it works. But at base, civic action has been regarded by its perpetrators as a publicity tool, as a safety valve, and as a weapon to facilitate control over the black population. Little effort is made to involve black people other than manipulable governmental personnel in planning and administration. If civic action arouses little popular support one could hardly expect more of the actual military operations of the SADF. Black South Africans have chosen not to join the promilitary bandwagon, and as the SADF is required to interact more closely with the black people, it is less likely that they will be drawn aboard.

Military Professionalism and the Praetorian Alternative

The SADF appears to be a state institution that seeks, if it can with minimal social dislocation, to change certain obvious features of South African society in order to conserve the essence

of what passes for the "South African way." But there are upward barriers as to how far such liberalizing tendencies can go
within the SADF, how far middle and even higher levels within
the SADF want them to go, and particularly how much they
can have an impact on the larger, less plastic society. Compared
to the bureaucratic and political elites, for example, the military hierarchy in South Africa has traditionally been less
closely identified with the political regime and the state. Although the SADF is conscientiously dedicated to the maintenance of order, it seems more independent in its particular
conception of the order to be defended. Indeed, throughout
the world there are numerous cases of militaries that dared to
challenge or to try to modernize precarious or unstable regimes.

The armed forces are usually controlled from two organizational foci. From within, a group of colleagues may oversee the
internal cohesion of the officers corps as a social and professional elite. Peer pressure applies self-imposed standards of
group behavior and surveillance. From outside, military discipline and control are subject to the political hierarchy of authority. These professional standards of conduct are judged by
the faithfulness with which officers follow directives from the
civil authorities.[8]

The SADF is serious about its image as a professional organization. It wants to please both its external superiors and to
conform to its own professional standards. The SADF hierarchy would like to be thought of as a nonpartisan, although by
no means a nonpolitical body. It wants to defend what it under-
stands to be the South African model as most probably embodied by the *verligte* wing of the National Party—not by the
Progressive Federal Party, the New Republic Party, the HNP,
or the *verkrampte* Nationalists. Enloe, perhaps prematurely,
wrote in 1975 that: "For the military the transition from Afrikaner nationalism to white nationalism has meant that the regime has grown uneasy with the idea of an army too narrowly

8. Amos Perlmutter, *The Military and Politics in Modern Times: On Profes-
sionals, Praetorians, and Revolutionary Soldiers* (New Haven: Yale University
Press, 1977), p. 2.

identified with just one white ethnic group."⁹ The military, it would appear, thinks of itself as having transcended that past, preprofessional characterization. In its self-image the SADF is a first-class combat organization with a skilled administration and "enlightened" social views. Among its white personnel promotion is reputedly gained by merit rather than ethnic affinity. Yet when difficulties emerge a deeply emotional Afrikaner identity can be expected to resurface.

Sometimes the external standards of behavior conflict with the self-imposed internal standards. One such discrepancy cropped up during the Angolan intervention in 1975–76. The SADF felt that it was made to bear the stigma of defeat unfairly. From its vantage the SADF (much like the United States forces in Viet Nam) felt that it had not been permitted to fight without fetters, and both the SADF and the government thought that South Africa had been betrayed by its Western and Black African "allies." Policy dictates from Pretoria vaccilated and the goals of the operation were misrepresented, leaving the SADF with shifting directives. The SADF questioned the need to go in, and once in it challenged the decision to withdraw short of unseating the MPLA government and taking Luanda. The entire affair was conducted clandestinely, with questionable logistic support and little open political encouragement. Considering that the SADF was not physically defeated in Angola, yet retreated ignominiously without victory, the worst feature of the intervention was the challenge to the SADF's credibility. The image of professionalism and combat invincibility had been tarnished, and SADF people thought the politicians, not the SADF, were responsible. There was by no means a "stab in the back" mentality, but there was considerable ill will between the SADF (and Defence Minister P. W. Botha), on the one hand, and prime minister Vorster and Gen. Hendrik van den Bergh of BOSS, on the other. In another alleged instance, as a reaction to the Soweto violence of 1976 members of the SADF general staff reportedly sent a memorandum to Minister of Defence Botha, implying that some

9. Cynthia H. Enloe, "Ethnic Factors in the Evolution of the South African Military," *Issue* 5 (Winter 1975): 23.

form of "military takeover might be necessary to bring about
socio-political changes."[10] Much of the divisiveness between
the SADF and civil authorities has been dissipated since
P.W. Botha took over as prime minister and especially since
Gen. Magnus Malan, an SADF insider, assumed the Defence
portfolio.

A professional, apolitical defense force is frequently regarded as an obstacle to military coups. Yet it is impossible to
buffer the military establishment from the tensions of the
larger polity. Especially if the regime regularly uses the armed
forces for purposes of general social internal control, it is increasingly likely that the armed forces leadership will want to
have some input in government policy, if not actually to shape
directly the order they are required to defend. Ranking personnel in a publicly visible military, such as South Africa's, will
apply perspectives and resources with a distinctive style to
problems of social fragmentation. Officers (and the ranks) may
be instruments of the state, but they are not *tabulae rasae*, not
just state actors.[11] They would like to play a more active role in
politics, too. What this has meant is that in the Botha regime
the SADF has become an identifiable and influential political
group, for the SADF a new and unfamiliar role in South African politics.[12]

The SADF leadership finds itself caught between professionalism and praetorianism. With Botha and Malan well
placed at the top, we can see the militarization of civilian authority and of the ruling elite. What this means is that those

10. This was disclosed by Dr. John Seiler in testimony before the United
States House of Representatives Subcommittees on International Economic
Policy and Trade in Africa and on International Organizations; U.S., Congress, House, Committee on Foreign Affairs, *U.S. Policy Toward South Africa*,
96th Cong., 2nd sess., 1980, p. 46. Dr. Seiler later said that this information had
been confirmed by at least three different people; *The Star* (Weekly Air Edition), 10 May 1980, p. 1.

11. Cynthia H. Enloe, *Ethnic Soldiers: State Security in Divided Societies*
(Athens: University of Georgia Press, 1980), p. 129.

12. Cf. Pierre van den Berghe, *South Africa: A Study in Conflict* (Berkeley:
University of California Press, 1967), p. 63; and Edwin S. Munger, *Notes on the
Formation of South African Foreign Policy* (Pasadena, Calif.: Grant Dahlstrom,
Castle Press, 1965), pp. 46 – 47.

who think in military terms are in control. This does not mean
that they always will opt for the violent solution, for they are
often more inclined than some civilian politicians to appreciate
the limits of militarist policies. If we recall the Botha years as
Minister of Defence, the situations in which he was thwarted in
his activist and offensive policies *vis-à-vis* Vorster and van den
Bergh would lead us to the conclusion that now that he is
prime minister, when pressures mount, the "surgical" strike,
the military thrust, are more likely to be considered favorably.
Pragmatism may indeed be in the seat of power, but it is a
pragmatism that leans toward "authoritarian reforms" that
would ruthlessly repress both the left and right. A civilian and
military junta is not out of the question. A "senior Nationalist
MP" has been quoted as saying: "The government would not
be able to meet future demands without giving the heads of the
defence force a definite say in the decision-making process in
the country, and that South Africa may ultimately be ruled by a
civilian-military junta."[13] But once it is less dependent on white
votes to stay in power, such a junta might try to defuse the
tension of a racist order. South Africa could become, in this
situation, a permanent garrison state. The civil and military
instruments of coercion have already been fused together, although bureaucratic disagreements between the SAP and the
SADF still fester.

In other respects the SADF and spokesmen for the military
perspective are ascendant. An elaborate military-industrial
complex is emerging into public view. The vehicle for the coordination of the SADF's views with those of other governmental
departments is the State Security Council. This statutory body
had been dormant under Vorster. With Botha it meets fort-
nightly as part of the prime minister's reorganization of state
administration. The State Security Council has become an alternative cabinet in that it takes important decisions. The government refuses to list the council's membership, but we know

13. As quoted in International Defence and Aid Fund, *The Apartheid War
Machine: The Strength and Deployment of the South African Armed Forces*, Fact
Paper on Southern Africa, no. 8 (London: International Defence and Aid
Fund, 1980), p. 7.

that SADF people are included and are active throughout its secretariat. In addition, the Botha and SADF tandem at the top has downplayed the policy roles of the National Party and of the Broederbond. The extent of the SADF's commitment to reform thereby becomes an important question.

It may be premature to say, as does the African National Congress, that we have witnessed "the transformation of military and paramilitary forces from being tools of oppression to becoming the central decision-making force within all facets of the government of the apartheid state."[14] But there is no question that the trend is in that direction. Whether it will run its full course will be worth scrutinizing. Will South Africans hold with Shakespeare when he laments: "When sorrows come, they come not single spies, but in battalions" (*Hamlet,* act 4, scene 5)?

14. "Army and Politics," part 1, *Sechaba* (April 1980), p. 20.

Index

Designer: Sandy Drooker
Compositor: Innovative Media, Inc.
Printer: Vail-Ballou Press
Binder: Vail-Ballou Press
Text: 10/13 Baskerville
Display: Palatino